The Salt Companion to Bill Griffith

WILLIAM ROWE teaches contemporary British and Latin American poetry at Birkbeck College, where he is Director of the Contemporary Poetics Research Centre. He has written on Maggie O'Sullivan, Lee Harwood, Eric Mottram, Allen Fisher, and William Carlos Williams and is the author of *Three Lyric Poets: Lee Harwood, Barry MacSweeney and Chris Torrance*, forthcoming from Northcote House in the Writers and Their Work series. His translations of contemporary Latin American poets have been widely published, and he has three books on Latin American poetry, including *Poets of Contemporary Latin America: History and the Inner Life* (OUP, 2000).

The Salt Companion to Bill Griffiths

Edited by

WILLIAM ROWE

SALT

CAMBRIDGE

PUBLISHED BY SALT PUBLISHING
PO Box 937, Great Wilbraham PDO, Cambridge CB1 5JX United Kingdom

© William Rowe, 2007

First published 2007

Printed and bound in the United Kingdom by Lightning Source

Typeset in Swift 10/12

ISBN 978 1 84471 249 6 paperback

Salt Publishing Ltd gratefully acknowledges
the financial assistance of Arts Council England

1 3 5 7 9 8 6 4 2

Contents

*Thanks to Harry Gilonis for his generous help
with checking textual details.*

Introduction*
Jeff Nuttall

Bill Griffiths' poems are dazzling. More than any work in English since Gertrude Stein they insist on being recognised as surfaces and structures. Statements are made. Stories are told. Places and people are described. A bitter anarchism is expressed, also Nietzschean yearning towards energy and joy. Yet statement, narration, description and expression are kept in check so that the poem is seen as itself, a poem, an artefact, an edifice with an importance over and above its subject matter. It is not the light and the landscape, the sense of motion of limbs or machine, the anger and the disappointments, the passions and hungers, which are magnificent. It is the poem itself which, in Griffiths' work, perpetually dazzles and astonishes in exactly the way the great stained-glass windows of European cathedrals dazzle and astonish before the eye has recognised whatever image is depicted.

People are reluctant to allow words to do this. The image of Christ may be presented in a thousand fragments of coloured glass because glass, light and architecture are materials in which structure is expected to take priority over content. But words in their day-to-day function are the vehicle of information. If priority is made secondary to their glory then a cautious and insecure area of the mind panics in case efficiency is lost in euphoria. To allow such a panic to determine the nature of poetry is to set poetry on a level with road signs and government white papers. Griffiths' work refuses such a levelling with aggressive vigour. Instruction manuals deal with facts. Poetry deals with excitement and joy. It may certainly inform but its first purpose is to energise, to exalt

* First published as Introduction to Griffiths section in *Future Exiles: 3 London Poets* (London, Paladin 1992: 157–8).

the spirit and kindle the eye. Griffiths' work is a vivid demonstration of this priority.

How does he do it? He uses a variety of language: prison talk ('its sick fucked-up / fish (that gave emselves up) jumped on the / hookz'); biker talk ('Hey, Blue! Tell? / What cars a'like racin' at you'); dialect ('sow'd as a tapioca most / 'at curds-up or cuts in the tabby sky'); literal translation ('no-yes grass's semi-audible sweet-howl'); ancient English ('Unlovely come I here some knight / That would with monsterdom fight'). The literal translation places English words in unusual syntactical positions which present the text as form a fraction of a second before the content registers. Similarly the colloquial passages use phonetic spelling, obscure nicknames, opaque references, to delay comprehension so that form makes its unimpeded impact ('the grand bagged billy's eyes / strained out from the glass-indoors / at quaint manner of its ledding / an' loud earth-up'). Throughout the text syntax is playfully and/or sometimes violently rearranged into an unfamiliar and unexpected order: ('Art being or being Our Art Art beginning And art / and starting-white hedge (be) doing Trigger tiger / wide-bayed snowy-up is Yolk-yellow (girl) see / deep Fella').

In the forms thus composed sound appropriates a major role. Rhymes, rhythms, alliterations, vowels accelerate, explode or dissolve in relentless, marvellously controlled sequences. Space and punctuation are used as silences, delays, percussion, or are withdrawn to achieve speed and smooth flow. Parentheses are opened but not closed. Sentences are begun but merge into other sentences before a full stop is inserted. A manipulation of phrase edges is used with a similar effect to that of Dada poetry. There are also similarities to the way in which a saxophonist like John Coltrane will rephrase a melody relentlessly, again and again, to find all the possibilities of a given handful of notes.

The sense, when it does burst through, comes enhanced, each image or event spun, polished, illuminated and celebrated by its membership of such a majestic galaxy. What filters through the myriad colours, chips of rainbow, frozen dew of forms, is light, the sun itself, life, sensibility and glory—'Locked in in the beauty, Locked into the beauty, Locked in in the beauty.'

Diorama of the Fixed Eye-Ball*
IAIN SINCLAIR

We haven't of late heard much from the poets about the London project. The language dandies have all left town. The years take their toll; practitioners, bored with the echo of their own voices in an empty hall, have abandoned us to the mercy of bullet-point epics, copyright to Her Majesty's Stationary Office. *Towards an Urban Renewal (Final Report of the Urban Task Force Chaired by Lord Rogers of Riverside)*, a thick yellow non-book of 328pp, has an unintentional resemblance to a telephone directory. Such manifestations, like Henry Kissinger copping the Nobel Peace Prize, put satirists out of business. But, in shape and size, this document also evokes, for sentimentalists of a certain age, the first edition of Allen Fisher's *Place* (Aloes Books 1974). Civic proposals, meditations on ecology, statistics, flow charts, varied fonts, doodles: committee forged anti-prose parodies the singular excavations and visionary riffs of unsponsored poets (Fisher, Bill Griffiths). For a number of years the city was the subject, urban scribes trained themselves to repossess the news, thereby saving the rest of us from collapsing under the weight of information overkill. Variously, Fisher as strategist and worker of systems, Griffiths as pre-emptive manic street preacher, alerted us to the duties and pleasure of citizenship. Now, thanks to a powerful downshift in consciousness, the hot poetic of the Sixties and early Seventies achieves its apotheosis as dead paper, spooked by the quislings of New Labour. Language is corrupted as the city embraces its entropic destiny. Living a written life within the circumference of the M25 is no longer a valid proposition. But Griffiths, born in London, a child of the north-west suburbs, is in remission; he has returned from exile. It is part of his new work, *Spilt*

* Preface to *The Book of Spilt Cities*, Buckfastleigh: Etruscan Books, 1999.

[3]

Cities, to test whatever coheres from that lively (shit-stirred) era, when mainstream (or even slipstream) publication took subterranean, subversive, or interestingly off-the-wall poetry into just enough bookshops to do the business. The proposition then was: London can be reclaimed, London can be described. The true life, worth reporting in diary, epistolary or conventional mode, could still be experienced. Primary models, such as Tom Raworth's *A Serial Biography*, record quite humble local observations. 'They were taking up the paving stones along the street.' This is not the opening of another futile protest, but the first movement in a swift chain of connected images—dream, the misreading of posters, how to walk—that build toward 'the final collision' of two preoccupied pedestrians. We remember the small things, the details; throwaway Polaroids and sensory conceits.

Plastic aliens in cereal bowls, bits of dialogue from films halfnoticed on latenight television. London was animated by its particulars, by the (self-conscious) ease with which the poets made themselves at home; smoking on the windowsill, clocking the song on the jukebox as they walked past the caff, watching the river. Time had not yet been privatised. Lee Harwood was a presence, passing through *Cable Street*. Chris Torrance cut the municipal grass in Carshalton and scribbled deliriously in secret notebooks. Bill Griffiths week-ended in Whitechapel prefabs, celebrating gang wars, rucks, rows, bloody 'domestics', in customised Anglo-Saxon and early Welsh warrior-speak. There was free movement, discourse. And enough ego to believe that small confessions, lyric seizures, blended with documentation, found facts, recognition of avatars and antecedents, were worth recording and processing.

Now (1999), confronting this heroic legend, pitching his voice(s) against an increasingly dystopian terrain, Griffiths finds that London has been cleaved, divided against herself, split like the hemispheres of the cerebellum. Treated with earth-fire and iron rain. Then tipped from the bowl, spilled free. (How much can be read into the dyslexic attraction of those twinned words: split and spilt.) The poet/bard has a preternatural ability to run multiple tracks, schizophrenic babblings (overheard, solicited, imagined), and to formulate a coherent argument. What is (noise) has been superimposed upon what ought to be (signal). An affliction of the eye turns stone to shadow, water to dust. Griffiths wrote to me that he 'unwillingly satirised those hopes of the 1970s that love would redeem the world.' Movement, out from the heart, is anxious. His language, under pressure, spits and surges like an unsecured hosepipe. Free-associating memories are tempered by fractured quotation, laws that have been learnt only to be broken. Through the trajectory of *Spilt Cities*, the poet presents the eye as a globe or egg or blind sun: 'Imagine you are an eye-ball. Open yourself.' He seems to solicit, as a means of redemption, Buñuel's razor or the psychotic rituals of Georges Bataille, prophet of visionary excess. 'A bell is the eyes.' 'Orb is perpetual.' 'This is the medium of the egg.' 'The one with the bloody eye.' 'The dots and eyes / is every-thing.' 'Each cheque / a wobble / of the dying eye.'

Forced visions. A knuckle pressed against the eye-ball. The eye reads everything except itself. Griffiths sets the inflamed monocular intensity of the private witness against the undirected sensationalism of the diorama, the tent-show stunt—as it [was] pitched by the unfashionable rhetoric of Tudor historian Sir John Neale, or by the promoters of the New Millennium Experience with their offwhite bubble on Bugsby's Marshes (aka the Greenwich Peninsula).

Are we to listen to the 'thing-voice in the dome' or to Griffiths' sharply-written polemic? There must be no heritage that does not acknowledge its own stink. That's the choice: to trust the report of a singular man (who speaks what he sees) or to let ourselves drift across an Imax panorama of over-clarified but meaningless detail. The poet refuses to collaborate in the 'malfiguring of the Past.' The Greenwich Dome is too mean a concept. It's a feeble analogue of J.G. Ballard's 'corporate sensorium'; the cup of an empty skull on which will be projected advertising slogans, political graffiti, bent statistics and broken quotations from the golden treasury. 'New dioramas of approximate, reality.'

Identifying the paradox, an invalid freedom of speech (nobody is listening), encourages Griffiths to let rip. That's the buzz. Uncensored intelligence jumping out of harness. He's talking to you and you'd better keep your ears pinned back. It's a performance: the narrative hesitates, breaks off, backtracks, pauses on a conjunction, exclaims, re-asserts, stalls, catches you unprepared. Contraries are so well worked—'disburst', 'uncopulant disengagement'—that we experience the dizzy-making vertigo of the shot that zooms rapidly in and tracks out at the same time. Negative capability, or some such. It's a much cleaner process than this halting note makes it seem. A proper response to *Spilt Cities* would be pure quotation.

'Something organic has snapped.' Griffiths projects privileged versions of urban experience (courtly pageants) against a system that is evidently in terminal decline: 'the norm is wrong.' Highangle surveillance sweeps reveal the extent of the carnage. The poet exploits a system of hyphens, derived from earlier models, praise songs, to bond together warring elements: 'burnt-bananaeyed fruit-groups', 'finger-suburbs', 'sleep-owl faces'. He works his apostrophes like dockers' hooks, hacking out unnecessary vowels, scoring the texts, straining for optimum pace and expression. Through momentum, he achieves prophetic instability. 'Purple meat mohawks, floods, / lipping at the perimeter.' Suburban exoticism invades the collapsed centre. Nothing is forgotten, everything is re-remembered. In stomping across Wordsworth's Westminster Bridge epiphany (sublime copywriting), Griffiths encourages amputated phrases to take flight. The sonnet is alarmed to find itself auditioning for an Objectivist anthology. We've misplaced our cultural markers. The riverscape has been tricked out with so many authentic fakes. This is the 'head-skull film' to which we are now addicted. Dud oratory. Commissioned buildings that nobody wants. Over-funded follies with an appropriate laureate to disguise their hubris. Griffiths, in his centrifugal frenzy, is the counter-Motion.

So the new poem becomes a pre-posthumous project, a forced vision like that enjoyed by the hanged man in Ambrose Bierce's *Incident at Owl Creek*. Choking, the flow of blood to the brain cut off, spectres of the past make their involuntary appearance. In *The Middle City* Griffiths returns to the suburbs, recovered perfumes: 'I was hauled out of the marigolds, / drunk with orgone scent.' Alongside the hell's angels, the strikers, the stricken, Griffiths runs this flickering home movie from the quiet foothills. Who else could successfully hymn the virtues of 'Ransome' petrol-powered mower of 1902 / soon adopted by Cadbury Chocolates / for their sports ground at Bournville'? A dream-restored culture of LCC parks and 'the last Aurochs' is floated. The poet understands the strange conjunctions of this undervalued landscape: 'a street will lead to Russian Orthodoxy / or a golf course.'

Griffiths is old enough to recall the same differences coming round for the second time. His songs are heroic but they shouldn't be confused, in their terse, broken-rhymed form, with modernist artefacts. They are not post anything. They both say and mean: 'Certainties / invented / and shaped.' If he opens with a cod-Shakespearean soliloquy (challenging the Nealite glossing of the Elizabethan period by reinventing himself as a journeyman Bankside playwright), he soon shifts from guying Wordsworth (the tourist) to fashioning his own Prelude of the London suburbs.

But suburbs (even when those suburbs were located in Hackney and Hoxton) were always a convenient location for asylums, houses where the deranged and the possessed could be hidden away. Now, along the rim the of M25, the colonies where the damaged dreamers of the inner city were once decanted are being torn down and converted into housing estates, suitable for reps and salespersons (convenient access to motorway system). Only the Italianate water towers survive; remote markers from which to formulate a new psychogeography. Other notable London poets, David Gascoyne and David Jones, paid their dues to the suburbs, to Twickenham and Harrow. They linked personal breakdown with what they saw as the psychosis of the city. (Eliot, the godfather of all metropolitan trauma, recuperated in Margate, 'On Margate Sands. / I can connect / Nothing with nothing.') Gascoyne in *Night Thoughts* downloaded his dream analysis (voices in the head), his drifts across quiet cherry-blossom avenues. Eliotic whispers ('I have sometimes gone out towards midnight') give way to something close to Bill Griffiths' diorama: 'A public park space from which one looks down / Upon the mighty Nocturne of the Capital / Whose twinkling panorama's spread below.'

But by the time Griffiths arrives at the final movement of *Spilt Cities*, his university/ prison is a sort of panopticon. A series of discrete cells built around a central eye. Freedom to move across the map has been curtailed in favour of bitter repression: 'a little subordination / for a lot of empowerment!' Physical horrors happen just out of sight, and are witnessed only by the perpetrators. Those who report these things risk 'a mouthbeating.' The concept of public accountability is outmoded, replaced by ever more freshly-painted offices of complaint. Judges judge the judges. The language system for recording this situation stutters on the edge of incoherence. The poet allows a run of cruel letters to fizz like bad electricity: 'fix // a fox / locked in a leap // a coniunx of prisoners / froz' / non-feel / (dessiclassicated) / / orbital frames / exact ill-alien / end.' Feral Xs and Zs, crossed and doped, sleep with eyes wide closed under forced lights. Sick halfrhymes and blood-pulse rhythms mimic the loud fugues of paranoia. Can the poet be as mad as the city? Griffiths is a master of the distorted monologue: Robert Browning after ECT. We are all now involuntary clients of the state. There is no public place for this public poem. 'Things march,' Griffiths asserts, 'that should've stayed in print.' Rupert Murdoch (a man whose face reveals the price of the bargain he has struck, Rex Mundi) wants to control all global communication, electronic, print, digital and chemical. One of his lesser assets is the Harper Collins publishing conglomerate. A group responsible for much vanity publishing on behalf of the Conservative party (blue propaganda); steroidal blockbusters by all the self-inflating nouveaux artistos, Lady Thatcher and Lord Archer and their ilk. Operations on such a water-brained scale allow the occasional anomaly to slip through the net. Paladin, a Harper Collins subsidiary, took on the publication (if not the promotion) of *Future Exiles (3 London Poets)*, a collection that featured a substantial chunk of Griffiths' work (along with Allen Fisher and Brian Catling). Murdoch's accountants moved in before any real harm could be done. The collection was briefly remaindered and then pulped. It is therefore a particular pleasure to see *Spilt Cities* appear in a form that makes Griffiths available once more to an audience outside the small press poetry ghetto. He is voices. And he is hot. Go with him.

'Every New Book Hacking on Barz' : The Poetry of Bill Griffiths.*

ERIC MOTTRAM

In the decade since his first appearance in *Poetry Review* for Autumn 1972, Griffiths has created a body of work second to none in its formal enterprise and necessary aggression against what this country has become, a deteriorated tyranny, both economically and culturally. A fair entrance may be made through a small book called *Miscellany*, which immediately demonstrates Griffiths' ability to create a language from common speech and street life which challenges the dull conventionalities of official poetry, the verse of a declined culture. Griffiths' tensions between literary scholarship and working-class and outcast life among the formally diseducated—the vulnerable—are here fused into a language of unique force and style, a voice opening up from suppression, breaking out and making new. 'Long Death of the Plains Indians Gypsies' uses Romany terms within this programme to bring home the fact that the bland language of Establishment poetics is in fact a language of rule which deliberately excludes the possibility of cultural renewal from any source except the controlling classes. *Poems for Ian Hamilton* (1975) is a careful excoriation of a ringleader and pet of the Establishment, whose literary magazine, subsidised to the tune of thousands of pounds from public money annually, failed both popularly and critically, and finally died unlamented. Hamilton reviewed for the *New Statesman*, a main journal of poetry control in spite of its alleged investigative/leftist politics, and broadcast for the BBC, a main regulator of what the country is supposed to believe is the only poetry around.

* *Reality Studios* 5 (London, 1983): 45-54

[9]

Where is he now? Such is the poetry-control: public funds administered for the Arts Council through Charles Osborne end up in private pockets, and nothing is done officially. So Griffiths' thirty-three brief poems which parody or complement Hamilton's *The Visit* include the line "I stomp inelegantly over your possessions (miles away) and you" within a series of examples of exhaustion of life which the power structure and its agents continue. The poems recognise the deathliness of literature governed nationally by self-elected and self-substantiated controllers, the new Grub Street, the new MacFlecknoes, their lies and their fakes:

> It's the weather flagellates: like a slice of sleet
> I only lick ....delinquent joker
> Of my fed-up family.
>
> *
>
> ....Sometimes I think or—
> Formulate—
> Think (maybe?) so calmly...
> While all the poets I've inhumed leer and limp about my garden.
>
> *
>
> Till I envy me,
> Neat chief top to the ranks of unreadable

But these are occasional verses, however necessary and accomplished. *Cycles* is a set of major texts written between 1970 and 1974 published together definitively in *Oblong Book* in 1976: The work begins with a characteristic fusion of personal, historical and contemporary, presented as a constellation in a language of elisions and disjunctures which draw in the explicative sensibility of any reader not entirely crass to the inventive imagination:

> Ictus!
> As I ain't like ever to be still but
> kaleidoscope,
> lock and knock my sleeping
>
> Within
> the complex of the fort against the French, Dover,
> 's mighty imperfection: fits to the sea,
> the moat (and ported, kinging the blue, closed, so built-made) and the
> salty grass and rubble of chalk
> growing

writing the chalk—kid
shout for separation

The ships, turquoise,
cutting open the sea
smiling killing
O.K.

The day opens up, is pale;
opens free, to me
my hands lightened, head

At running in the sun
I thought
this serious, my world is.

Here was the new voice and project of a poet paying attention to every aspect of the craft, leaving the Hughes/Thwaite/Dunn establishment far behind in their careless and safe variations and repetitions. The prosody itself is part of Griffiths' tensions between free self and authoritarian society, between contemporary and historic and archaic. The highly controlled measures resist authoritarian mathematics of the incessant Establishment iambic and build a stance against all imposition. The language and the syntax invent a new pleasure for the reader trained for and open to receive the exhilarations of the new rather than the familiar minor pleasures of the Hardy/Edward Thomas/Donald Davie line, or the enfeebling, whining, clever ironies of Auden and Lowell, or the likes of a later scion of the Establishment, Craig Raine, proclaimed from the TV screen by Melvyn Bragg, an Arts Council man, as the poet of a New Poetry. Griffiths' music, already at this stage, is really his own; the performance is invented within the inheritance of essentially modern poetics generated out of the "tradition of the new" from Mallarmé and Hopkins onwards. But at the core of the deployment of skills lie the facts and causes of actual imprisonment in Dover borstal—"Prison's the future, Mike, just the alternative"; "grave police music", the class nature of the law, art against the uniforms of the State, the sense of a social system, "memorising" the individual in its categories out of which you step at your peril. Dover is a complex site, therefore, and it includes other kinds of invasion, a number of kinds of violation of self and boundary. The prison screws are part of the site of control violence and violation. The cell is where you are memorised. The poetry moves in its cycles to other British sites; the themes expand and the prosody changes:

> NOW CORFE; TOTTERS
> AT ITS LUMP AND SUMP
> TOUCH AND CHURN THE RUBBISH
> YOUR SMALL STERILE YELLOW LIMED BIRDS
> WILL HAVE KIDS IN THEIR BEAKS BY YOU

Ships and the recurrent shapes of the Lady move energy out in a journey from enclosure into potentiality:

> Chrize she sez you got me
> ever?
> (stuck?)
>
> starz eye to eye
> slep wiv sheepz
> curly smell lambs
> river I got up woz yello a lot of mist, shiny
> these last animals
> making hole wallz of animals
>
> hey! cant you hear the steamer ?....

Nature functions, as in Blake, as varieties of plant and creature inno-cence, the context of our moral life in the State we toady to or bang against:

> on this sea-lion ticking & thinking keeping going, grey with grinning
> demonstrating God and God's castle
>
> i would plant it
> seeing fish like plums
> the penitent thief who got paradise ('an enclosed park')

The exuberances of the poetics constitute—here and throughout Griffiths' work to come—an eloquence in itself a criticism of immoder-ate arrest and stasis in social and religious hierarchy ("good afternoon, god's policemen"). Any British poetry that is at all innovative proceeds from the margins which assault the self-appointed regulators, is placed with all that is politically and culturally subversive of the Centre and its control manias. Section 16's "justice" has become mere Punch-and-Judy under Master Judas, and the prosody retaliates:

az in a crowd
black, the butterflies to her head
. . .
& golems
        of kitten, car,
& at noon, fiurworx
like loony pals ova ruby—
mediatin & placating
. . .
magic iza science
every herb iz ina book
every new book

hacking
on barz
the near-lazule hate,
if that ESCAPES.

War with Windsor (1972–4, 1976) is a set of texts in the experiential area of gang living. Again, the sheer inventions of their forms constitute a poetic challenge. In the four columns of Text 1—the short measures moving laterally into each other at certain points, to be read vertically and/or laterally—Angels and organisers involved in police confrontation are examples of a wide context of British custom and law, confrontations of behaviours which also exemplify the 1970s and 80s: "It was brilliant I breathed it/And Angels az kinging & joking az catastrophic". "Into Prison" (used in *Cycles*) is a prose-poem of paragraphic units pointing proper analogies between church and prison walls, the chaplain as warder and therefore a state-church agent. The world of Angels and prison is one "you court folk" could never imagine, let alone understand—and Text 3's thirteen numbered units gives the ambivalences of victim/law/judgement of criminality:

4. Bev as the sea wave wake
See this is Angels getting the booting of their
Life in Scrubs
This is Johnny
This is me picking up snout bits in Brixton

12. Stood with my hands for an hour
From the edge.
. . .
(Are you tired yet
said the detective ?)

In Text 4 trapped wild animals are paired with the zooed up animals the
State prefers in one of Griffiths' best social lyrics:

> Close up wolf about my mouth
> He would go in
> Sit in his cave, like me,
> Smell at the daylight.
>
> Animals an' criminals
> Among of the legs of the animals
> Criminals hands in belts
>
> Jesu 'pecker
> My eyes is loose with worry.
>
> I've stood
> Like a polar bear
> In court—no one will move
> At the white
> Till all the wood stank.

"Long Death of the Plain Indians Gipsies", now placed here, contains
Hitler's attack on Romanies as a form of US whites versus Indians
(Griffiths has translated Romany poetry)—an image of any persecution
towards deliberate elimination. Text 5, "War with Windsor"—and the title
takes in the Crown as the constitutional centre of law—is a statement
from a victim—flat factual rhythms for violent action, the action of violation. The police need to frame Angels and "druggies" for their careers, but
this is not understood for action by their victims. It is the poet who understands that the "Crown" is the courts and the House of Windsor at the
head of the class structure's wealth and rank. The Windsors "only reign
elexion and getting god's grace", a contract which is broken "in regards
mercy in regards the laws and in regards holy laws, everyday" (An
appendix documents the work from newspaper reports and a book on
the bikers). The poem reminds the British that the Crown rules by
"consent and law and is not the image officially promulgated. Text 6,
"LATCHMERE: (Remand)"—"solitary—no—lead-lifting/tongue/tight as tap
//fuse your fucking heads"—precedes "Zookeeper" in which the title has
won, and against the reassembled syntax of new prosody challenges the
iambic authoritarianism of state poets under the Crown:

> Tempestu-
> ous a ocean-token
> to dolly air 'at's a'
> waste-with-magic or

whirled curls/pearls
face it all bright, grim....

And the sequence ends appropriately with the God who reinforces the
Crown and its agents:

> till the roof's groaning and plausible w' the words of a god
>
> shaking and tramping, eager t' its guillotine, I'll keep you.

One of the changes in the republished text of "War with Windsor" adds
to the story of how Johnny Prez was imprisoned in Pentonville, and the
poet's entrance into vulnerability:

> for a bit I saw something so different from non-stop black streeting, in
> the-snow for like lemon-awning and the bright sounds I heard I set off
> away from everyone to start all new when I was charged for carrying a
> pencil-knife do was remanded to Brixton and told this is what the govt
> thinks about *writers* so I wore my colours when they sent me back to
> court.

So the poet is brought, as we all may well be at any time, into the law's
militancy—and the appendix's documentation is extended to include a
fuller indictment of the Crown's powers under law—"the contract
between god, king and people". This contract is "actionable in its
breach" but there is "no fixed procedure" (Griffiths cites his references),
which leaves the statute law "subject to political reinterpretation"—that
is, prisoners injured in police custody, imprisonment without trial in
Northern Ireland, the death of a prisoner in Dover borstal refused investigation, solitary confinement for a *remand* prisoner, disobedience, and
Colchester military prisoners forced to "slaughter animal-pigs w/
wooden hammers as a punishment". Elected democracy is hypocrisy;
resort must be made to Lockean principles of revolt:

> A world of this sort hardly needs an elected (in law, monarchical) govern-
> ment to conduct it. Perhaps chaos is all govt can give you (all power of
> coercion a twisting round to kill as a magic to fend array or exaggerate
> the actor's own human death-likeness.)
>   So it is open to each (as each is reckoned in common law to be bound
> by fealty) unless that good govt promised is found, to withdraw his fealty
> from monarch and law with good cause.

This is immediately followed by a translation of a Romany's song in
which a gipsy protests against being drafted for a soldier.

CUM PERMISSU (1973) commemorates "one year's free residence"—i.e. squatting—with a translation of a Welsh battle poem by Taliesin, and a text in an invented language,[1] spelled partly phonetically, as a challenge to standardisations. *Eight Poems Against the Bond and Cement of Civil Society* (1975) begins with a text whose first line says "And the compass/idea/ being/city/interim" and ends with "And the guy's buckle under his navel/Glared into/the edge of my eyes". Between lies a set of units on frame/ kaleidoscope, gods, "the fitness of things" challenged, uneasy relationships in which a game of dominances is played out. One poem is a condensed paraphrase of "the" crucifixion scene, again a set of units in a strongly paratactical structure which takes up common syntax and shakes it out into possibilities. These eight poems show Griffiths' risking actions clearly replacing imposed conventions, the city of words, with invention, a new code of terms: "And held models of the Earth made from brown glass/And smashed them, for sunbursts." "Conan Sets a Drift-Wood Man on George Wightman" opposes the comix hero against a minor but active figure in the Establishment campaign to destroy the National Poetry Centre once it had at last entered the Twentieth Century, and there are poems on "the unsettling of the status events" and on the current plague of police riots, Justice Melford Stevens, internment, and so on, stemming from *A Journal of the Plague Year*.

These early 1970 poems developed Griffiths' acute and detailed sense of the precise points at which social pressure is exerted against the individual, and an ability to discover a disruptive poetics to embody the scene. It became clear that beyond this site the metamorphoses of energy, and the nature of truths revealed oppressively within what all authority calls fact and which manifests those transformations. His radical reassemblage of syntax and invention of formal procedures began what is now one of the most striking of recent British poetic ventures. The basis is the poet's necessity to act on a language and its forms which has deteriorated through boss usages.

One of the major works for 1978, *The First Three Novellas of the Second Row*, indicates in text and instructions for reading, Griffiths' developing concern for techniques of performance, which has also drawn him towards soundtext performances with other poets, notably with Bob Cobbing. Voices speak here within improvisatory methods, and the notations of the text are scores for performance (the musical analogies

---

[1]   The facing text is in fact in Old Welsh [Ed.].

explicit in some of the titles—barcarolle, hymn). The virtuosity of the structures requires particular performance skills for proper fulfilment, a demand which would of course infuriate the bland readership of the Davie/Arts Council state poets. "Novella One", structured like a triptych altar-piece, opens with "Priapics", invocations to the god of procreation, gardens and vineyards, the god of seasons and change, and the goddess of fruitfulness, the turning point of fruitfulness and "dead wood", in an urban lyric sited in parks, recalling orchards and gardens, decay and reconstruction. "The Garden of Earthly Delights" consists of images in metamorphic conditions, like those in Bosch, as the title infers. The grotesque enters nature—a recurrent Griffiths theme: the unnatural and natural formations of energy, the voluntary and involuntary conversions of energy into form, including those of justice and poetry, children in the guardianship of responsible or irresponsible adults:

> Great sunlike unsober field of
> milk-shadows, men and war-walls
> unsteadied and
> all panning one way
> eroded, silent, wry-tacking, servantile,
> leading the child like a loop-serpent
> to the sea-point and spray
> key-traced, corneted and opaque, mild blue /
> blind yellow
> moving and not making, moving

The "Barcarolle" introduces Griffiths' usual enemy:

> the lord that looks along
> all the levels of the oceans
> eats the workforce
> happy as rails

Nature, statues, masks, buildings and ruins, the main apparatus of this section, come together in "Between Passage", texts for three voices voicing dominances—a huge domed head, a desert impersonality, the transposition of the poet to a gazing stone head. "A Hymn to the boy Jesus and his sister Ayesha" is a challenge to death—"skeletal horsemen, crown on bone", military scorched earth, "encaged fathers", a tarred badger. Jesus moves with the Angels—and not in the extreme sense of *Scorpio Rising*:

> If you know laces and zip, you cld see life a laugh of money / work.
> Three youths set out to challenge death, they come to an area of temples
> slewed over and choked galleries.

The theme, again, is power—apes of the sun, "the sunworx the point of repractice. // The kingdom of protection", skies of varied clouds forming a language density as varied, dominant and flimsy as any other over-all system, and the explosive prisoner as image of breaking bounds, and being bounded (the Whitechapel site returns here). The summary is Griffiths at his best:

> the cold roll of the river
> the judged spark of cold stony flesh
> the solemn spinkle of bells toward a sun
> vast dimensions
> pinewoods & pure roadways choose on,
> don't check you

Parts one and two of "Novella Two" use parts of letters from expeditionary soldiers in conquering armies in El Dorado to their women at home—treasure they will be deprived of, armour, blood, gold, the Prince—plus a set of letters from Wormwood Scrubs. Part three takes up contemporary exploitation as robbing the giant or dragon's hoard; property is theft is the substance; the basis is *Beowulf*. In part four a pastoral family is the primal horde coming across gold (the basis is the Tutankhamen tomb robbery), and part five gives the ocean as treasure chest of chemicals and ores for exploitation. In "Novella Three" brief units are connected in tracks for performance—that is, improvisation plus directions: the gist is a take on sections one and two in terms of control, authority, boundary crossing and escape, including a rescue from drowning, possibly a suicide, treated by police authority with characteristic suspicion. The tracks increase in complexity.

By the time this work was issued, it had become clear that Griffiths might suffer from a limited if important range of materials, that his inventive forms were staving off a certain repetition of obsessions. But *A Preliminary Account of Nordrhein-Westfalen Etc.* (1978) is a step away, a delightfully conceived book of designs and texts recording an experience of a German place as a recognition of "Germany" as culturally received: Köln, Saarbrücken, Paderborn, Wagner's *Ring*, elements of teutonic power and vulgarity at the service of hierarchy; old scripts, biological textbook sketches (of *V. Germanica*, etc), sardonic reflections on the use of *Gastarbeiter*, "a German syllabary" with amusing lexicographical transpositions (streetghost—argumentativeness; seawoof—jetsam; retchfussy—furry-toed), the ingredients of a herbal remedy surrounded by fragments of music on staves (a polka), "Kinderscenen"—a gently witty interfacing of German directions for music performance with pastoral and romantic scenes, somewhat in the manner of Schumann (a number of his tempo and mood directions are quoted), a trap for anarchists, a brief scheme of language reform, West Berlin—"as an empire holds, causes of cancer around me", East Berlin—"suddenly, he was stranded in a universe he could not fathom. Without warning, he became a strange fowl in an even stranger land"—and so on. The book is an exercise in critical orientation, detached but still a way of observing where the predatory and hierarchical impinge on the vulnerable self: the poet as foreign labourer in the full sense which Griffiths' poetry continuously demonstrates.

Formal virtuosity is developed again in *For Rediffusion* (1978), with the primary function of enabling the passionate, critical voice to detach from mediocritising society (and its poetic Establishment), summarised during the third of the "Texts for translation into Icelandic":

POWER = IDEAS + UNDERSKIN + ENERGY + COMPLETED TIME −
COMPLETED TIME
DEATH = UNDERSKIN − ENERGY
UNDERSKIN − DEATH + ENERGY
ENERGY = UNDERSKIN − DEATH

and during "Text for Referral into French: Chaim Soutine":

Frenzy, pulse, immediacy; tactile closeness, as the hot new blood of a goat, red with shining, the very light, the very brightness, the fire by day and night also a reddish and blackish redness. Inedible blood of Passover; red of gladioli.

Black—combining especially to strengthen green, to strengthen red, gains an engulfing potential. Later subordinated (merged?) to blue-green.
As earth, all black, but all virtues, the savour of them that live wisely here on earth or the glosses of Moses say it betokens the holy men of this world.

These poems join others in the book to manifest Griffiths' landscape of unity upon which God and his police intrude with spurious eternity and authority, the liquor of Nelson's pickled body drunk "seriously, as a marriage", and examples of contemporary injustice. The urge to innocence is strongest in this book, acting as moral desire, not stated in rigid terms but enlivening throughout. Nor is it mere nostalgia, or Blake's reliance on children, sheep and sparrows, but the desire for release from oppressive authority which instigates violence and violation and instils guilts. The valves, wiring and aerial of a telly become the structure of defective power. In "Text for translation into Russian", a Catholic church is given as "little evidence for God a nebulous/political figure in North Europe"; colleges are "a dead vivacity"; the Old Testament Paradise in a window is a whip to labour: "In the decline of serfdom, not only bewilderment/ not only criticism"; actual society is the decay of technotronic trades:

> training as TV repairer, panel-beater for crashed cars/real contempt for art/the exaltation of dead art/there ought to be no function now of ornamentation and old detail/that hides or repels or makes unreal/ we are seen as a great and grave country/ swollen by the gigantic past/rigging its prices by destroying food/and needing a lot of entertainment.

The old police story—a man so injured that he cannot speak in court is "accused of assaulting a policeman"—is followed by a note against the monarchic state's injustice and hypocrisy: "There is no constitution and therefore a citizen has no rights in law": the second and third "Texts for translation into Russian" provide extended documentation. "Journeys" is a triple-columned text of magic and legendary islands, the paradigm of enclosures, malignly attractive paradises where energy is present as controls: "compulsive laughter and compulsive weeping, places where you must run round and round like in squared walks under the sky, and all the varying taboos of theft—behaviour and travel—caution ...traps that await the dead as much as the living". "Self-preservation" is therefore the only realistic need in a false paradise garden of codes, litter and prisons: the monarchical injustice state.

Transactional Poems (1980/1) is printed on a single large sheet—an indication of the impossibility of good contemporary poetry being published by capitalist presses and the sheer expense of self-publishing for a poet with scanty funds. In "The Influence of Swedenborg on Training", a court-martialled soldier is in Colchester prison—"another nick inside the nick / . . . complete isolation / . . . that's for people that's really uncontrollable"—is placed in parallel with "Divine punishment" in a God-controlled world—the systems interlock; angels are government administrators : there is "the strictest order in heavenly societies / . . . it could be called maximum / . . . universality and stability"—"in the afterlife / . . . useful service is the ground / . . . of heavenly happiness / . . . those who are unwilling are / . . . compelled / . . . to labour / . . . without regular procession / . . . of hours days / . . . and years or bodily progression"—"so the Lord turns all / . . . punishment / . . . to good use / . . . & by degrees the man is elevated". Human life becomes "personnel"; the USA cannot be distinguished from Prussia—"marching and jumping / like newsprint / and a system of mirrors / seriously tilting state to state /chucking up flags and catching / piloting is the word / and the song!"

The Ideal Home Exhibition shows the imperial Roman influence on apparent democracy—the laid-out totality, "the equivalent of kit-form" (ready for kit-inspection), and "the whole show could be readily over-looked from a special balcony" (which refers back to prisons and to Roman gladiatorial arenas). "The Influence of Corrective Environments" and recycling as training leads to "Jehovah Mimicks Victoria": "that there be no complaining in our streets / / The law of the Lord is perfect / the statutes of the Lord are right". No other poet has so completely dramatised the state of Britain in the 1980s.

His latest work is *The Nine Herbs Charm* (1981), part of "an Anglo-Saxon manuscript on medical matters", written down c.1000 AD, a text whose origins predate Christendom, now edited and translated into verse units. Griffiths' note reports the Anglo-Saxon concept of disease—"the shell of the body was penetrated"—and cure—"to make contact with, control and dislodge whatever evil influence has stationed itself within the body". Poetry in such a context is an analysis towards a therapeutic state, without relinquishing the right to be complex: "Like many another magic ritual, it is made as difficult to enact as it can be made". The verses are "designed to be broadcast and intensify the power of the herbs". The homeostatic action is usually to be found located in the writings of this gentle and scholarly man who writes within the heavy energy controls of his society. His language is broken, shifted and reshaped as a means to prevent the diseased and aggressive, the system-atically entropic, from becoming increasingly destructive. His work is placed at the disposal of no ideology; it is the farthest removed as possi-ble from propaganda. *A Note on Democracy* (1979) is his traditionally anar-chist description of things as they are, the prose core of a body of poetry acutely aware of poisoned power, clear evil, and the legalistic nature of the hostile environment. The variety of his texts testifies to his determi-nation to be generative. The Tarot he devised "to replace the inflexible sets at present hawked out in the name of cult and occult, to encourage you in preference to make a set for your own," has one guide: "If in doubt, prefer your own interpretation". *A Note on Democracy* is a protest against any government that takes itself as fixed fact: "A fact (like a species) is not immutable; its selection and directional presentation is highly individual". As Arendt writes in *The Origin of Totalitarianism* "all ideologies contain totalitarian elements" because they seek "to make the world consistent, to prove that (their) supersense has been right". In Griffiths' text the electorate is "simplified" into institutional order through an archaic system of mythical values: "While technology has proceeded from flint to atomic and micro, the system of government (not its bureaucracy, but its basic decision-making power-processes) is fundamentally unaltered since 1,000 or 10,000 BC. Prisons and rewards are part of state corruption by coercion; the system of modern living has become also a state of unappeasable panic," and within that hysteria the individual democrat can achieve nothing, unlike "the revolutionary (who) stands a fair chance of ending up a victim of justifiable homicide." Crime is therefore "any action by which someone in power causes injury to someone under his control; reciprocally, no action by anyone against a 'superior' in the system can ever be a crime." The utopian condition would be "a constant machinery to prevent the reemergence of status. The counter-force and the counter-emotion of fraternity". In *Transactional Poems* the "Roman tradition" continues the "border and classification of all experience within rigorous, if artificial, schemes". Their "Celtic or barbarian attitude", on the contrary, is "humanity… viewed from a personal viewpoint (to which) the abstract concept of the state (is) irrelevant". Monarchy is simply the obvious sign of the Oedipal state and its "absurd charade", without "serious debate". Secret action is the rule. Human beings "tease and harrow" others. Democracy is a "non-word" since "no govt system can be equated with the people it also governs".

This is the anarchist tradition of Blake, Godwin, Shelley, forward in our own time to Paul Goodman—a long tradition in opposition to the transformation of people into soldiers, prisoners and personnel. This is Griffiths' field of action in poetry and politics, the bases for the set of four "praise songs" of 1977, which remain the most useful short introduction to his skills (*Poetry Review* Vol.67 Nos.1 & 2, 1977, and not reprinted together in book form). "The Praise Song of Judge John Lyle" shows the judge confiscating his victim's "pride and joy, his two nickel-plated revolvers with maplewood handles", but then gloating over their being dumped in Lake Michigan: "there is no other way to deal with a certain class of criminal…." Melford Stevenson likewise appears as a judge enacting pique and revenge beneath his wig. Sir George Everest, a pathetic Home Office official, parodies the self-defensive, prevaricating language of power under enquiry—"I have not a copy with me", "not personally cognizant", "in some cases it might be desirable", "usually he does but sometimes he does not"—and fused in his character is George Everest, the India surveyor. "The Praise Song of William IV" begins with a mockery of self-substantiating authority:

> It was William, who set and instructed them as cast-iron robots, the effigies of himself
> and his brother and father in their
> special temple at Kew....

Bill Griffiths' ten years of texts, mostly self-published, represent an exemplary enterprise which increasingly becomes an essential rhetoric against that British system of decayed assumptions—in both literature and law—which has brought the country to its present state of deterioration. Griffiths' poetry analyses chaos with a clear head. As Whitman once wrote:

> Here the theme is creative and has vista. Here comes one among the well-beloved stonecutters and plans with decision and science and sees the solid and beautiful forms of the future where there are now no solid forms.

The Secret Commonwealth*
CLIVE BUSH

Griffiths has the whole range of sound and rhythm. His pace is *moderato* but it is a *moderato* tense with its own fragility. It is a deliberate wry speech with a hint of mockery in it. But it is a mockery without malice and conceals a slowness which paces meaning and sound as a Zen master archer draws the bow. There is a visionary light in the voice which dazzles as it did for Samuel Palmer in a strong encounter with the world. The world itself is viewed dispassionately, which only highlights more the things which threaten it. There is an old passion here: the passion for independent vision, deep learning, the slow uncovering of the unexpected, the courage of range and inventiveness in a world which against Blakean single vision, is declared radically multiple in all its perspectives whether artistic, social or political.

In performance the powerful, slightly hunched body seems to need those famous heavy boots to remain rooted to the ground. An effort to be gentle and wondering tenses every syllable, image and line. There is a melancholy also in the sound, not the ego-flattering melancholy of the authoritarian, but a melancholy which, moving from wit to wistfulness, touches with a staggering virtuosity of rhythm, phrase and image the wastefulness and brutality which has followed the death of the nineteenth and twentieth centuries' democratic ambitions. It is the gut sadness of the powerful revolutionary emotion of shame accompanied by a music in the line which has been hardly equalled by any other English poet in modern times.

* pp. 291–303 From ch.3 ('*Dance hymns on a semi-stable planet*' : Bill Griffiths'), pp. 211–303 in *Out of Dissent: a study of five contemporary British poets* (London: Talus, 1997).

[24]

One of his latest works is *The Secret Commonwealth* (1994) which he introduces thus:

> *The Secret Commonwealth* is the title of a book by Robert Kirk, published in the late C17. Superficially this is a silly work, placing elves and fairies at a semi-corporeal level between angels and humans. But then if we did not swallow monstrous impositions and reject an equal number of clear human facts, would we be able to participate in the social reality of the 1990s?[1]

The world of the imagination puts the facts in brackets. And that "superficially...silly" has to be carefully unpacked. For Robert Kirk's work has a genesis and history which makes it peculiarly amenable to that combination of mysticism and practical anarchism that characterises Griffiths's own work. The work exists in manuscript, the first extant version is rare and dates from 1815, and an important edition which drew attention to the work for a later generation was edited by the great Victorian folklorist Andrew Lang in 1893, at a time when in Lang's words, "it appeared to give a generation that seems to have lost faith, both in the the Pentateuch and the Apocalypse, something that may be worthy of belief."[2]

Given Griffiths's interests, it is not difficult to see what attracted him to this work, with its multiple chronological levels of real and implied chronology within a multiple reading experience of late seventeenth-century prose, of a radical use of folk-lore and myth exploited by Romantic writers, particularly Scott. There are also its Celtic and Border materials, its late Victorian reception in the mindbody debates and in the emergent disciplines of anthropology and psychology, linking it with Griffiths's own interests in Darwin and to his own "histories" of the solar system and of the soul.

A word on Lang himself will help connect these diverse matters more closely. He was notorious among his great folklore contemporaries: "his fecundity and wit were the despair of his contemporaries, who writhed at his thrust in morning leaders, weekly and monthly reviews and

---

[1] Bill Griffiths, *The Secret Commonwealth* (London: Oasis Books, 1994), p.3. Further references to this work follow in the text.

[2] Robert Kirk, *The Secret Commonwealth of Elves, Fauns and Fairies*, commentary by Andrew Lang, introd. R.B. Cunningham Graham (1691; rpt. from 1893 ed.; Stirling: Eneas Mackay, 1933), p.12. Further references to this work follow in the text.

columns...."[3] Profoundly influenced by E.B. Tylor at Balliol College, Oxford, he devoted himself to an anthropology of folklore mainly turning his wrath on the celebrated Max Muller, particularly against the latter's excessive universalising explanations for myth in solar cosmology. His great achievement was to enlarge "the concept of folklore from Tylor's restricted sense of European peasant traditions to the oral inheritance of all races."[4] In the 1880s his work curiously parallels and predates that of William James in its attention to "psychic lore," and he became president of the Society for Psychic Research in 1911.

In his introduction to Kirk, Lang praised the minister for defending folk materials against the charge of witchcraft: "Mr Kirk of Aberfoyle, living among the Celtic people, treats the land of faery as a mere fact in nature, a world with its own laws, which he investigates without fear of the Accuser of the Brethren... he shows nothing of the usual persecuting disposition." (p.23) Lang points out the rich ad hoc hypotheses Kirk produced in his defenses, from Platonic doppelgängers to explain ghosts as second selves, to quotations from the American Increase Mather's *An Essay for the Rewarding of Illustrious Providences* (Boston, 1684) as evidences of poltergeists, and laments that M. Charcot and M. Richet do not help much in the "matter of veridical second sight." (p.74)

In the spirit of Kirk, Lang took seriously the social narratives. Kirk as a fairly orthodox Calvinist generously recorded an alternative metaphysics to that of Christian eschatology, the faerie believe "that nothing perisheth, but (as the Sun and the Year) everything goes into a circle... that everything in the Creation moves... to the utmost minutest Corpuscle that's capable to a Receptacle of Life."[4]

In many instances, it becomes clear that Kirk reads the Bible for its magic. Indeed his charm lies in his sympathy and modesty. On the key issue of second sight (visionary /hallucinatory seeing)—Kirk is not sure which—he says:

> These are matters of Fact, which I assure you they are truly related. But these, and all others that occurred to me, by Information or otherwise, could never lead me into a remote Conjecture of the Cause of so extraordinary a Phaenomenon. Whether it be Quality in the Eyes of some People into these Pairts, concerning with a Quality in the Air also; whether such Species be everywhere, tho not seen by the Want of Eyes so qualified, or

---

[3] Dorson, *The British Folklorists*, (Chicago: University of Chicago Press, 1968), p. 6.

[4] *ibid.*, p.212.

from whatever other Cause, I must leave to the Inquiry of clearer Judgements than mine. (p.98)

Noting that women do not have it much and that those who emigrate to America tend to lose it, Kirk concludes that "this Sight is not criminal, since a Man can come by it unawares, and without his consent; but it is certaine he sies more fatall and fearfull things than he do gladsome" (p.99).

What Griffiths takes from his reading of Kirk is further sympathy for people without official language, a sympathy for their untold tales, a dehierarchising of orthodox explanation for anything which relies on the authority of absolute power, a reinforcement of the claims of poetic vision over the banalities of second-rate science, a promotion of the same kind of imaginative choice before the necessities of the men of profit that he put forward in *A Century of Self Service? (1995)*, and an acceptance of a kind of Keatsian negative capability in order to find a space for freedom. Griffiths's *The Secret Commonwealth* asserts that all these things are connected.

The poem begins. Is it like a child's ramble, a walk along the coastal path at Seaham, or is it the beginning of a denied epic, a dangerous permitted path among the caprices of the gods, or a journey to some visionary world of "second sight" in which the poet sees the real among the fantastic representations of psychopathologies of everyday life? The afternoon stroll suggests lineage with Coleridge's conversation poems, but the structure is an occasionally interrupted monologue serving a concentrated attention to details of a visionary landscape. In a favourite Old English double strong beat, and double noun word-building, it begins:

Well, we quitt'
the sand-blade shore
up cliffs (coast)
there like a ghost-map the marls slide
amazing some of us
(see our plant-blue eyes).
There are whinny-bushes
'n' a struggle for sandwiches
'n' bare gaps
'n' a g'eat round of spoil
(floods 'n' skids, grab 'n' rubble). (p. 5)

Thus the poem sets out by coming in via a map of the unseen. The ease of effort at climbing is paramount and *marl* (a generic poetic word for earth) is a clay mixed with carbonate of lime used as fertiliser.[5] It is also cognate with French "marner" which means to rise beyond the level of the tide. So there is a sense of incoming here, or beginnings, as well as a sense of the history of the earth in continual movement and as an object of wonder: that is for those with eyes to see. The "whinny-bushes" (gorse) suggest that intense aliveness, sound and movement characteristic of the vegetable as well as the animal kingdoms. The semi-allegorical interpretation invited by the poem's start in medias res suggests a larger and omnipresent struggle for subsistence (not existence) and the place of will and decision inside it. The dene in the cliff walk is then offered as both "glacial gash" and "pretty thing" opening up a convergence of times, youth and age, inside an anxiously subverted romantic prospect. And the imagined child's game has sinister overtones:

> for I got edgy in the low altitude—
> imagine them—the foot-high tribe of indians
> wi' lurky ambush
> rose-bows/ash-arrows/trip-vines.
> And
> Trevor pointed a dog-slide down:
> That's where they pushed me."
> *A phantastic imitatione of the actiones.* (p. 5)

The child's world and the world of Kirk's analogously "indian" little folk converge to suggest danger of a psychological or even moral kind: the fear of the dog-slide, not one of the many extant dog-combinations but one richly suggestive of all those expressions analogous with going to the dogs. But it also suggests, as well as the precariously domestic wild, the mechanical tool (dog) for gripping, for precisely not sliding, hence intensifying the threat. Kirk's line (italicised) by decontextualistion also suggests Aristotle's classic definition of tragedy with the addition of phantastic to its invocations of pity and fear.[6]

---

[5] Griffiths note to author, 31 July, 1995: "The sub-strata here are limestones."

[6] "A tragedy, then, is the imitation of an action that is serious and also as having magnitude, complete in itself; in language with pleasurable accessories, each kind brought in separately in the parts of the work; in a dramatic, not in a narrative form; with incidents arousing pity and fear, wherewith to accomplish its catharsis of such emotions." *Aristotle on the Art of Poetry*, trans. Ingram Bywater (Oxford: Clarendon Press, 1920), p.35.

The name of Aristotle suggests the function of classification and helps read the next lines:

A hierarchy of facts containing
Things of congealed air,
of an alien expression
a missing matrix-folder. (p. 5)

Unpacking the Aristotelian classificatory logic of poetry and nature, with its separation of nature and the self, is one of the subtexts of the poem and Griffiths is clear about the consequences of this philosophy's alliance with the "big-people." What Griffiths challenges here is what Roger Sperry called the "natural cosmos of science," a view which was also challenged by the late Paul Feyerabend defending "the mythical, intuitive, mystical or otherworldly frames of reference," which fall outside the hegemonic description of Western humanities and scientific orthodoxy.[7] The nightmare could be read in many ways. It is the closed world of science-fiction movies with their metallic atria and control-desk lounges operated by semi-robotic monsters who explore, in narra-tives of uncomplex, and largely pietistic ethics, hostile and uninhabit-able spaces:

Somewhere over the spine-science seafloor
patrol
dead holly-nail hand
seeded with obliteration
is a war
and the life-engine changes
opposing/colluding/gathering
and the main-aim self-maximization
limpet metallic giants show. (p. 6)

Griffiths links the religious iconography ("dead holly-nail hand"), and makes the implied Christ/mass analogous with the practices of positivist scientism, which is the dominating ideology of those vast numbers of western experts who think they have none. "Opposing/colluding/gath-ering" is the managerial discourse of those who are quick enough to denounce demagoguery or "witchcraft": "Food is fury/and dreams are demons" (p.6).

Against this there is a fairytale dream of the "golden boy and garnet girl" who sleep "ear to ear/in the mouse hole/in the plow share" as the

7   Paul Feyerabend, *Farewell to Reason* (London: Verso, 1987), p.26.

poem swings violently between technological nightmare and nursery rhyme fantasy. The place of the human subject is clear for "as strange misbehaviours/we move about." (p.6) Struggling to find the words, Griffiths tries the Michael McClure solution of visionary unity in which romantically the scientific-technological view of the world becomes without mediation a poetically unified and visionary cosmos:

Strange lights, mauve, warm,
the ginger halogen
and the strident shiny river
circling, zodiacal/pins of
the place of flesh-face
run/mammal-grass (p. 6)

Attractive though it is, the English poet demurs. The Zodiac animal-star cosmos may just be too easy an animation of the world for our time. The new age is not so simple. In a dramatic moment of political and eschatological reflection Griffiths asserts:

Am I a liar then?
Why, the whole forest (tube-limb /leaf/aperts/
    glowy-globe /patter & rattle/white face/its tin
    slopes)
is thick with reminders
like Who is Who
and how Someone is Someone
and What Nothing Is.

Me and my lost litter,
My words. (p. 7)

"Litter" is variously defined as equipment for carrying by men or animals (often for the wounded as a stretcher), fragments, discarded scraps, mess, and offspring. His "words" are all of these, his place of rest and comfort, his refuge from wounding, his fragments shored against lying unities, his own children. As the science-fiction nightmare closes in, "the grotesque multipede/rearin' over the capsule and ship/as in the Venusian jungle," (the trampling of the multitude—all those equal "feet" indistinct, undifferentiated, the poet's nightmare, allied to untrammelled desire), the poet needs at least Kirk's seers with second sight:

And there becomes
The unusual universe
apparent to a second sight

having their visive faculties entyre
seem to see
the atomes in the air, alternative people
their apparell and speech is like that of the people and countrey
but having no set teaching
they throw great stones, pieces of Earth, and wood at the inhabitants. (p. 7)

Griffiths is not creating some cosy New Age alternative vision here, but using a critical utopian dream of a different world which claims choice and freedom against the reduction of the human body to a nexus of scientifically described forces, genetic chains:

Being exampled to be free to decide to do
equals fizzy brew. (p. 8)

For this madness is analogous with the madness of the lost discourses and peoples of Kirk's folk world under British threat and Calvinist orthodoxy. The "mad," the "drunk," the insane are caught in the grip of other image makers, for occupational therapy and as categories of value-laden Latin nomenclature:

allow
someone
who sees you as mirror-makers

we are painted
night-lady-scented narcissus
and heliophiliac daisy (p. 9)

The search for certainty is there in the use of alien language to fix category: a priori idea as the metaphysic which guarantees certainty. Alternative worlds are easily dealt with. But the strange language of the folk who "talk turk/orders are given in something gothic" do not quite mirror the action of the rulers in reverse. The excluded are defined as such to be "stubborn":

to be broken by medical ethical action
and you end up agreeing
new sets of prejudices
and new cancerous stances (p. 9)

Griffiths knows that we are complete in any case and wandering into foreign words and keys is not a mark of dislocation. Here is one of the finest passages of the poem:

Sweetly we swirl and sleep,
complete
and there is schumannesque sandy security
in the fremd keys we wander into—
Ut
Fa
Bis
Moll
There are tins in the store
and we curl and kip

As tho the rest
(call it Baphomet or Daniel)
the bringer of benevolence
the tacit kings and queens of cards

Why, the exclusion of the data,
the embryo of fact-swatch
alone half-a-world

...

A tree	a road	a pail of water
a cloud	a cocoon	a bead of amber
a protein	a process	a performance (pp. 9–10)

Performance, music in motion is the "key," for the names of keys are
only shifts within movement of a continuous modulation. The shifting
sands are not the opposite of some Christian rock, but a condition in
which we move. In Griffiths's world of visionary wonder nothing is a
priori foreign, nothing strange ("fremd") unless it be the strangeness of
wonder. The alliteration of "swirl and sleep" and "curl and kip" at opposite ends of the sound register are casts at common experience, remind-
ing one of Blake's figures in motion, and the entire sound pattern and
disruption/flow of the opening section is virtuosic. They also seem
amenable to an interpretation in terms of Blakean contraries. Are "curl
and kip" (with variable historical meanings of disease and whore house)
indicators of the life process hermetically sealed, as indicated by "tins in
store", and is any prophet, true or false, a false key in the whole game
which they dominate: power without modulation?

The poet attacks the world of atomism, and Blakean malignity of
reasoning and comparing. Swatch (and its recent Swiss-originated
brand-name use to designate cheap watches as fashion accessories
cannot be ignored) means a specimen or example and also a line of

water between a sandbank and a shore. The key conceptions indicted in "fact-swatch" are to do with the deep nature of specimen (the problem of metonymy), problems of boundary and shifting edges within thinking itself.

In linguistic terms Griffiths draws our attention to states of affairs not guaranteed necessarily by the common-sense structure of the sentence, but of the implied sentence, paradoxically endlessly evasive within an apparent strategy of strict adherence to rule. Nor is the word for Griffiths a lexical entity but a "semantic kernel", in Ricoeur's term, which gives more than half a hint for getting at the meaning of "embryo of fact-swatch."[8] It also seems to echo William Carlos Williams's "(the multiple seed, packed tight with detail, soured,/is lost in the flux and the mind,/ distracted, floats off in the same scum)" as an example of what you do with the facts, who defines them and on what terms within the systematics of common potential.[9] Example must be paradoxically prospective not retrospective. That "half a world" is positive and negative at the same time: it is what is available if we don't play the games of sentence in every sense (legal, verbal), but it is also what is denied by the cruelty of partial vision, the world divided and ruled in the bureaucratic social games of authority in the late twentieth century.

The connectedness of visionary appearance is posited against the atomistically divided world of authoritarian power. The poet breaks to rediffuse a different world within the givenness of system itself. Griffiths reclaims the malignant words for his myriad systems:

limbs and flowers
a new thing and a list
(exhaustive/magical/totalled)
a corporation by analysis (p. 10)

It almost seems like a commentary on Williams's "by multiplication a reduction to one; daring; a fall; the clouds resolved into a sandy sluice".[10] But Griffiths's sandy security is here ''Schumannesque'' and the focus on creative agency is less metaphysical than the American poet's fractured correspondences.

The vision is terrifying, however, as the persistent new life of the earth itself becomes irretrievably damaged. Good or bad attempts at

---

[8]   Ricoeur, *The Rule of Metaphor* (London: Routledge, 1986), p. 129.

[9]   William Carlos Williams, *Paterson*, (New York, New Directions, 1963), p. 2.

[10]   *ibid.*, p. 4

"exhaustiveness" are placed against the claims of biological exhaustion. Griffiths, in a most moving sequence, outlines the terror of being without agency, that despair of the Darwinian revolution:

> Am the
> frail, trialous body
>
> depleted,
> beat that was my first beat,
> out of the heart,
> staring air.
>
> But the old
> that wears way
> is heart-beat
> a flat something, a rate
> of exhaustion at the multiple
>
> for the dying yards
> are stone-clear
> grass-trim-plot
> heads grow
>
> Sips ripples round
> on swirls
> on leaf-deflected faces
> ink
> trumpet-jump-up/trumpet jump-down (pp. 10–11)

How to distinguish the breath and heart of the poet from that "economics" of the knowledge of the body's death itself: its flat rate, its equal terms, its pseudo-democracy of even time and "cost"? These are the issues that Griffiths addresses in these last pages as he comes forward with every mood from despair to humour to wonder. The "earth-fry" persist, however, but not from the point of view of the wreckers. They are singulars not plural, a potential of the multiple, not a specimen within the statistical holocaust of a greenhouse effect.

And with extraordinary density the last pages bring the themes into yet ever more complex dispositions, but with a "key theme" of the lightness of air, of breath, of music up and down, as if agency itself floats in how we breathe and speak. It is a magic world in motion gathering the commonplace into a particular glory:

> and
> the fusion

the sliding 'side dirt-orange
the god
'n' kid chuntering round the room
wi' horns bubbling

The rose of sun arising
sparkles on the genitals of stone
of mountains moving

are scents.
nights.
nox. (p. 12)

Everything is animated. The sacred is embodied in the child, the young, and celebratory, not the sacrificial being of desire. Horns bubble with drink or sprouting. The movement of the sun is flower because it is rose and arising at the same time, suspending the logic of syntax in a redefinition of time. Like a latter-day Samuel Palmer, Griffiths's vision moves mountains through poetic faith. The aural convergences delicately augment the sense: "are scents" suggests ascent and assent. And the full-stops indicate completeness not termination: the constituents of the potential classificatory Latin name for a flower, broken, re-ordered into the suspension of all foreignness glimpsed between the particular-universal of native "nights" and the general-singular of "nox."

Griffiths's work, therefore, combines a virtuosity of lexical and syntactical play in the service of an always rhythmically lively line. He circumvents that drive to centre which authority mistakes for order in the choice of his materials, which includes a deep knowledge of the actual history of the English language itself. He is a poet with a very strong sense of history, particularly the history of power and its effect on its victims and the dispossessed. Sceptical of all ideologies, religious, scientific and political, his poetry rewrites the history of society and religion and preserves a dynamic tension between a sense of freedom which turns from death and from the malignly-encoded discourses of desire itself, towards an acceptance of the unpredictable ways of the imagination and civic responsibility. Linguistic and musical skills revivify the language, the combination of old English and Romantic/Victorian materials reinvents a living culture in the former, and curbs a sentimentalising nostalgia in the representation of the latter.

But perhaps Griffiths's greatest ability is to combine the severest of ethical judgements without losing a sense of open intellectual, social and historical curiosity. He walks with a kind of grace through this polluted, economically and socially distressed island, which has never faced up to its crimes of empire and whose historically-developed instincts for class privilege and secret power have still only been minimally challenged. His poetry revives a sense of wonder within the wreckage and in so doing reconstructs a new poetry beyond the limits of cynicism and irony. His materials and techniques lie far from fashionable concerns and are the stronger for it. To be sure his work depends on the twentieth century's concern with visual, syntactical and narrative rupture (and the range is from Pound to concrete poetry and improvisatory performance techniques), but these ruptures are redeployed within multiple rhetorical variations derived from a wide range of literary genres, from oral and performance-related traditions, from folklore, and from philosophic and scientific dialogue. In performance the voice itself never fails to address its materials with a true Schubertian moderato, but it is deceptive in its intimacy and nonchalance, for there are worlds at stake in the technical virtuosity of the offer of the poem's pure song.

Bill Griffiths:
A Severe Case of Hypergraphia
PAULA CLAIRE

At Bob Cobbing's Sixty-fifth Birthday Celebration, held upstairs at the *White Swan*, Covent Garden, London, the afternoon of 30 July 1985, Bob, Bill and I performed as *Konkrete Canticle*, the sound poetry group Bob had inaugurated with me plus Michael Chant in 1971 to make a record for the Arts Council of Great Britain Touring Exhibition *Concrete Poetry*.[1] Later, Michael got engrossed in conducting the Scratch Orchestra, so Bob invited Bill to take over from 1977 onwards. In the main, we three improvised together on each other's poems, but Bob had a new work, *Van Gogh: an Annotated List*, a found poem comprising pages of annotations in a catalogue of a Van Gogh exhibition he judged more appropriate for two male voices. Bill had a suitably manic look in his eye—there is something about the intensity in his face which has always reminded me of Van Gogh—I remember I checked he had two ears when I first clapped eyes on him in his panoply of leathers and chains when he walked into Bob's experimental poetry workshop at The Poetry Society (then at 21 Earls Court Square SW5) circa 1971—fair frit I was until he opened his mouth to read and I knew he was only a poet like me and Bob. Anyhow Bill darted about holding up each imaginary painting— whoops! upside down—he straightened it to great applause as Bob dead-pan delivered the cataloguer's sublime verdict, something like 'this is a painting of sunflowers…in it we see a vase containing… sunflowers.' It was a scene of high comedy by two brilliant performers which

[1] organised by the Stedelijk Museum, Amsterdam in November 1970, sponsored by the ACGB on tour to the Walker Art Gallery, Liverpool; Museum of Modern Art, Oxford; City Art Gallery, Belfast.

entertained everyone greatly, so when the following day in a newspaper I spotted an article by 'a leading American neurologist' boasting he had discovered the cause of Van Gogh's 'phenomenal, obsessional output: Geschwind's syndrome,' a disease of the temporal lobe, the main symptom being 'hypergraphia, an endless compulsion to write, draw, paint and produce graphic material,' I declared this gem a found poem and dedicated it to Bob for his birthday. [2]

Konkrete Canticle: three individualists with hypergraphia in common. A fascination with the nature of language in its widest sense, that waggling of the tongue wriggling the stylus expressing all languages, all utterance in its gamut of sounds and rhythms from gutteral to musical, all ways of writing it down—scripts, scribbles, graffiti, making of marks— all texts, all textures, codes, designs and signs: the VERY CORE of Poetry Itself. Scientists were obsessed with getting to the heart of the matter, elementary particles; we sound and visual poets equally obsessed with the **stuff** of words what are they made of. You can't take words for granted. They are living organisms, perpetually permutating, evolving and dissolving in the saliva of the mouthbrain. The crucible for dynamic research on the subject was the range of experimental poetry workshops run by Bob at The Poetry Society from 1969 to 1977. At that period Bob was working both with permutated word patterns and an ever-increasing diversity of visual signals—images from photos and adverts treated through his duplicator; engrossed in exploring the vocal interpretation of fragmented words, the response to a multitude of different fonts and markings. Letterforms merging with blobs were spewed out by his eccentric mimeograph machine on which he produced all the publications of his Little Press, Writers Forum...and we vocalised *everything*. I became hyper-alert to pattern and de/sign. My frequent Tuesday meetings at Bob's flat in Maida Vale, 1970–71 to try out his and my latest poems for various performances together ended up at his weekly evening experimental poetry workshop at The Poetry Society. The leaflet for these workshops, instigated as a result of the Autumn 1969 Poetry Society Conference on contemporary poetry techniques at York University where I first met Bob, announced weekly workshops in 'visual poetry; electronic poetry; poetry and movement; free-formed music and

---

[2] *VAN GOGH : SYMPTOMS* (No 272 in my first annotated catalogue *Declarations Poems 1961–9*, International Concrete Poetry Archive Press No. 30 Oxford 1991). Recorded by *Resoundscore*, Paula Claire: voice, Peter Stacey: saxophone. ICPA Cassette 1: *The Fellowship of the Green Parrot*, 1986.

poetry' which soon became a focus for the vibrant exchange of ideas among a growing number of poets committed to live performance involving the extension of poetic forms; and attracted experimentalists from abroad such as Ana Hatherly (Portugal) and Sean O Huigin (Canada).

Those were extraordinary days at The Poetry Society, shown in the programme of events and the contents of the quarterly *Poetry Review*. The Autumn 1970 magazine contained a section on visual poetry curated by Peter Mayer, including my *Chartres Windows: Winter*, a typewriter text proposed as a blue/red slowly changing neon structure, poem for free improvisation by many voices. The next guest editor was Adrian Henri, with a cover and two pages from *A Humument*, a treated text by Tom Phillips which is now a classic. In Autumn 1971 for four years poet Eric Mottram, later Professor of Contemporary American Literature at King's College, London, took over as Editor and intensified the trend to openness and catholic taste. You need not do more than glance at the covers and flick through the pages of the dozen magazines from Vol 62 No 3, Autumn 1971 to Vol 65 No 4, Autumn 1975—that had as cover my *Cucumber Wilt* × 500, a photomicrograph I perceived as a sound score—to see that a radical change had been wrought. Alongside the traditional linear, narrative poems were pieces pushing the boundaries: a gamut of sound poems, visual poems, poems experimenting with vocabularies... Three poems of Bill's, among his earliest, showing a startling use of words, appeared in Autumn 1972; and a further selection indisputably demonstrating his original talent covered fifteen pages in Vol 65 No 1, 1974. As a climax to the experimental workshops, from 1974 to 1977 Bob organised an annual International Sound Poetry Festival there in that capacious first floor drawing room, with major international exponents alongside the workshop regulars: Sten Hanson (Sweden), Henri Chopin and François Dufrêne (France), bpNichol (Canada), Jackson Mac Low (USA) to name but a few.

It was Bill's regular attendance at these workshops and involvement in publishing work through his Pirate Press both with Bob's Writers Forum and at the newly formed Print Shop of which he was the first manager (1975–6) that made him so conversant with Bob's work and mine, and such a congenial colleague in the group. The way we gelled is evoked in an article I wrote about my improvisations at these workshops:

To the experimental poetry workshop at The Poetry Society on 22 May 1973 I took various stones: jagged flints, pumice, sea-smoothed pebbles, a hunk of granite... and a group of us, including Bob Cobbing, Bill

Griffiths, and Jeremy Adler, responded to the textures, markings and shapes of these concrete objects. These different stones drew out a much wider range of sounds than conventionally-used language: all kinds of fragmented vowels and consonants; cries, gasps, whispers, yells, whistles—in fact all the sounds which unite us with the birds, insects, animals and sea creatures and the elemental sounds of wind and water.[3]

STONETONES was documented by 8 photocollages and published by Writers Forum in 1974; it was performed at the 7th International Sound Poetry Festival.[4]

'The birth of the 'new' *Konkrete Canticle* was at a performance in the great hall of the Akademie der Künste to celebrate the DADA aspects of contemporary sound-poetry as part of the 27th Berlin Festival (18 September 1977).'[5] Our presentation in the Sound Poetry concert included Bob's *Alphabet of Fishes* (1967), comprising Cornish vocabulary and illustrations; *Jade Sound Poems* (1976, 1st performance), vertical lines of unusual fonts; my *Stonetones* 1973/4, vocal improvisation to text-ures on concrete objects; and Bill's *Forming Four Dock Poems* (1974, 1st performance), stark minimalist text set in the landscape of the page. Our performance combined with improvisation on an array of simple musical instruments was videoed by the University of Hanover.

We used to meet at Bob's flat in Maida Vale to rehearse. In those early years we really did rehearse, as far as improvised work can be said to be rehearsed: we made ourselves familiar with each piece by juggling together, exhilarated in the knowledge that every time the piece would be different. As the years went by, however, Bob got increasingly averse to any preplanning: finally he would thrust his latest work, unseen by us, as we went on stage, in order to snatch the very essence of pure utterance it was his dream to express—it explains why I have no detailed performance lists after 1984. We three performed each other's texts but rang the changes with two male voices; or Bill and me; Bob and me; then sometimes singly—I when alone always invited all present to join

---

³ *The Use of the Voice in Sound Poetry*, my article in *EAR Mag*, New York, Fall 1981.

⁴ *The Notation of my Sound Poetry*, *Open Letter*, Spring 1984, Fifth Series No 7, pp 56–74, published by bpNichol, Toronto, Canada.

⁵ *Sound Poetry: A Catalogue for the Eleventh International Sound Poetry Festival*, Toronto, Canada, 14–21 October 1978, editors: Steve McCaffery, and bpNichol, Underwhich Editions, The Coach House Press, Toronto—an invaluable source book: 112 illustrated pages.

in, the essential characteristic of my work since I began performing in 1969. I think the value to the audience was that between us we covered a very large area of experimental work. What I enjoyed, as writer and performer, was the open-mindedness I could rely on in my colleagues. It was taken for granted that whatever material anyone proposed, was utterable: no-one baulked; and this allowed us all to forge ahead with exploring the possibilities of interpretation not only in words and their forms, but in the area I term 'the gestation of language', i.e. signs, marks and text-ures wherever found, challenging meaning to become meaningless, yet finding always fresh significance. What Bill says about words in his *Introduction to Found Texts* in *Pyrofiche 3*: 'their potential as sound, rhythm, and symbol... and as pattern-blocks and semantic codes...laughs at limits' inspired *Konkrete Canticle's* approach to interpretation and improvisation.

In the mid 1970s a mighty storm brewed up at The Poetry Society between those who held traditional ideas about poetry, and the 'invasion' by the experimentalists exemplified by Bob and his workshops and Eric's editorship of the *Poetry Review*. Sufficient to record that a schism occurred, and Bob and everyone interested in extending the forms of poetry left; hereafter for some years Bob's performance base was the London Musicians' Collective in Gloucester Avenue NW1, a very dilapidated building, but with the advantage of a large performance space. There at the International Sound Poetry Festival, Saturday 13 May 1978, we tried out a range of new material. I remember Bill's *Journeys*, a found text, the three columns denoting the three voices reading simultaneously—an ingenious plait of sound, and *History of the Solar System/ Fragments: A History of the Solar System*, a complex found material piece with vocabularies relating to the sun and planets, in a concertina-fold format which made it easy to switch from text to text rapidly when creating a sound collage. This is when I presented *Cabbage Brain,* slicing open a red cabbage with a carving knife to reveal the dense convoluted cryptic patterns within, *Konkrete Canticle* and the audience vocalising with gusto. Aficionados, that crowd.

Bob then organised an A4 flier for *Konkrete Canticle* and distributed it widely. As a result, several performances were booked. We were invited to the International Sound Poetry Festival, Toronto, Canada, Sunday 15 October 1978, at the St Lawrence Centre, organised by bpNichol and Steve McCaffery. Bill wrote to me suggesting poems of his. I have my performance sheet hand-written by Bob, annotated by me with the estimated timings. On the menu was Bob's *Alphabet of Fishes*; I presented three of my *Stonetones* followed by Bill's *SUN-CARD showing sunrises*, a chapbook format Bob published having nabbed hold of my unofficial copy with my handwritten suggested vocal responses using varying speeds of hand-beating on the mouth and chest. The graphic material for interpretation was various rubbings of striations from brass, potent images, each with a nail embedded like a sun disc. Then came the major piece *Ginetic Gingles*, created specially: I had found an eye-catching advert consisting solely of a large cursive capital letter 'G' followed by an 'i' and part of 'n'. I pounced on this and made a poem sculpture *Gingle* by drawing four sets of curving lines on it, photocopying it onto card and cutting out the indicated sections. The resulting tentacle-like paper structure could be mounted 3D on coloured card, hung on string as a mobile or waved about as a hand poem whilst expressing in sound the sweeping lines of the letterforms. Bob and Bill took up the challenge and both made sound poems: Bob's connected with the origins of the word 'gin'—from Geneva—and chants on the ingredients in gin: coriander seeds, angelica root, orris tuber, almonds, lemon peel, liquorice and juniper berries; Bill playing with the permutated patterns of sound in the word. We ran round the aisles of the raked auditorium, sounding the poem texts, waving my hand-poems and tossing many of them high over the audience who grabbed them and waved back, joining in our chants: we had attained our goal: the sheer exhilaration of utterance—drunk on words. Bill's *Long Elephant Song* was next; then two intense poems of mine, *Magma* and *Plutonium*,[6] scorch-mark poems made with a soldering iron onto cartridge paper with the theme of elemental energy. We walked off sounding Bob's chant *MRN MRTN BRMRN*.

During our stay we visited Niagara together, the Canadian Horseshoe Falls side. The ritual of visiting the Horseshoe Falls made an indelible impression on us all: to my puzzlement male and female were compelled right and left, like in a Greek Orthodox church, to robe up in enveloping black mackintosh capes and black wellingtons. The august white-bearded black-shrouded figure of Bob emerged looking like Zoroaster himself. Then we went out to the viewing platform, spectacular, roaring, baptismal indeed; but I preferred standing behind the Falls themselves, where apertures had been cut through the rock, every bone in my body vibrating with the force of the water—that was sound poetry itself! We all created poems about it. *NiagarA* by Bob. *NiagarB* comprised Bill's hand-poem sculptures *The Horseshoe Falls (Niagara)*, rectangular,

---

[6] set of 8: *E.I.E.D?* published by Writers Forum, 1978.

printed inside and outside with word list performance texts and two illustrations. Later, a second version was made in German with two different illustrations for our Münster visit. I produced *NiagarC*,[7] snippets from a book detailing the weird feats people felt compelled to enact on the Falls, usually ending in death, combined with pen sketches of the tumult I had made on site. These we presented at the Lyric Theatre, Münster, during our visit to participate in *Speech Beyond Poetry*, Münster Museum, then West Germany, 19–21 May 1979.

Next was a *Konkrete Canticle* performance at Goldsmiths College, University of London, Tuesday 14 November 1978. We presented a whole evening of pieces, seventeen in all, including all the Toronto material, accompanying our voices with bells, gongs and little drums. It demonstrates the range of styles we encompassed: all present joined me in *Air Luggage Labels*, a found poem advert showing a fistful of airline luggage labels with abbreviated destinations, providing a piquant variety of condensed place names. Bob and Bill had both written chants during the Canada visit; then I invited everyone to join in the 'scores' I handed round of my *Silverbirchmorse*,[8] rubbings of the morse-code-like markings on the bark of silver birch trees in Oxford and Manitoulin Island, Lake Huron where I had performed in a school with Sean O'Huigin, Bill accompanying me on his potato flute. Bob and Bill did *NZ*. Then Bill on his own with *Cock Robin*, the rhyme he had fragmented and rearranged in different sound patterns. The first half ended with Bob's powerful *Sumerian Hymn* with bells and gongs. After the break was more Toronto material, then Bob's fierce non-verbal *Winter Poem* was worked on by the three of us, voices and wide-swung bells. Bill's *ISCHL* followed, a complex verbal piece of found material relating to an epic sea voyage scored for 'three intermittent voices.' My *Nucleus Divides* explored the graphic similarities in the shapes of a dividing cell revealed by powerful microscopes. Bob and I then performed his jazzy *Gail Song*, an intricate set of permutations on the names 'Gail' and 'Bob' we had first recorded on the Arts Council Record and wowed the Dial-A-Poem scheme with in 1972. Next Bill and I combined voices on his *Shunting Poem*; he his *Museum Poem*, a found text 'neon display of cycle of minerals' from the Royal Ontario Museum visit before we all finished off the evening with the

---

7 the Niagara sequences were all published by Writers Forum in 1979.

8 Writers Forum April 1979.

riotous *Ginetic Gingles*. Our confidence in each other allowed us to ring so many changes of voices and instruments in a hectic evening.

Hard on the heels of this was a thereabouts similar programme for Cambridge University Poetry Society, Trinity College, Cambridge, Thursday 16 November 1978. The night was cold: brilliant stars in a clear sky, the moon just past full. Bob had agreed we could present my *SPACE III*, its basic text 'space void dark vast star start startle stab' exploiting the vowels sounds, in up to nine languages showing their Indo-European roots which I had presented with fellow poets along a narrow canal during my Venice Biennale visit two months earlier.[9] When I saw that night sky, I told Bob the setting was perfect: the quad at the end of our indoor session: my colleagues did not demur. So out *Konkrete Canticle* went, faithfully followed by our audience who had joined in earlier in my participation pieces, spreading out round that great quad of Trinity College. I will never forget the arcing sounds of the basic text, embell-ished with French, German, Italian, Croatian, Greek, Turkish, Farsi and Arabic pouring out in mighty sound waves into infinite space. Suddenly the places crawled with bulldogs 'sshhhushhing' furiously. OK: all smiles we made for the lodge at a measured pace, still chanting to the stars as bulldogs yapped at our heels, the voices of the students echoing us on our way.

Another cluster of performances occurred in the middle of 1979. A friend of Bill's, Manfred Sundermann, who attended some of Bob's workshops when staying in London, helped to have us included in the international exhibition *Sprachen Jenseits Dichtung* (Speech Beyond Poetry), Münster Museum, 19 May 1979; with a different performance programme at The Lyric Theatre on 21 May. The large foyer of this modern Museum with an upper level and open stairs to work on was a gratifying space through which to cast our sound webs; we moved around extensively on my *Circuits*[10] which juxtaposed microchip diagrams, the *Book of Kells* illuminated capitals and Middle Eastern carpet designs, all perceived as lines of vocal expression, intensely coloured by the musicians from abAna, Paul Burwell and David Toop, who Bob collaborated with a considerable amount at this period. They also made a vivid contribution to Bob's *Jade Sound Poems*. Bob and Bill

---

9   *Materialisation of Language*—Exhibition: more than eighty female international sound/visual poets; catalogue; allied performance, Old Salt Store, Venice, curator: Mirella Bentivoglio.

10   Writers Forum Chapbook 1979.

were very cooperative in helping me with *BREAD*, I had created specially. We toured the bakeries to purchase superb local breads: craggy white, sunflower and poppy seeded, wholemeal, rye and black to display at the performance including a birdcage Bill found as home for a spiky hedgehog loaf. Our three voice chants were the words for bread, knead, dough, yeast, loaf, the last connected with lord = hlaford: loaf-controller; lady = hlafdige: loaf-giver, in Old Norse, Old English, Old German, Old Frisian and Modern English to appreciate all the ancient linguistic connections. Then everyone present munched the loaves. Bill's *Lament for Charlemagne*, a Latin hymn fragmented into powerful sound clusters expanded dramatically in that space, but how we would have loved to make a recording of it in the ninth-century Charlemagne Chapel we all visited in nearby Paderborn, which has a profound resonant acoustic we tested impromptu.

The impetus we felt in Germany carried us through the Cambridge Poetry Biennale, 10 June 1979. On the same bill as Ginsberg, so a mass of people, a great incentive to go full blast with *YEDOKETAWARO* (Bob), *Circuits* (me), *Number Structure* (Bob), *Four Winds* (Bill), *KWATZ* (Bob), *Elmlament* (me), *Basil Bunting* (Bob), *Jeremy's Constellations* (me), *Moons of Jupiter* (Bill). Bill's two hand-poem paper sculptures *The Four Winds* and *The Moons of Jupiter* (both Writers Forum, 1979) are intriguing items to work from. They have paper folded simply to make four 'wings', so you must rotate the poem to perform it. *The Four Winds* were symbolised by different textures Bill had made with screen printing, whereas *The Moons of Jupiter* had photocopied photos of the surface of the moons of planet Jupiter recently transmitted to earth, cut up into the letters in the names of the moons. They elicited subtle and haunting sounds. Bob's *KWATZ* (1968) was a dramatic piece we all relished, a poem with recognisable sentences(!) describing the discipline undergone by students of Zen: when they think they have finally achieved their spiritual goal "KWATZ!" the Master cries, striking them with a stick to destroy their equilibrium and force them to start at the beginning yet again. *Elmlament*[11] is a set of drawings and rubbings I made of a 'king elm' in Oxford that was suffering from the disease that destroyed over four million elms in England at that time, the title providing the sung refrain. My new piece, *Jeremy's Constellations*, was dedicated to Jeremy Adler because when in Münster he gave me a Golden Delicious apple: he

[11] Four pages published in *RAWZ*, Magazine of visual poetry, Chris Cheek, London, 1977.

saw me scrutinising its skin peppered with tiny black pores and said dourly, "I suppose you will make a poem out of it." I traced all its markings to document it, but in performance I use actual apples, that's what concrete poetry means. So we staccatoed all the marks, then ate the apples, giving the rest out for consumption. We did Bob's tribute, *BasilBunting*, a lyrical eight herb words; eight bird words; ending with the word-play *Bill Jubobe*, based on François Dufrêne's eulogy on Cobbing.

On to Brighton College of Art, for the Brighton Festival event, 21 July 1979. YEDOKETAWARO, *Sea Shanty* (me), *Moons of Jupiter*, *Basil Bunting*, *Sha ma na* (Bob), *Spiderunes* (me), *Four Winds*, *Sumerian Hymn*. It was at this event we had our only serious heckler. This chap started to shout: "NOT PROPER POETRY," unaware that we considered any vocal response a valuable contribution. To show him the marvellous potential in every phrase, we did a quick improvisation on his words—that got him incensed. "GIBBERISH!" We were thrilled with the compliment. The more words he flung at us, the more we permutated their sounds with enthusiasm, not to mock him, but hoping to communicate the sheer joy of utterance. The audience, students mainly, were in paroxysms. Alas, he went out in a huff. It was not until the last work he suddenly appeared again, perhaps thinking he had taken enough lung-fulls of sea air with which to blow us away. Unfortunately for him we had embarked on Bob's great sonorous piece *Sumerian Hymn to the Sacred Mushroom*, a chant of all the words naming the hallucinogen sacred to the shamans of the ancient tradition, a poem Bob was so devoted to I call it his signature tune. Our heckler's diatribe was soon swallowed up in Bob's ferocious startlingly deep growls "sOOOOOOma," my high swoopings "hh AY oooo ma"—whilst twizzling an African bead drum to release its staccato outbursts—and Bill's dogged concentration on maintaining the bones of the chant. Then, to add the final dimension, Bob picked up his bull roarer, a tribal instrument on a long string which, when whirled overhead ever faster, expresses a cosmic howling, the while threatening to decapitate anyone in its flight path. An enormous whirlpool of sound sucked everyone into its vortex—like that fairground ride where a huge drum goes so fast that the people in it are finally stuck to the side with the energy of the movement, experiencing a perfect Zen nothingness. 'KWATZ'! *Konkrete Canticle* had done their job.

After this great run, our performances were occasional, partly because Bob was so involved in a multitude of projects; but the stark fact was the increasing difficulty in finding funding for poet-groups. However, he invited us to perform at some of his events at the London Musicians' Collective every year between 1984-8 where we continued to present our latest work, experimenting with many different performance triggers such black rubber spiders, savoy cabbage, bubble-blowing, ...A particularly memorable event for me was at Bob's New River Project programme there on 14 February 1987. My diary relates we gave a powerful performance of my new chant *Not the Painting By Goya (Cat. No 307)*, a thanksgiving for the fact that someone who shot at me with an air rifle when I was admiring the rising new moon on my balcony by the Isis, missed. That day Bill told me about the fire on his boat and I wrote: 'Bill very philosophical about loss of manuscripts.' Finally the LMC became unavailable, so for a while Bob moved to the Torriano Meeting House, Kentish Town, London, where on 10 December 1988 we gave a programme alongside Writers Forum book launches: *Histoire D'E* by Mirella Bentivoglio (Rome); *A London Odyssey* by Betty Radin (London).

In 1990 Bob was asked to curate a small exhibition of concrete poetry at the Arts Council Poetry Library: Bill and I both contributed; and *Konkrete Canticle* gave a performance in *The Voice Box*, the Library performance space. Bill's exhibits were pages from *Forming Four Dock Poems*; *The Four Winds*, *Suncard* and *Moons of Jupiter*. We presented those works of Bill's, and some of my first foray into computer visual poems produced on an Applemac, *Mindblown 1& 2* and *Cedar*, a chant of the botanical and English names for cedar, and improvisations with cedar cones, pieces of wood and five cedar seeds representing the five letters in the name. Some of Bob's work on show we performed, including ink-splurge *Flute Trees*; computer visuals and an early piece, vortices of typewriter texts *Beethoven Today*. We also gave a short burst at Bob's Seventieth Birthday Celebration at the ICA, London, 6 August 1990, a great gathering of all those most interested in and committed to the experimental scene, when we improvised to my birthday poem for him, *Plumes for Bob*, a sound interpretation of the markings on an actual long tail feather of a cock pheasant, the booklet comprising photocopies of three pheasant feathers.

What turned out to be our final performance as *Konkrete Canticle* was a film made by Marcus Bergner from Melbourne with a grant from the Australian Arts Council upstairs at Bob's current workshop venue, the *Victoria* pub in Mornington Crescent, London NW1, 25 July 1992. *Ata matuma* (Bob, 1970), 'distorted text'(Bob); *Performing Four Dock Poems* (Bill); *Ode* (me), *Fellowship of the Green Parrot* (me). I remember it as a high-octane event which has been captured by a set of colour photos I have, taken by someone whose name I can't find a record of. (*Illustration, pp. 221, 222*). They capture the essence of our exuberant three-way collaborations: throwing ourselves into the fray without hesitation, knowing we could rely on each other. In the upper four photos we are improvising to my poem *The Fellowship of the Green Parrot* comprising the words of its title, their sounds, and the ear-splitting squawks the feathers elicited, donated to me by the green parrot who lived with Robin Crozier, another extraordinary poet and endlessly inventive visual artist whose work also features largely in my Archive.

In late 2004, plodding along in the mammoth task of at last cataloguing my Archive,[13] I tackled all the items of Bill Griffiths—over two hundred entries taking up nine A4 pages—amongst the largest holdings of any individual I have. These were acquired in two ways: by exchanging work we did as members of *Konkrete Canticle* during its lifespan 1977–92; and by a large deposit, much of it originals, Bill made to my Archive when he left his parents' home to live on his boat on the canal near Uxbridge in 1987. That gift was to become particularly important because when the boat needed some emergency repairs and was taken into dry dock with all his belongings in it, a fire broke out, singeing his manuscripts and destroying some—uncanny, as fire imagery is key in his work—all his projects, documented on microfiche, were entitled 'Pyrofiche.' The sheer variety of experimentation in the works in my Archive guarantees that they will inevitably find their level. Everything is grist to his mill, as exemplified in *Pyrofiche Nine: Visuals*, where found material from adverts, brochures, comics, photos, old postcards, is collaged or treated with watercolours; cut shapes of text sewing-machined onto the page trailing clues of cotton; there are cartoon scenes painted in watercolour; gold textured wrapping paper cut into shapes dancing rhythmically over pages; rolls of screen-printed sponge dabbings to provide textures for letters such as in his elegant *Clarinet Score* illustrated in the Münster Catalogue.

---

[12] International Concrete Poetry Archive Cassettes 1–5: see <u>Declarations</u> Listing pp. 57–8.

[13] Founded and officially opened by Mirella Bentivoglio (Rome) at the Oxford Poetry Festival, March 1980; first called International Concrete Poetry Archive with my Little Press ICPA Publications, founded 1983; name changed to International Sound and Visual Poetry Archive, 1998; then, on legal advice in 2004, for perpetuity, the Paula Claire Archive of Sound and Visual Poetry. Items not otherwise sourced in the text are drawn from this archive.

Looking through the range of texts seen in *Pyrofiche Three: Found and Multivoice Texts*, 1979, of which my Archive contains the set of working originals, the title page names eighteen found pieces, twenty-two multivoice texts and ten observed/action poems, the sources and techniques are diverse in the extreme. *From the Charge of the Light Brigade* exemplifies what a visual poem can achieve (*Illustration, p. 219*). Just one phrase, 'valley of' from Tennyson's poem is embedded in a mass of rushing '((((('. The effectiveness of the proliferation of these one-way brackets depends on their being hand-written, so each one is slightly different, expressing the unique action of its making: it comes to represent each individual, each brandishing his weapon, carried headlong 'INTO THE…' That's the opening that precipitates the poem into its headlong dash to death. Perceived as a sound poem, Bill calls it 'an echo text…the point is to make an interesting, changing rhythm.'[14] The multivoice piece *Waterfall Poem* (*Illustration, p. 219*) presents another device of visual poetry: a typed text that disorientates by placing the 'verses' at right angles to each other making a patchwork that demands to be deciphered; but this can only be done by swivelling the page and making a determined decision which 'patch' of text to read, and in what order. This very action forces the readers into a dynamic engagement with this dialect found text. *An Index to the Possibilities of Divination by Urine* is a hand-written chart providing adventurous performers with many possibilities. Its layout is a deliberate challenge: parts of the text are 'landscape' with a key to the text alongside; but another key runs in the opposite direction; with a further sentence requiring the page to be swivelled… yet the sentence is unfinished. The content is bizarre. The chart of the different colours of urine is followed by the possibilities of interpretation a) to z)—rhythmic possibilities in these staccato sounds—with surreal 'answers' provided in the key sections, e.g. 'beware of short people.' 'as are gall and honey,' and 'search near fireplaces' - ah! the fire imagery again. In the observed section is a three-page 'score' of wavy lines inspired by thunder claps; and a poem made up of rhythmic sound patterns formed by a chart of matches played by the Blue Jays. Wherever we look, the poet urges us to see poetry.

His many studies of Old English, Welsh and Icelandic texts make him familiar with the tradition of cryptic utterances and runic signs. He brilliantly invents his own in the precise black ink pen drawing with the hand-written instruction 'make up into a four-sided baton'(1980)

---

[14] Letter to Paula Claire 3 Oct 1978, proposing his pieces for the Toronto trip.

(*Illustration, p. 220*) conjuring up a magic world akin to Klee's, where a multitude of sprouting signs convince us to enter a mysterious world of coherencies. Tiny images of war—castles in flames, are echoed by hearts on fire; pikes and axes, letters and numbers, a phoenix, a sweep's brush, a Christmas stocking, an oil lamp…the invention seems effortless. At the opposite end of the scale is the monumental *Pyrofiche Six: Flame Fiche*, February 1980, a tour-de-force of creative use of torn paper recycling a large colour football match poster spread across fourteen A4 pages in seven rows totalling ninety-eight collaged pages. I'd love to see this work, 2.95m wide × 2.06m high, displayed in units on a wall. The poet's instructions when accessing its display on microfiche say: 'view frame by frame, noting cross-frame continuities, or: move rapidly about the viewer to achieve flame-flicker, especially if wall projector used, as of ritual e.g. Balinese, fire.' The fierce yet controlled action of tearing particular shapes—for instance, some are specifically curved; the discipline of creating 'cross-frame continuities' on such a large scale (I would have liked more to heighten the explosive effect); the fragmenting of language signs and the representational images on the poster, mostly upside down as if hurled to earth in an archetypal Fall, produces an abstract work of elemental energy: the enigma of wholeness in fragmentation.

Finally, my favourite: *Fire Fiche*, a work of the same period, is a visionary watercolour *(45cm w × 30cm h)* of many small flame-like shards painted in brilliant yellows, oranges, reds, touches of bright green; in some of which black rune-like signs appear, energised by an Aztec terracotta (fired earth) figurine of the sun god instructed to be stood in front of it (*Illustration, p. 221*). When photographing the work for this book, I suddenly realised that these meticulously designed and vividly painted shapes echo the macro text of *Flame Fiche*. They are the micro version of it, a demanding technical achievement. Does this suggest the ritual ball game in honour of the sun divinity in whose furnace—the ultimate glory hole—manifest the primal poems of language, the game, the dance?

Bill's reputation for innovative word-based poetry is established in his published work; but his hypergraphic output of a whole range of poetic experiments, including the use of colour, spanning the repertoire of communication signs in their broadest sense that he deposited in my Archive demands to be appreciated alongside his other achievements. He will, when the entire spectrum of his work comes to light, be recognised as among the most gifted and tenaciously inventive British poets of his generation, with distinctive integrity as a performer.

Earl's Court Squared

SEAN O'HUIGIN

1

I first met Bill in the autumn of 1975. Having just moved to London from Toronto (having previously lived in London in the mid 60s) I contacted Bob Cobbing and went to his Experimental Poetry Workshop at the National Poetry Centre in Earls Court Square.

When I arrived, Bob was the only person there and mentioned that a very interesting young writer (or words to that effect) would be coming shortly.

And he did. A rather tentative Bill Griffiths, slightly bearded & blue jeaned with a halo of wispy blonde hair.

I don't remember who else was at that session. I expect Peter Mayer, who was then teaching at Goldsmith's College, and possibly Lawrence Upton and Jeremy Adler.

For the next three years the weekly gatherings were the central part of my time in London and the focal point of a great deal of adventure-some and innovative "literary" activity.

I'll quote from Bill's own rememberings of the workshops... "The procedure as I recall was we would take form a seated circle, and take turns round the circle to read or exhibit something new—and perform it, solo or with help from those present (varying from reading a text to musical performance, etc.) Bob or others seldom made critical comment, but constructive ideas on how to improve the performance would sometimes be made. It was essentially the positive encouragement of these sessions I remember...such sessions were often a window for new poets to have their work appreciated—and sometimes printed/published, when a body of work was built up over a period of time."

This was exemplified by the growth and commitment of people like PC Fencott and cris cheek. I also recall a saxophone player, Rozanne Marks, who came to a number of sessions and would "jam" with the readers. Canadian poet Herb Burke, an older performer, was especially influenced by music in his work.

There were so many others who were involved either as regulars or drop-ins that I couldn't possibly mention them all (even if I could remember).

It was during those years that the London versions of the Swedish TextSound Festivals took place. These brought together an inspiring group of artists from Europe and North America. Much, I must say, to the bemusement of the establishment of the Poetry Society.

Poets such as Sten Hanson from Sweden, bpNichol from Canada, Henri Chopin (French but living at that time in England) were just some of those taking part in the Festivals along with Bob, Bill, myself and younger workshop participants such as Cris Cheek & PC Fencott.

One of the exciting things was the wide variety of approaches to SoundText performance that took place. From Bob's movingsinging-dancing pieces based on his abstract mimeo/xeroxed texts, to Chopin's multilayered taped manipulations, Sten's vibrant "readings" of his work and the group collaborations of Lawrence, Cris & PC as the group JGJGJGJGJG.

dom sylvester houédard, Paula Claire, Jennifer Pike, Lilly Greenham, Svante Bodin, bill bissett, all presented completely different takes on the use of Sound/Voice work.

2

My own area of interest was, and is, in multivoice texts. Sometimes word based, sometimes using colour coded language based visuals, sometimes projected on screen and performed with electronic accompaniment.

From the early sixties, when I first began to think of myself seriously as a poet, the interaction of voices intrigued me. I expect it was a way of dealing with, and expressing, the voices that inhabit my own head and don't seem to want to go away.

My earliest attempts were "straight" poems scripted for two simultaneous readers using different texts which occasionally echoed of certain words or phrases. An example from my book "BLINK (a strange book for children)", in which a child wakes one morning to find that from each eye they see a different world:

```
Example—from your   from your
        left eye     right eye
        everything   everything
        you see      you see
        is in        is in
        the city     the country
```

I also did a lot of work in Toronto with then electronic music composer, Ann Southam. She would treat & multi-layer my readings producing atmospheric tapes which were used for multi-media performance, dance works and a record, "SkySails".

I quote from a review of "SkySails" in the occasional review of visual poetries and language arts *contexts*, spring 1976… "So fused together are the sound and text that it's impossible to focus on one without the other—they carry each other along, leading sometimes to a completely nonverbal abstraction, othertimes to a more subdued and controlled, almost prosaic, concreteness."

One of my other approaches was to give each member of the audience one or more bits of paper with a line for them to read, then exchange with someone else and keep going until they got their own line back again at which point they would stop. I think my "DOCTOR" poem was one of Bill's favourites.

```
Example—IS THERE A DOCTOR IN THE HOUSE?
        ARE YOU THE DOCTOR?
        HAVE YOU SEEN THE DOCTOR?
        HAS THE DOCTOR LEFT?
        etc.
```

Bill was my regular partner in the two voice pieces as well as taking part in my more abstract bits. The multi-voice work was my main contribution to the workshops.

Bill's own interests at the time included translating the Gilgamesh legend, devoting a work to Mary Anning and some Hell's Angels reminiscences.

Bill was very involved with the Cobbing printing enterprises and eventually the Consortium of London Presses became ensconced in the basement of the Poetry Society, including a printing setup which produced work for Bill's Pirate Press and others such as Lawrence

Upton's Good Elf, Fencott's el uel uel u, Jeremy Adler's Alphabox and various others.

Bob's Workshop group became involved in a nasty confrontation with the Poetry Society and the Arts Council by trying to get recognition for the more experimental works and to open up the Society to a broader range of creativity.

At the same time, the first Poet's in Schools programmes grew out of it all with Bob, PC Fencott and myself being amongst the first and most popular of the performers.

Bill printed a small collection of my work through his Pirate Press and I contributed some visuals to his *Gilgamesh* and *War W. Windsor* issues.

Unfortunately my fading memory has clouded over much of the activity and many of the people involved in the Workshops. I do recall a constant bubbling of creative energy, many nights of scotch with bread and cheese at the hotel next door to the Society and many open eating get-togethers at my own flat over the years.

I spent many times at Bill's various squats, being one of the few not to have been savaged by his lovely, but vicious, little black dog Douglas. I even managed to get his squat mate Alf to help me build a poetry generator at Vauxhall Manor Secondary School where I became the first Poet in Residence.

I still have a large collection of tape recordings from those days. I can't bear to think what condition they're in now but I'd love to be able to listen to them again.

I returned to Toronto in 1978 and helped organize the first Canadian SoundText Festival. It was a great privilege to bring Bob and Bill and others to North America for the first time and to send them out across the country to enhance our awareness of the huge variety of poetic approaches to language that were and are still happening.

I didn't see Bill again until 2005 in Cork where I now live. He managed to get out to spend a day with me. I have to say, when I met him off the train it made me laugh to see that we, who once were young…

Pirate Press: A Bibliographical Excursion
ALAN HALSEY

One day (or year) a researcher with sufficient time and (I hope) an ample grant will attempt to make a full descriptive bibliography of Bill Griffiths' publications. This excursion aims at no such thing: I mean only to record some impressions of reading the work in a few of the editions produced by Griffiths himself. There is no doubt that he is a signal example of a poet dedicated to maintaining control over the appearance of his work, often re-presenting it with a shift into a new context; in some cases this involves revision in the commonly accepted sense, in others it is more a case of re-vision—the text reproduced verbatim but in a different page space and/or variant setting, and so arguably and in some sense a fresh work. Griffiths has used two imprints which can be distinguished chronologically and technically: Pirate Press principally from 1971 to 1980, mostly produced on ink duplicators with some use of silkscreen and offset litho (although two later books carrying the Pirate imprint were made by photocopy); and, from 1989, Amra, sometimes appearing in offset paperbacks but more frequently in A5 pamphlets produced by photocopy or computer-printer. I confine myself to the Pirate editions partly for brevity and partly out of fascination with Griffiths' idiosyncratic use of the ink duplicator as print medium. Compared with photocopier and computer-printer the ink duplicator is or was a stubborn machine. The new technology brings a welcome ease but with that a less expressive print surface (which Griffiths, needless to say, disrupts in characteristic ways). But I will concentrate primarily on the smellier and more tactile business of books made with typewriter, stencils and black ink which squelched out of a Gestetner tube.

~

In the mid-70s I was living a secluded life in Devon, unaware that a poetry war was about to erupt in Earls Court. I did occasionally read a Sunday paper, and happened to find an article by Jeff Nuttall which praised Bill Griffiths. And so I sent off an order for the two volumes of *Cycles*, 1–7 and 8–16. I can't remember what I expected to receive; what arrived was strangely exciting. I'm not sure exactly why, although the opening lines would be sufficient explanation

> Ictus!
> as I ain't like ever to be still but
> kaleidoscope,
> lock and knock my sleeping

since I had no idea that anyone in England was writing like that. The word order in the second line is worth thinking about—'ever like' would seem the more obvious choice but 'like ever' springs the rhythm and tautens the patterning of hard 'c' and 'k'. But it was more than the words themselves (and I could quote many other passages which seemed to me then, as they do now, a revelation). The production of the two volumes seemed so entirely right, a species to itself, embodying the sense of anarchy and disruption evident throughout the writing. Description doesn't help much: a cataloguer would say 'mimeo, A4 landscape, double column text, card covers printed silkscreen'—conveying none of the sense of reading a text which with its typographical irregularities and what may or may not be misprints gave the impression of a masterwork in typescript, somewhat erratic but palpably determined in its transgressions. Even now I'm not sure whether an edition of the complete *Cycles* in standard paperback would convey the same excitement and immediacy—there has yet to be such a thing. Nor do I know to what extent the exigencies of the medium account for the uncommon effects of this edition—was it simply that single-column text would have been a problem for the stapler? (Unlikely.) Poetry in double column, offering in the manner of a newspaper a horizontal as well as a vertical axis to the reading eye, was unusual in the 20th century and will probably remain so in the 21st; and the numerous 19th century examples were aimed at the polite bookshelf rather than the committed reader. But *Cycles* wants no such etiquette; its demand is to be read, urgently.

≈

There is a history to be written of the part played by the ink-duplicated book in the development of the new poetries of the 1960s through to the mid-80s. It would be a graph of a distinct era which is rapidly fading into the past—I doubt whether any young Anglo-American poet would now contemplate publishing his or her work in this way. I have seen it stated that the era began with Ted Berrigan's "C" Press, publishing its first book in 1963. This would roughly coincide with the first ink-duplicated editions from Bob Cobbing's Writers Forum. There are in fact earlier examples such as Gael Turnbull's Migrant but it is true that "C" Press led the way for the several New York presses which in ink-duplicated editions issued the early works of the second-generation New York poets. It is notable, however, that their books are relatively conservative in design, the formats modelled on the commercial paperback—the ink-duplicator is used for purely economic reasons. Economy also dictated many aspects of Writers Forum editions but Cobbing showed much greater ingenuity in inventing designs and formats which would reflect the 'concrete' nature of his texts: the design becomes an aspect *of* the text, closely involved in its composition, rather than mere carrier. Since many Pirate Press books were co-published with Writers Forum we can see this attention as Griffiths' main debt to concrete poetry—relatively few of his works fall within the category of visual poetry as such, although the notion of text as score for multi-voiced sound plays a prominent role and presents a constant challenge in terms of layout. The double-column landscape of *Cycles* is in fact only a slight deviation from the norm. The folded leaves of the 1974 edition of *War W. Windsor* or the long concertina of *A History of the Solar System* (1978) offer an embodiment of text which only the rarest commercial printing could supply.

∼

'Pirate Press began with single-sheet handouts in 1972, small duplicated booklets 1973-74, duplicated booklets and litho booklets 1975–77.' (Footnote to *Conversation / Bill Griffiths / Cris Cheek, Saturday Morning 4*, 1977.) The earliest booklet I have to hand was issued in 1973[1]: *Masses-Texts/Allied Texts*. This is of very simple design: 4 quarto sheets stapled at the spine, front cover printed silkscreen with title and line-drawing of a

---

[1]   No date is given. Here and elsewhere I follow the checklist sent to me privately by Bill Griffiths in 2005.

mask-like head; the author's name does not appear. The anonymity contributes to the impression that we are reading here a provocative piece of street-literature, anarchist by inclination and much concerned with the legal nomansland at the edge of civil society. In fact the first poem, *Mass*, bears an epigraph from the Hell's Angel Frank Reynolds, recorded by Michael McClure: 'The psychologist would say, "You hate cops, you hate cops, you want to kill cops, the button says the only good cop is a dead cop".' *Mass* was one of the poems issued as a handout in 1971[2], as were other poems here: *Bill Compton* and *To Tom Saunders on his Imprisonment*—the latter to appear, along with *To Johnny Prez. Hells Angels Nomads* and *LATCHMERE: (Remand)*, in *War W. Windsor*. The booklet is an early example of Griffiths' recontextualization, amounting here to a kind of manifesto, a refusal to acknowledge an individual 'self' bearing responsibility to a society with whose judgments it is not complicit:

> That is it a mind I mean
> When I say that is good or very right
> Or beautiful   as we act it   Light and Eye
> Alone now
> I did not believe (know) to say right was capital
> (that is, not: Thought)

Masses-Texts / Allied Texts sets the ground for an interrogation which Griffiths developed on a larger scale in *Cycles* and has been a constant theme extending into later works such as *Star Fish Jail* and *Durham: a visit to Durham Gaol*: on the one hand a challenge to the demand for imprisonment of any kind of malefactor and on the other a consideration of the degree to which imprisonment is the potent image of all our situations in a polity which redefines 'democracy' as best suits its latest need. The prose text *Into Prison*, also to appear in *War W. Windsor*, is annotated here as '(draft of third Cycle on Dover'. As an example of the craft of Griffiths' verse, by which I mean the achievement of its apparent spontaneity, we may compare the first paragraph of *Into Prison*

> A prison looks like houses or usual Youre nothing going in just watching
> And a prison looks like rows with roofs of housing you look like a laye dog
> getting in hey master A prisons like houses piled up a couple Blocks and
> Octagons They make a real note they say is baiting of me So but there aint
> no housing ever got walls or doors like these or backgardens of barbwire

---

[2]   Sic, following the 2005 checklist, *pace* the statement in *Saturday Morning*.

with the opening stanzas of *Cycle 3: H.M. Prison Brixton*:

> To the sickish kids
> nothing. all the epileptics
>
> Prison
> like houses
> going in a sort of late dog
> watching, hey master
> all built, blocks, octagons
>
> waiting in a room
> There's Charlie with his fists strained;
> balls big as teapots

The revision of his prose, on the other hand, tends to be additive. The second paragraph of *Into Prison* in *Masses-Texts / Allied Texts* reads

> I was in the street then not to their liking I am waiting how long I took off my leather not joking Not donating Got my prison clothes Take my shirt off to queue and strip for the doctor so as to tell the truth yes

And in *War W. Windsor*

> I was in the street and a knife Thats not the chaplains liking thats not to no ones liking I am waiting how long I took off my leather not joking Not donating Got my prison clothes Take my shirt off to queue and strip for the doctor so as to tell the truth yes who yelling

～

I have not seen the edition of *War W. Windsor* published in 1973.[3] The 1974 edition (Pirate with Writers Forum) is A4 format, portrait, with a visual text by Sean O Huigin on the cover. Two more pieces by O Huigin appear on single leaves punctuating the Griffiths texts; geometrical/lettrist in style, printed in blue, they suggest modernist buildings of somewhat sinister design—the third with its right angles based around the forms E, F, L and T is reminiscent of 'prisons like houses piled up a couple Blocks and Octagons'. Griffiths' texts are printed not on A4 but trimmed A3, folded at the fore-edge so that the

---

[3] '1973 *war with windsor* was a quarto side-stapled booklet with silkscreen cover, but contained only a sample of what was to become WWW later' (email from Bill Griffiths, 7 September 2005).

folded leaf conceals the text appearing on the A3 recto. Opening the book, which has no title page, the reader is confronted with *Into Prison* on the leaf which folds out to reveal *Text 1* and *Text 2*: the device simultaneously suggests that these first numbered texts are themselves either imprisoned or in hiding and that the reader should not be overly attached to any notion of order—*Into Prison* both precedes *Text 1* and follows *Text 2*—order imposes its own imprisonment. *Text 1* is allowed the full range of the A4 space; deservedly, since it is one of Griffiths' most spatially complex poems. The lines are arranged (with occasional transgressions) in four columns, inviting at least this reader's eye to read downward column by column; allowing for extreme disjunction the text does very nearly work this way although the eye soon learns that a horizontal reading skipping across columns is more pleasant to the ear. Here is the opening passage:

air around	Marigolds	raw	sun-hoarding
Empty of angels	Its orange tree	reaching	geometrically
rat's fur on'is anarack	soft & minds	at the grey	warm wind turns
tongue & nose	does the millstone	riding on donkeys	the scooter awry
some curled in	or sweat in the	in the laps of	set pattern
round & round	territories than black brick	knee, knuckles	of signeury

—but standard typesetting with variable spacing radically changes the visual effect created by the fixed spacing of an old-fashioned typewriter. Perhaps for this reason the text appears in neither the Coach House (*A Tract Against the Giants*, 1984) nor Paladin (*Future Exiles*, 1992) selections. It is an early example of a Griffiths text as score: I imagine the performance would be by five voices, one reading horizontally and the others from the vertical columns.

The folded leaf on the second text page presents a blank. Opened it reveals a tableau of three longish poems—*Text 3. To Johnny Prez Hells Angels Nomads*, *Text 4: Animal* and *Long Death of the Plain Indians Gipsies*, a trio of subjects who are in different senses and for different reasons outlaws— followed by a short poem, *Magistrate*, which within the enclosure of the leaf forms a judgmental coda—this is the magistrate who 'put up the kid face to death'. Animals clearly fascinate Griffiths and appear in many of his poems. They are 'outlaws' without being formally outlawed; they live outside human jurisdiction, although human jurisdiction does affect their lives and they have no choice in the matter. They live in human consciousness and at the same time far beyond it; they seem to us deeply emblematic but we suppose they inhabit a world without emblems. *Text 4* directly associates the animal and criminal, the wit of the piece nicely balancing its angry alienation:

> Close up wolf about my mouth
> He would go in
> Sit in his cave, like me,
> Smell at the daylight.
>
> Animals an' criminals
> Among of the legs of the animals
> Criminals hands in belts.
>
> Jesu 'pecker'
> My eyes is loose with worry.
>
> I've stood
> Like a polar bear,
> In court—no one will move
> At the white
> Till all the wood stank.
>
> [...]
>
> Little pig pealing
> For a small church tower
> You're mighty quarrelsome
> Pretty bricks ("Caesar's")

The third and last folded leaf presents the Appendix to the long prose text on its A3 recto, *Text 5. War With Windsor.* The Appendix mostly quotes the text's newspaper sources—the reader is invited, if s/he wishes, to read the sources first, with the implication that the text will not be affected either way. The war between rival chapters of Hells Angels is narrated in London slang, casual in appearance but always with a glint of self-amusement and faint ghosts of allusion:

> The real war was Essex'. One of them blasted w/ a shotgun on Chelsea Bridge, and we was to help them against Windsor. Levi I remember & one other. They had a caravan on the North Circular and their speaking & planning was well O.K., sunshiny.

The frequent use of place-names to identify both locations and the gangs' identities is bound to remind us of the names of battlefields peppering our history books—all those bloody skirmishes so definably local but set to determine the ownership of England or at least of its crown. A biker gang is not, after all, what we usually associate with the name 'Windsor'. And so the text does end

> And now it is time to say to the kings and queens of england, you only reign by elexion and getting god's grace [...] and now say have you too broken that contract in regards mercy in regards the laws and in regards holy laws, everyday.

Or, as the leaf turns back to show the Appendix's version:

> Fealty, or the link between monarch and subject is revocable, as are all feudal ties.

And then the leaf turns fully over to reveal the only true verso in the book, showing *Text 6: Latchmere (Remand)* and *Zoo-Keeper*. The latter is an extraordinarily lively poem, beginning with a wild burst of animal energy

> tempestu-
> ous a ocean-token
> to dolly air 'at's a'
> waste-with-magic or
> whirled curls/pearls
> face it all bright, grim

but ending with that ambivalent notion of 'keeping' by which a keeper is simultaneously guardian and gaoler

> there's scarce grail-flower
> not in the pots, not in the tins—
> not in the windows, walk, bins—a bagatelle
> till the roof's groaning
> and plausible w/ the
> words of a god
> shaking and tramping, eager t'its guillotine, I ll keep you

∽

The 1976 reprint with the slightly variant title *War W/ Windsor* appears in A5 portrait and although it lacks the ingenuity of the 1974 edition it finds new resolutions to the problems of layout. O Huigin's visual texts seem more sinister in black and white, particularly the third as it hangs from the left-hand margin. The reader needs to turn the book 90° to read the landscape settings of *Text 1* and *Into Prison*. The Appendix reproduces the original newspaper cuttings in facsimile and the print is further varied in that a few poems are offset from their printings in the sans-serif then used by *Poetry Review*. Offset paste-ups from magazine publications are used in a number of Pirate books at this period; *Reprinted and Current Poems (I)*, 1976, another double-column A4 landscape, is wholly produced in this way.[4]

Pirate issued several A5 portrait pamphlets in 1975. The texts are generally less ambitious than *Cycles* and *War W. Windsor* but Griffiths' handling of this commonest format of high-street printing is characteristically witty. The anonymous *Poems for Ian Hamilton* has a cover design mostly picked out in little triangular lozenges, one of which forms a love-heart. The brief poems parody the tediously domestic poems of the Movement in its death-throes—the author's father fittingly enough seems to die several times and has to resurrect once to provide the subject for yet another 'poem'—but Griffiths' linguistic exuberance is too quirky and apparent to maintain the pastiche. The pamphlet is offered to Hamilton (a literary Caesar at the time although he probably by now requires an identificatory footnote[5]) 'with the bright idea that I too might get some poppy out of the seeming lottery by which public funds are distributed', says the 'Prefatory Episstle' (sic). Griffiths seems to have enjoyed the bibliographical conventions of the 18th century at this time; the cover of *Eight Poems against the bond and cement of civil society* (also anonymous) is set as or perhaps copied from an 18th century title page. The strongest poem here is the first, *Dead "Wessex" The Dog to the*

---

[4] The Johnny Prez poem shows several changes and additions in the 1976 edition of *War W/ Windsor*, including the re-placing of the lines 'Are you tired yet / Said the detective?' to conform with the *Masses-Texts / Allied Texts* version. Section 7 is omitted, perhaps accidentally, but restored in another version, now entitled For *Johnny Prez Nomad Hells Angels*, in *Bikers* (with John Muckle, Amra 1990). The poem is not divided into numbered sections here; the first six lines are rearranged and there are a few other small revisions and additions. The original section 6 (beginning 'And love / Works to mix you up miscates the soul') is omitted; section 7 shows variants, most notably 'Underhumanly' for 'Underanimally'. There is a substantial addition, a 19-line passage beginning 'No / Christ straight / kid-clear / white / ice-head / the stranger' inserted between the original sections 4 and 5. The poem reverts to the 1974 version in *Future Exiles*.

[5] 'Hamilton, Ian, see REVIEW, THE (2)', The Oxford Companion to *English Literature*, Fifth Edition, reprinted with corrections (twice), 1985.

Household (reprinted in *A Tract against the Giants* as *Compass Poem*), with its use of a canine (albeit ghostly) perspective—

> And the guy's buckle under his navel
> Glared into
> the edges of my eyes

a persona which is more fully developed in another pamphlet from the same period, *The Gesta Alfredi: Rex Anglie*. This sports a striking hand-lettered cover design, printed sideways with pleasant annoyance. The author is identified as 'Bill Griffiths Esqr Poet' and Pirate Press shows its logo. The 'Matetials' (sic) are identified by make, size and weight; we are told that the book has been produced on 'A B Dick 320', 'Text typed directly onto paper plates with Imperial Typewriter / Printed Friday 30th May 1975' by 'Bill Griffiths and Bob Cobbing at the Printshop of the Consortium of London Presses at the National Poetry Centre 21 Earls Court Square as a pilot printing work on the new equipment of the Poetry Society'. This pastiche of the technical information detailed by private presses to convince their clients of their product's quality does, of course, carry a political point and in the light of later events at the Poetry Society it now seems a banner with distinct historical significance. The texts are among Griffiths' funniest, using a story-telling technique reminiscent of a comic-book. The *Narrative* in numbered paragraphs is presumably derived from Asser's *Vita Alfredi*, improvised freely around jerky syntax probably founded on literal translation—

> 1. The chief duty of atheling (he-sez) in youth is keep touch to all things about. Make them as real so you won't dream the day so you don't stop the minute of any day (I can he-sez I can go on wherever) you do not break the bridge-out. So it will not matter about being generous or the loss of battles but you lose command of the external clarity it is your crown gone (he-sez) and laughs about so his tears dribble about the flower-beds.

There is a child-like manner throughout this telling, perhaps emphasizing that kingdoms (won or lost in a sprout-fight) are playthings to kings, but this is balanced by an undertow of admiration for Alfred the scholar and translator. Balanced too by the views of Alfred's dog, Sigefer, who offers a coronation poem (nicely resolved in the page-space: when the narrow-lined text hits the bottom margin it reverses upwards and upside-down in a parallel column) but in his third contribution 'revokes his fealty':

Not named me as slave. I did homage to no sovereign or if I had could
revoke it—but I am to be held in legal bond to the sovereign! Outland!
Called to look at the failure—how us-less-than-us got laws and the same
way negates a failed-creator; called to the improvement well i think i am
becoming a god
So I read books and more on the fairness of prison-governors policemen
the psychiatrists and teachers autobiographies.

I see *The Gesta Alfredi* as the most succesful of these A5 pamphlets, the
texts filling each page and fulfilled by their placement. It is a surprise to
find it in *Oblong Book* (1978), a compendium of A4 landscape printings,
'retyped and revised' for the purpose. The paragraphs of the *Narrative* are
unnumbered here and turned into small rectangular blocks, side by
side above and below, as best fits the page. The poems and other
passages are similarly arranged. The visual effect of some pages is of
certain manuscript books in which text is fitted wherever space and the
transcriber's script permits, a technique Griffiths used increasingly in
the late '70s and early '80s.

~

The double-column A4 format is put to good use in several of the translations issued by Pirate in this period. 'Translation' is in some ways a
misleading word for these editions since it might imply a consciously
'literary' version in one language of a poem originally written in
another. These books are for the most part printings of the poems in
their original (mostly 'North Atlantic') languages alongside English
versions presented word-for-word, without syntactical change: the
double columns of A4 landscape are particularly effective in presenting
this form of parallel text. The most ambitious volume, at least in size, is
Beowulf (1975, 2nd impression 1977, translation by John Porter with
Griffiths introduction); I find I can read the Anglo-Saxon with relative
ease in this edition although I know little of the language. The early
Welsh of *Llywarch Hen* (1978)[6] presents more intractable problems to
which Griffiths offers some ingenious solutions. The relation between
his own poetry and these translations deserves consideration, both for

---

[6] This carries the imprint 'Writers Forum' but shows all the hallmarks of a Griffiths
production. A 'literary' version by Griffiths had been published by Tern Press in
1976.

the embodiment in his own work of translated material and alien syntax as well as for his frequent use of devices such as consonantal patterns derived from the Anglo-Saxon and Welsh which the strict translations do not aim to reproduce. I'm passing over this aspect of Pirate publishing too briefly here, for reasons of space, but it represents a dedicated effort to re-introduce with very limited resources some rare texts—a checklist is the least it deserves:

> *Gisli's Saga—the verses* (trans. John Porter) 1974
> *The Gododdin* (trans. Griffiths) 1974
> *Beowulf: Anglo-Saxon text with Modern English Parallel* (Porter) 1975/77
> *The Grave Stanzas of Urien* (Griffiths) ?1975
> North Atlantic Texts 1 (Griffiths and Porter) 1975: includes *Caedmon*,
> *The Spider*, *The Ruin* and *The Runic Poem* in parallel text, with freer versions
>   of *Wulf and Eadwacer* and a passage from *Beowulf*
> *The Story of the Flood from Gilgamesh* (Griffiths) 1975
> *Aron's Saga* (Porter) 1976
> *Llywarch Hen: In Welsh/English* (Griffiths) 1978

~

It seems worth considering three Pirate books from 1977–80 as a group: *Twenty-Five Pages, A History of the Solar System / Fragments: A History of the Solar System* and *The First Three Novellas of the Second Row*. *Twenty-Five Pages* is an uncomplicated production, quarto sheets, portrait, stapled into card covers, and has more resemblance to a conventional poetry collection than most Pirate books. The title is reflected in the manner of page numbering—the words 'Page 1', 'Page 2' and so on appear at the head of each leaf, lending an air of naivety—it suggests the way a child might number the pages of an exercise book at the same time as it conveys a nonchalant attitude, as if the pages have been numbered after being assembled at random. In fact it forms a quite cohesive collection of mainly single-page poems which follow a sequence simply entitled *Sequence* and a longer work: *The Twenty-Fifth Anniversary: Six Sections on the scheduled Visit of the Queen to Paderborn*. Familiar Griffiths themes are here worked out on German territory, particularly the question of sovereignty; the law-giver in this case is not Alfred but Charlemagne, whose relations with papal authority offer perspectives on claims of temporal and spiritual power. The first section is a playful macaronic, a few English words jumping in and out of the dominant German. The second consists of a prose travelogue—'Paderborn the outstanding site of 200 springs in the chalk, the crossed paths of the Hellweg and spoke routes to 500 years before the missions and the reaching of Charlemagne [...]'—beneath which runs a passage from an English version of the Paderborn Epos, beginning

> 44 Eager for the hunt the people enter the wood
> 45 A brown bear is scented
> 46 After a long chase the exhausted boar [sic] turns
> 47 Charlemagne tackles him and kills him with a sword
> 48 He says Fortuna promises that this day will be joyful for us by her auguries and she will favour our enterprises

The Epos is picked up again in Section Five and ends with the meeting of Charlemagne with Pope Leo, before whom Charlemagne's army 'prostrates itself'. Meanwhile the travelogue continues in the verse of Section Three, where the poet watches an airshow, perhaps a rehearsal for the arrival of the Queen. The flypast has become the standard English display of sovereignty; here it is seen as a kind of airborne calendar, as if an assertion of dominion over time:

> To the south of Paderborn ("Paths'-stream")
> 4 parachutists fall to my left, like
> four bad weeks, then an aeroplane, slow, also shiny,
>   lands to my right for
> August, another, September. Then
> a glider wheels about on my left, another aeroplane
> lands to the right, very serene will be November, also
> December, a glider landing on the correct side.
> Finally October comes down gently to my right.

The airshow continues in the central column of the tricolumnar Section Four. This central column is a poem by Geraldine Monk, splitting in two a Griffiths poem concerning 'The four / beasts of the God / Ram and cat/ mastiff and bear'. This is another text as score for performance.[7] Section Six resumes 'the meeting of the Head of Europe and the leader of the Church on Earth'

> Till Power assists Power
> assists and reduces.
> It is time to wake tricks to the hills. New.

---

7 Monk remembers a performance in which her poem was read by Bob Cobbing, with Griffiths reading his own text simultaneously.

The sequence ends with a rollcall of future German female saints in heavenly splendour; if the traveller is 'he' then it seems he has not himself ascended:

> eyes hard, of aquamarine
> his loops spongey, tangerine
> coils of green
> his ears bright new cream
> as he raced and spun, ignite, above a just maroon mud.

A History of the Solar System / Fragments: A History of the Solar System is perhaps Pirate's most original large-scale production. A4 sheets folded to A5 have been machine-sewn into a concertina which when fully open measures approximately 14 feet. The text is printed landscape, in red, with green covers in which an arrow has been sewn as if to say 'Open here'. This is a work I enjoy very much and understand very little; that it encodes an arcane music score is suggested by the picking out of the tonic sol-fa in text i:

> There bubbles of fire planetary scent or cinder that means doubt in progress or no way is our source of centres' systems degree. Therefore there creation and foremost place were of all complicated questions so emphatically pre-eminent, that it jibes and enquires of the designations quoted if they fairly represent practically our Earth's best direct relationship to the Almighty, to doubt if the great solar system unquestionably revolves happily through our large scent of death, so to make acted out by force the neo-sacral punchy functions of domain, as type of Carousel, Hyperion and Ymir (bits of white brain, bits of grey brain, bits of black brain pumped up as clouds).

There is a play, then, on the music of the spheres but this is performed within a solar system which has been largely demystified. The sun is still seen as the 'fusionally-powered centre of the system' but its symbolic role as Governor when 'What I aimed to see / Is Science, Fact' is held in question: as soon as 'one personified governing force is no longer safe' we need to address the 'anarchical' nature of things 'in the absence of any erstwhile sanctuary' on Earth. Earth itself is described as

> A very useful, semi-stable planet; the only emotional planet; it is both circular and oblate, pear-shaped or infinitely symmetrical; almost everything of it we know, misleads us.

The text, I think, follows the misleadings, staking out a mazy path among competing symbolisms and baffling perspectives. The penultimate fragment remarks 'But I haven't shown yet the carousel': this would be a simple model but its descriptions stutter in a repetition of 'it it is it is the it is the'—horse, billows, skin, crown, the reverse, horse again, the blue, acts, the centre ...the last fragment recalls the sun-boat from Egypt:

> Lord of bright-red, of bright bandage, of the binding of a fast jolt
>   a glad heart ...
> Of the Sea stamp-to-toss, like viril'st of crewmen, bumpst boat over
>   the back-disk of Apophis, bad sand bar ...
> Lord that attaches on heads, makes the neck one again, unmakes
>   wound and thread-work, You
> Tow me ... diffi-difficult land ... where there topsy, turvy stars
>   fall 'n their faces 'n' cannot rise, chaoted, c'lapsed,
> Tows ... guides the wierd boat, directs

The First Three Novellas of the Second Row (Pirate with Trumpet Press 1979[8]) is a simpler production, trimmed A5 landscape stapled in card covers, but its neat page setting (made on a varityper, a slow and clumsy ancestor of the 'golfball' electric typewriter) shows considerable versatility in laying out a complex text. The novellas are in part, again, scores for performance, moving from relatively conventional verse to prose via the double-column *Shunting Poem* in which the left-hand lines echo the right-hand, through 'Texts for three intermittent voices' (triple-column prose blocks) and finally the score for *Novella Three* in which the voice connections are made along asterisked lines which configure the Roman numerals I-XX. The reader is also told that 'The cloud section is intended for a large number of voices, [...] improvising'. This is a complex text in all respects, grounded in Ovid's *Metamorphoses* and beginning with an improvisation on the tale of Vertumnus and Pomona; we see that *Shunting Poem* is similarly improvised around the tale of Echo. Metamorphosis seems an inevitable subject for Griffiths and to a great extent all his work is imbued with it.

> King emperor now
> dry copper cough
> red stemmed redflowers
> and mark the process

---

[8] The book is undated. The checklist states 1980 but the copy I am using is inscribed and dated 8.8.80. Griffiths planned a volume called *Novellas of the First Row* consisting of '*War with Windsor, Pippin,* etc., but I never got round to reprinting them' (email, 7 September 2005).

what is the essence of
why shld not Nature
take
a sudden leap from
like a destruct of colour
structure to structure?

~

With *The First Three Novellas of the Second Row* the main series of Pirate books comes to an end. Much has been written about the fierce disputes at the Poetry Society in 1977 and it is often suggested that the most serious consequence was that Eric Mottram ceased to be editor of *Poetry Review*. The poetry Mottram would have continued to publish did, however, find new homes; on the other hand the loss of the printing equipment used by the Consortium of London Presses meant there were books which were never published at all. In the *Saturday Morning* conversation Griffiths remarks that the Consortium 'gave me a period when i could print continuously.' When Cris Cheek asks him 'what kind of directions can you look to for support to continue your activities?' Griffiths replies simply 'i can't.' Significant Pirate publications in this period include *Oblong Book* and *Quarto Book* (both 1978, both reprinted with amendments 1979). These are compendia comprising sheets from earlier printings. I have a copy of the third edition of *Oblong Book* to hand: it includes *Cycles* (the single-volume edition published in 1976), *Reprinted and Current Poems (I)*, the resetting of *The Gesta Alfredi: Rex Anglie*, a resetting of *Six Walks Around Tenby* (a letterpress edition had been published by Earthgrip in 1976), the collection *Idylls of the Dog, King & other poems* (1975) and the concrete text *Forming Four Dock Poems* (first published as an A5 pamphlet in 1974). I have two copies of *Quarto Book*. What I take to be the first edition comprises *Twenty-Five Pages, Spook Book* (1977) and *Arons Saga*. The other is dated 1979 and has a cover label & title page portrait by Robert Clark; the contents are identical except that *Arons Saga* has been replaced by a miscellany of shorter poems, some offset from magazines. The loss of the facility to 'print continuously' seemed to encourage Griffiths in his search for new techniques including non-book formats. Around 1980 he transferred all his work to microfiche, which he recommended on the grounds that it could be read on the ceiling by a reader lying on his back, perhaps in bed—no more stiff necks and aching elbows! He also produced photocopied A3 broadsides onto which he fitted large quantities of text, often pasted up as previously remarked in the manner of a manuscript or even a scrap book; some of these show entire works—*Paracycles*, *Five Praise-Songs*, *War With Windsor* (with some lines printed vertically in the spaces between columns), *The Gesta Alfredi* and *Joanne-Marie's Swimming Manual*. These are reproduced from typescript or magazine typesetting. There are a few others reproduced from holograph, a method Griffiths was to pursue in later publishing. *Transactional Poems*, dated 1980–1981, seems to have been published for the first time in this form and so far as I know has not been reprinted entire—two of the poems appear in *Future Exiles*; the layout, defined by ruled vertical and horizontal lines providing each text with its own box, has an elegance all its own. Another broadside shows a shortened form of the prose sequence *An Account of April and May*, *Account of the End* and *Start Text* in manuscript; typewritten editions had previously appeared from Lobby Press and Pirate. Finally, on a sheet exceeding A3, there is a version of the complete *Cycles* set out in tiny manuscript. (There are revisions and excisions—'all the epileptics', for example, does not appear in line 2 of *Cycles* 3.) This is specified 'PP 81', 'Pirate Press 1981', although some of the other sheets are designated 'from APT POST'.

The mid-1980s were a thin time for Griffiths publishing. *Further Songs & Dances of Death* appeared from Anarcho Press in 1982; and in 1984 *Materia Boethiana* from Galloping Dog and The Poetry Bookshop, and *A Tract against the Giants* from Coach House. A revival begins in 1987, and *The Bournemouth* carries the Pirate imprint in conjunction with Writers Forum. Griffiths' control over the production of his work picks up again in 1989, following his move to Seaham and establishment of the Amra imprint. 'Pirate Press' appears for the last time as the publisher of *Morning-Lands*, 1989. Trimmed A5 landscape, this chunky text is repro-duced by photocopy from Griffiths' script—not the handwriting used on the broadsides but an open form of lettering, an irregular hand-drawn sans-serif filling each page and most of its lines. In the *Note on Lay-out* Griffiths remarks that 'The lines of varying length of Old English verse were written continuously; & I adopt this system, blocking in the last syllable of each "line" as a halt.' It is yet another example of his restless exploration of the diverse ways of expressing a verse-form through its visual appearance. *Morning-Lands* makes a proud coda to Pirate Press.

Bill Griffiths and the Old English Lyric
ROBERT HAMPSON

I. Two Fragments

In *The Medieval Lyric*, Peter Dronke introduces his discussion of the Old English poem *Wulf and Eadwacer* by recalling Charlemagne's capitulary of 789. This ordered that 'no abbess should presume to leave her convent without our permission, nor allow those under her to do so…and on no account let them dare to write winileodas, or send them from the convent'.[1] 'Winileodas' are literally 'songs for a friend': they are secular lyrics, women's love songs, part of a popular vernacular tradition.

Clive Bush begins his invaluable extended account of Bill Griffiths's works in *Out of Dissent* with an extract from an interview with Bill Griffiths by Paul Holman, in which Griffiths recalls the experience of being arrested:

> I was picked up by the police and remanded in Brixton for possessing a small knife, which I was currently using as a pencil sharpener. The problem was that, because of my injuries, I couldn't speak very clearly and this was taken as a sign of aggressive non-co-operation. I was put in solitary and did not appreciate the experience of being locked up in a wing where all you had all night was continual screaming. Eventually, a psychiatrist came and told me that, if I didn't give up my ambitions to write and get a sensible job, the court would send me to prison…[2]

---

[1] Peter Dronke, *The Medieval Lyric* (1968) (D. S. Brewer, 1996), 91.

[2] Clive Bush, *Out of Dissent: A study of five contemporary British poets* (London: Talus Editions, 1997),213; interview with Bill Griffiths by Paul Holman (14 September 1993), *The Haiku Quarterly*, 10 (1993), 30.

II. Wulf and Eadwacer

My title refers to 'the Old English lyric'. I should make it clear at this point that, in this essay, I will be referring to *one* Old English lyric (not the genre). The 'Old English lyric' I have in mind is known as *Wulf and Eadwacer*. *Wulf and Eadwacer* is a 19 line fragment in the Exeter Book. As Ruth Lehmann points out, among surviving Old English poems, it is metrically unique.[3] First, it has a refrain, but the refrain is a line and a half long, not just a single line (as in *Deor*). Secondly, seven of its 19 lines are (unusually) of more than twelve syllables. Thirdly, there are four half-lines with double alliteration that take the place of full lines; in each instance, they are preceded by one of these longer lines. According to Lehmann, these short lines are without parallel in Old English poetry.

The structure of the poem is very clear. As most critics read it, the divisions of the poem are marked by the regular introduction of Wulf's name and then the final address to Eadwacer. There are the opening lines, which I will say more about in a moment. After these opening lines, the second stanza deals with the present situation ('Wulf is on an island, I on another'); the third stanza deals with the past ('When it was rainy and I sat weeping / Then the bold warrior would take me in his arms'); the fourth returns to the present (' Wulf, my Wulf, I am sick with longing'); the final stanza addresses Eadwacer and turns towards the future.

The title given to the poem derives from the names of its two main characters, *Wulf and Eadwacer*, but the identity and relations of the characters is problematic. This is where some of the difficulties of the poem begin to arise. The poem is generally read as some kind of love triangle or tangle. But, as Louis Rodrigues points out, some critics read Wulf as an outlaw and the speaker's lover, with Eadwacer as the 'tyrant husband'; others take Wulf to be the outlawed husband and Eadwacer her gaoler who has (perhaps) forced his attentions upon her (depending on who we decide is the 'bold warrior' who took her in his arms)'.[4] However, it is also possible that there is neither a Wulf nor an Eadwacer: John Adams, for example, interprets Eadwacer as meaning 'guardian of the home' (rather than as a proper name) and reads it as an epithet

---

3 Ruth P. M. Lehmann, 'The Metrics and Structure of *Wulf and Eadwacer*', *Philological Quarterly*, 48 (1969), 151–65, 152. My discussion of metrics and structure is largely drawn from this article.

4 Louis J. Rodrigues, *Seven Anglo-Saxon Elegies* (Felinfach: Llanerch Publishers, 1991), 17.

ironically applied to the absent 'Wulf' (rather than introducing another character).[5] More radically, W. J. Sedgefield, in an early article, argued that the poem wasn't about humans but about dogs.[6]

The difficulties of the poem derive in part from its fractured and fragmented, highly allusive narrative. They also derive from the uncertain meaning of certain words and the poem's resulting densely polysemous nature. Patricia Belanoff notes 'the polysemous quality of disputed words, phrases and punctuation' and demonstrates this by reference to Arnold Davidson's translation which maintains the range of meanings of the disputed words.[7] We can see from this composite/variorum translation the multiple meanings present in just the first two lines of the poem. The first line reads: 'It is to my people as if one might give them (a battle /a sacrifice/ a gift/ a message/ a game'). The second line, which follows paratactically, doesn't help the reader to select from that range of meanings since it merely generates another range of uncertainties: 'Will they (receive/ consume/ oppress/ relieve) him, if he comes (with a host/ in violence/ in need)?'[8]

Peter Baker has shown how most of the readings Davidson suggests for the first line are erroneous and that ' *lac* probably means nothing more than "gift"'.[9] Lehmann, too, thinks the first line 'gives little difficulty in translation' (157). For her the problem lies, as often in this

[5] John F. Adams, '*Wulf and Eadwacer*: An Interpretation', MLN, LXXIII (1958), 1–5.

[6] W. J. Sedgfield,'Old English Notes', *Modern Language Review*, 27 (1931), 74–5. According to this interpretation, the narrator is a bitch, and the narrative involves an affair with a wolf and stolen puppies, but ends with the realisation that it was all a dream, at which point she falls asleep again beside 'her faithful mate, Eadwacer'.

[7] Patricia A. Benaloff, 'Women's Songs, Women's Language: *Wulf and Eadwacer* and *The Wife's Lament*', in *New Readings on Women in Old English Literature*, ed. Helen Damico and Alexandra Hennessey Olsen (Bloomington, IN: Indiana University Press, 1990), 193–203, 197.

[8] Arnold E. Davidson, 'Interpreting *Wulf and Eadwacer*', *Annuale Mediaevale*, 16 (1975), 25.

[9] Peter S. Baker, 'The Ambiguity of *Wulf and Eadwacer*', *Studies in Philology* 78 (1981), 39–51, 41. He notes that 'battle' is derived from a misinterpretation by Bosworth-Toller of a passage in *Guthlac B*; that 'message', also found in *Guthlac B* is a metaphorical extension of the meaning 'gift'; that 'game' is imported from Old Norse and is not attested in Old English; and that 'sacrifice' is an attested meaning, but would require 'a more ceremonious verb' than gifan.

poem, 'in the…application of the line to the story' (157).[10] She then goes on to list a number of major interpretative problems in the remaining eighteen lines of the poem. I have already mentioned the problems with a *epecgan* and *on þreat* in the second line. Baker suggests that the former can be translated 'either "to feed" or "to kill"' (43) and the latter perhaps as an adverbial phrase meaning 'violently' or, more plausibly, as 'to a band of men' (43). Lehmann concludes her discussion of this crux by producing what she calls a northern meaning ('They will oppress him if he comes at last') and a southern meaning ('They will accept him if he comes into their company'): northern and southern, of course, on etymological grounds rather than different approaches to hospitality (158). Line 9 she describes as one of the 'most vexing' in the poem since *dogode* is not found elsewhere and has no satisfactory etymology (160). Bosworth-Toller glosses *dogian* as 'to bear, suffer'. Lehmann points to a later Scotish word meaning 'to lose brightness or freshness; to fade' (161). The *beaducafa* who comforts the speaker poses a different kind of problem. There is no difficulty about the meaning ('battle-quick' /'the bold warrior'), but there is about the referent. Is this a memory of her past life with Wulf? Is this Eadwacer? Or could this even be one of the 'fierce warriors' of line 6? Similarly with *laþ* in the following line: *laþ* means 'harm, evil, trouble', but does it refer to her psychological state, her mixed feelings about the 'comfort' she receives, or to the outcome— the trouble that came from it—whether in the form of Wulf's exile or the child referred to later in the poem.

There are also uncertainties about the poem's generic affiliation. It was once known as 'The First Riddle' because of its enigmatic quality and its position in the Exeter Book immediately prior to the first group of Old English riddles.[11] Nineteenth-century scholars generally argued that the answer to the riddle was 'Cynewulf'.[12] In the twentieth century, it was generally grouped as one of the 'elegies' of the Exeter Book, along with 'The Wanderer', 'The Seafarer', 'Deor', 'The Wife's Lament', 'The Husband's Message' and 'The Ruin'. But the 'elegies' themselves have been assigned to different genres.[13] And *Wulf and Eadwacer* has been

[10] Cf Baker: If the literal meaning of line 1 is plain enough, the interpretation of it is exceedingly difficult' (41).

[11] Rodrigues, 17.

[12] Lehmann, 151.

[13] S. B. Greenfield and D. G. Calder, *A New Critical History of Old English Literature* (New York, 1968), 281.

described as a love poem, a dramatic monologue, a *Frauenlieder* and (usefully for my present purposes) a lyric.[14]

It is the enigmatic nature of the poem that lies behind some of the uncertainties about its genre. I described *Wulf and Eadwacer*, at the start, as a 'fragment'. This is because some scholars have suggested that a couple of lines are missing from the start, perhaps addressed to Wulf (since that seems to be one way in which the divisions of the poem are marked), perhaps addressed to '*min hlaford*' (my lord/husband).[15] These missing lines, it is argued, would clarify the relations in the narrative. Peter Dronke, however, states that the opening of the poem 'concisely sketches the narrative setting, with an allusiveness characteristic of Germanic poetry' (92). For me *Wulf and Eadwacer* is as much a fragment as ' Kubla Khan', where the fragmentation takes place within the poem in the fractured and allusive narrative.

Peter Dronke, by implication, locates *Wulf and Eadwacer* within the continental secular vernacular tradition of women's songs. For Patricia Benaloff, picking up on Dronke's work and the earlier work of Kemp Malone, *Wulf and Eadwacer* is significant precisely because it presents the female voice; it is not female emotions filtered through a male narrator (as in *Beowulf*); it is an expression of 'the feminine in a literary milieu seemingly dominated by heroic male action' (193). She also emphasises how the narrator projects herself 'out of the present and into the past' and out of the present 'confining' location into others (196). Benaloff thus attempts to locate a suppressed female voice and a suppressed or marginalised female subjectivity in the poem. However, this needs to be set against other features of the poem: the syntactic fluidities—in particular, the pronominal uncertainties—to which she also draws attention; and the repetition of whole lines and half-lines, which, as she notes, 'create aural linkages which weave their own pattern through the narrator's words'. Above all, there is, as she puts it, a tension 'between the set patterns and customary linguistic contexts of words in Old English poetry' and 'the intermittent disruption of them' that contributes to the poem's emotional impact. Pronominal uncertainties, syntactic fluidities, patterns of aural linkages, and the disruption of customary patterns and contexts are all features of Griffiths's poetry. They also

[14] See, for example, Lehmann, 151; Kemp Malone, 'Two English Frauenlieder', in *Studies in Old English Literature*, ed. Stanley B. Greenfield (Eugene: University of Oregon Press, 1963), 106–17; Dronke, 91.

[15] Lehmann, 159.

work against the recovery of a unifying voice or a unified subjectivity that Benaloff attempts.

III Griffiths and Translation

During the 1980s, Bill Griffiths studied Old English at King's College, London. He gained his doctorate in 1987 for a scholarly edition of Old English translations of Boethius's *De Consolatione Philosophiae*. He has also published various translations from Old English including an edition of *The Battle of Maldon* (Anglo-Saxon Books, 1991), an edition of *Guthlac B* (Spectacular Diseases, 1986), *The Land Ceremonies Charm* and *The Nine Herbs Charm* (Tern Press, 1986–7), and *The Old English Poem 'Phoenix'* (Amra Imprint, 1990). His published poetry also includes translations from Welsh, Romany and Assyrian. Translation is an important part of Griffiths's poetic practice, and, in his translations (versions he would call them), Griffiths allows the target language to be affected, disrupted, by the different linguistic and poetic practices of the language from which he is translating. Griffiths awareness of other language uses then also impacts on his handling of English in his own work.

To take one example. Bush juxtaposes the Penguin translation of *The Epic of Gilgamesh* with Griffiths's. The Penguin translation reads:

> With the first light of dawn a black cloud came from the horizon; it thundered within where Adad, lord of the storm was riding. In front over hill and plain Shullat and Hanish, heralds of the storm, led on ...

This could be from any language: any sense of cultural difference has been smoothed, erased. Griffiths's translation, as is his common practice, includes the original for comparison. His version is an interlinear translation, but I will omit the Assyrian:

> (when) something-of-dawn (was) in view
> came from the-edge-of-the-heavens (a) cloud black Adad in inside-it thunders
> Nabu and Sharru went in front went heralds (over) hill and plain

As Bush observes, Griffiths's version gives the reader 'some access to an unfamiliar poetic form'. More important, 'it emphasises the oral quality of poetry which in turn reminds us of its origins in interactive public theatre' (216).

In *North Atlantic Texts* 1, co-edited by Bill Griffiths and John Porter, there is a translation of *Wulf and Eadwacer*. This translation doesn't, in fact, allow

the target language to be disrupted significantly by the original language—
beyond the neologism 'murder-keen' to describe the violent inhabitants of
Wulf's island (*walreowe*), the similar neologism 'seldomcoming' for Wulf's
rare visits (*þine seldcymas*), and 'food-lack' for *meteliste*. In each case, Griffiths
draws on Old English methods of word-formation to produce more
precisely accurate vocabulary for his translation. What is most striking
about the translation, however, is the way in which it emphasises the
fragmentation of the original text. It breaks the poem down into 16 fragments: the poem is a series of utterances rather than the enactment of a
unified subjectivity. Furthermore, the way in which the poem is arrayed
across the page both emphasises the fragmentation and draws attention to
those 'aural linkages which weave their own pattern through the narrator's words' that Benaloff mentions. Thus the layout places the lines 'They
will want to capture him if he comes with a troop' and 'We are unalike'
directly above their second appearance. This serves to make even more
problematic their application to what immediately precedes them. The
fact of repetition is emphasised at the expense of the already minimal
sense of narrative continuity. The layout of the poem, the particular disposition of its fragments across the page, also encourages the reader's eye to
find other routes across the page-space than those indicated by the
numbers. Thus, for example, the diagonal movement enacted in fragment
8 ('I / have yearned/ for my/ Wulf/ with a farreaching longing') carries the
reader onto fragment 12 (' Wulf, my Wulf/ the longing/ for you,/ for your
seldom-coming/ has made/ me/ ill') with its obvious subject rhyme. One of
the most radical effects of this increased frgamentation can be seen in the
final fragment ('Man can easily tear apart/ that/ which/ was/ never joined,/
our song together'). This is recognised to be a challenging ending in the
original. What this translation does is sever the apparent connection with
Eadwacer. It might still refer to Eadwacer, but it could equally apply to the
narrator's relationship with Wulf. At the same time, the increased fragmentation of the original can be seen to be acting upon a permission
granted in these lines: the sundering of a song. These are not, I probably
don't need to say this, fragments shored up against a ruin. As Lynne Keller
says in a different context, in relation to Robert Creeley: this is not an
attempt to 'represent in imitative form a shattered order; rather, he
attempts to re-enact a non-order inevitably structured by language itself'.[16]
For Griffiths, as for Creeley, fragmentary structures highlight 'the provi-
sionality and arbitrariness of all orders' (256).

---

[16] Lynne Keller, *Re-making it new: Contemporary American Poetry and the modernist tradition* (Cambridge: Cambridge University Press, 1987), 256.

IV The Poetry of Bill Griffiths

Griffiths's first poems to appear in print were three poems in *Poetry Review* in Autumn 1972: the poems were entitled 'from "Cycles on Dover Borstal"', 'Terzetto: Brixton Prison', and 'To Johnny Prez. Hells Angels Nomads'.[17] Peter Middleton has discussed the first of these, later called 'Cycle 1: On Dover Borstal', at length.[18] He rightly notes the brilliant first line: the single word 'Ictus!' It is both strikingly dramatic and wonderfully condensed. The past participle of the Latin verb *icere* (to strike), *ictus*—i.e. 'struck'—refers, in medicine, to the beat of the pulse; in prosody, to stress on a particular syllable; and, in the phrase, *ictus solis*, to sunstroke. 'Ictus!' thus has the opacity and polysemiousness of some of the problematic words in *Wulf and Eadwacer*, bringing together violence, the body, poetic rhythm and the sun—all of which are important features of the poem that follows in what Middleton terms its struggle 'to articulate the relations between self, language and power'.[19] As the day 'Buckets a strong yellow', there is a moment of self-realisation:

> At running in the sun
> I thought
> This serious, my world is

As Middleton notes, this is a realisation both of the self and of the self as situated in a particular world, but it is immediately countered by the anonymizing pressures of prison, instanced by the prisoner objectified as the addressee of the guard's commands:

> You're you
> And I ain't anyone but you

The final part of the poem plays a sense of overwhelming external power against memories of agency, intimations of personal action, as

---

[17]　*Poetry Review*, 63.3 (Autumn 1972), 226–31.

[18]　Peter Middleton, 'Who Am I To Speak? The politics of subjectivity in recent British poetry', in *New British poetries: The scope of the possible*, ed, Robert Hampson and Peter Barry (Manchester: Manchester University Press, 1993), 107–33, 125–7.

[19]　It is also, perhaps, relevant that, in 'The History of the Solar System' (1978), Griffiths uses the sun as control and the solar system as an arbitrary system of power.

part of the poem's presentation of Dover as a site of invasion, as the site of what Eric Mottram termed 'a number of kinds of violation of self and boundary':[20]

> The flower was forced open by the sun
> Is yellow of bad brass
> Like I beat it golden-black.

The motif is picked up later:

> I think on the pattern of an action
> Till the gold of the answer I can beat anyway

There is the same ambiguity as before: the search for an area of personal agency, in this case the making of an artefact or artwork, which tips into a suggestion of violence, only to be answered by the greater violence of the institution:

> God trumpet you
> Screaming as elephants
> Dog, fist, ground
> God of a hiding.

The poem involves an attempt to find 'lacunae of possibility' within a social world perceived in terms of de-humanising pressures and institutionalised violence, that is, within the authoritarian society that Griffiths's other works also serve to expose.

However, the poem I really want to focus on is the third one I mentioned: 'To Johnny Prez. Hells Angels Nomads'. The poem is divided into 13 short sections. As in *Wulf and Eadwacer*, there is the sense of a fragmented, irrecoverable narrative. As with the first poem, this poem weaves between glimpses of freedom (or, at least, pleasure) and the legal/authoritarian apparatus of the state in a nuanced and constantly self-undermining manner. Thus section 4:

> Bev the sea waving waking
> See this this is Angels getting the booting of their life in Scrubs
> This is Johnny
> This is me picking up snout bits in Brixton

---

[20]   Eric Mottram, '"Every New Book Hacking on Barz": The Poetry of Bill Griffiths', *Reality Studios*, 5 (1983), 45–54, 46.

The first line sounds like a holiday memory or holiday photo, and the successive lines sound like the commentary to a set of holiday photographs, but, if these are snaps, this certainly isn't a holiday. The sense of freedom and pleasure invoked by the first line gives way to the violence and degradation of prison.

Similarly section 5:

> Johnny begot, beading of black Jack-club
> Aiming out, watch run, making around cornering
> Dance kick at drums, can-banging
> Death-douce

It describes a motorcycle manoeuvre, taking pleasure in a display of skill (like dancing) and localised control. It is a game of kicking at a drum, but the dance kick invokes the 'dance of death', and the section that begins with begetting ends with the sweetness of death. There is a suggestion, perhaps, that the taking of risk is already half in love with death. As for love, the next section continues:

> And love
> Works to mix you up miscates the soul
> Love is
> Shooting blood out of a bloke
> Red-laking; is
> Being shut in the breasts of her.

As Bush points out, Griffiths, like Wilhelm Reich, believes that living is based 'on the three pillars of love, work and knowledge', but he is also aware that 'only a tiny part of our emotional range is compatible with the operation of the state' (224). For Reich, the authoritarian discipline of the state thwarts 'natural sociability and the pleasure of work'; 'the compulsive sacredness of the family' thwarts 'the love of husband, wife and children'; and the 'compulsory suppression of sexuality' provides energy for mysticism and the 'irrational.'[21] For Reich, one feature of this 'emotional plague in social life' is 'to escape the difficulties of responsibility and the actualities of everyday life' by seeking refuge in brutality (among other things) (MPF 382). 'Emotional plague' in these lines finds pleasure in violence, turns sex into another prison.

---

[21] Wilhelm Reich, *The Mass Psychology of Fascism*, 375.

V The Lyric

In the preface to his book, *The Medieval Lyric*, Peter Dronke observes:

> The poetry here presented is so genuinely varied that I hope to be
> forgiven if I do not begin with a definition of the nature of lyric itself. (10)

Instead, he hopes his book will add to our understanding of 'what a lyric
can be' (10). In *The Idea of Lyric* (Berkeley 1982), W. R. Johnson described
the lyric as 'the most unstable of generic impulses'. Chaviva Hosek and
Patricia Parker, in their preface to *Lyric Poetry: Beyond New Criticism*,
similarly note 'the difficulty of actually defining what constitutes a
lyric'(13).

In this penultimate part of the essay, I want to address this generic
question by considering the idea that there was a particular concept of
the lyric that was dominant in criticism in the second half of the twentieth century. This concept of the lyric, I will suggest, doesn't fit *Wulf and
Eadwacer* and doesn't fit the work of Bill Griffiths. I want to look at two
moments that seem pivotal in the production of this idea of lyric poetry:
the first involves the Victorian interpretation of Romantic poetry; the
second was the moment of New Criticism. And I want to use a third
moment, the October 1982 Toronto symposium on 'Lyric Poetry and the
New New Criticism', as a lens to bring these into focus.

Tilottama Rajan, in a paper called 'Romanticism and the Death of
Lyric Consciousness' presented at the symposium, brings together these
different moments. She begins by observing how 'From the late nine-
tenth century onward the Romantic period has been characterized as
the age of the lyric, by traditions as different as Victorian criticism and
the New Criticism' (194). Stuart Curran and Herbert F. Tucker both
instance J.S. Mill's 1883 essay 'What is poetry?' as an important contrib-
utor to the Victorian recuperation of Romanticism. Curran argues that
Mill's essay, along with John Keble's lectures as the Oxford Professor of
Poetry (1832–41), 'redefine poetry as the mere expression of lyrical
emotion, an art of spontaneous overflow empowered by an aesthetic
clearly derived from what were mistakenly conceived by these writers to
be Wordsworth's notions of his art'.[22] Tucker similarly notes Mills's priv-
ileging of lyric as being the essence of poetry and his description of

---

[22]   Stuart Curran, *Poetic Form and British Romanticism* (Oxford University Press, 1986), 207.

poetry as 'feeling confessing itself to itself, in moments of solitude'.[23] Tucker further notes a sentence Mill deleted from the essay when he republished it: 'That song has always seemed to us like the lament of a prisoner in a solitary cell, ourselves listening, unseen in the next' (228). As he observes, this attempt to define the lyric actually shifts the lyric into the form of the dramatic monologue.

Rajan argues that the Victorian reading of Romanticism (which she maintains is at odds with the actual practice of Romantic lyric) prepares the ground for New Criticism and its approach to the lyric.[24] She cites Frank Lentricchia's account of the New Critical view of 'poetic discourse as the creation of a free, autotelic subjectivity'.[25] She compares this with Hegel's account of the lyric poet as asserting himself/herself as 'a self-enclosed subject' in a 'subjectively complete world'.[26] This is not, Rajan goes on, the eschewal of the external world, but rather what the lyric poet portrays 'is not objective fact, but "the echo of the external in the mind"'.[27] Jonathan Culler, in 'Changes in the Study of the Lyric', offers a similar account of the New Critical view of the lyric, but also notes its wide currency and influence. Thus, M. H. Abrams, in his *Glossary of Literary Terms*, defines 'lyric' as 'any fairly short, non-narrative poem presenting a single speaker who expresses a state of mind or a process of thought and feeling'.[28] The effect, as Culler notes, is to encourage us to treat the lyric 'as if it were a dramatic monologue' (40).

The readings I have so far offered of *Wulf and Eadwacer* and 'Cycle 1: On Dover Borstal' have stayed quite close to this 'dramatic monologue'

---

[23] Herbert F. Tucker, 'Dramatic Monologue and the Overhearing of Lyric', Hosek and Parker, 226–43, 226. Tucker is quoting from John Stuart Mill, *Essays on Poetry*, ed. F. Parvin Sharples (Columbia, S . C . , 1976), 12.

[24] Rajan argues that Romantic poetry itself 'is in the process of discovering a poetic episteme radically at odds with the New Critical one which it is credited with initiating': 'The interdiscursive nature of the Romantic lyric problematises the mode by revealing the traces of another voice within the seemingly autonomous lyric voice' (195).

[25] Frank Lentricchia, *After the New Criticism* (Chicago, 1980), 109.

[26] G.F.W. Hegel. *Aesthetics* (Oxford, 1975), 2.1132, 1120.

[27] Rajan, 196; Hegel, 2.1133.

[28] M. H. Abrams, *A Glossary of Literary Terms*, 4th ed, (New York, 1981), 99.

model. However, it is instructive to compare these poems or 'To Johnny Prez. Hells Angels Nomads' with, for example, Thom Gunn's 'On the Move' or 'The Unsettled Motorcyclist's Vision of his Death'.[29] The titles of these poems on their own indicate their different stance. Gunn's titles offer a distanced, thematised reading of the poems; Griffiths offers a location and a dedication as titles. Gunn's poems are both monologues and, although they both offer themselves in terms of a conflict between the will and the natural, the natural is already subjected poetically to the lyrical ego:

> The firm heath stops, and marsh begins
> Now we're at war: whichever wins
> My human will cannot submit
> To nature, though brought out of it.

In *Wulf and Eadwacer* and in the poems by Griffiths, there is an emphasis on dislocation and discontinuity rather than coherence. Certainly there is not a sense of a subject or a consciousness that dominates the poem and provides the basis for coherence. In Griffiths's poems the subject is, in various ways, at the mercy of the environment, both natural and social, and is subjected to state institutions. The subjective voice is placed within an intersubjective space, the space of history, law, personal relations:

> Are you tired yet, said the detective?

The subjective voice emerges from, negotiates, dissolves into 'a perpetually shifting intersection of textual surfaces' (Rajan 203) in an art of elisions and disjunctures.

The transformation of lyric into dramatic monologue and the emphasis on the 'solitary mental life' as the overall container for the contents of the poem has an obvious effect on the way the reader approaches the lyric.[30] Thus Culler argues that it encourages us 'to attend to sound patterning when it has a bearing on the attitude of the speaker; and… to interpret puns as wit, though that by no means exhausts the possible functions of the play of signifiers in lyric' (40). In both cases, the patterning of sound and the play of signifiers are subordinated to the 'mental

---

29   Thom Gunn, *The Sense of Movement* (London: Faber, 1957).

30   Jacques Derrida, *Speech and Phenomena*, trans. David B. Allison (Evanston, Illinois: Northwestern University Press), 22.

life' of the narrator. By contrast, Northrop Frye, in his essay 'Approaching the Lyric', asserts that 'the lyric turns away, not merely from ordinary space and time, but from the kind of language we use in coping with ordinary experience'. Andrew Welsh, in *Roots of Lyric* (Princeton University Press, 1978), similarly describes lyric as 'less a particular genre of poetry than a distinctive way of organising language' (21). Frye explains: 'the lyric...so often retreats from sense into sound, from reason into rhyme, from syntax into echo, assonance, refrain, even nonsense syllables'. This echoes Benaloff's account of the effect of the repetition of whole lines and half-lines in *Wulf and Eadwacer* that 'create aural linkages which weave their own pattern through the narrator's words'. It relates also to the aspect of Griffiths's work which I hope has been apparent in the examples I've given, but which I have not otherwise drawn attention to: the obvious concern for rhythm, for the sound of the words.

VI Cultural Margins

I began with two fragments and I want to end by returning briefly to the issues I intended them to raise. First I want to pick up the quotation given by Peter Dronke by attending to Marilyn Desmond's reading of *Wulf and Eadwacer*.[31] Desmond begins with the erasing of women from Anglo-Saxon literary history (574), and the reluctance to acknowledge the presence and importance of women in Anglo-Saxon culture (575).[32] She claims that 'Anglo-Saxon social structures encouraged women to occupy significant positions within the hierarchical structures of the culture' (584), but 'gender' excluded women from 'occupying equally with men the central positions of power' within the dominantly martial and masculine ideology of the *comitatus* (585). Accordingly, she reads the elegies of the Exeter Book as the utterances of cultural exiles 'whose

---

[31] Marilyn Desmond, 'The Voice of Exile: Feminist Literary History and the Anonymous Anglo-Saxon Elegy', *Critical Inquiry*, 16 (Spring, 1990), 572–90.

[32] She notes, for example, that Michael Lapidge, in the first chapter of the *A New Critical History of Old English Literature*, ed. Stanley B. Greenfield and Daniel G. Calder (New York, 1986), 'ignores the participation of women in the "textual communities" of AngloSaxon monasticism' (576).

very expressions define the cultural reality of her marginality' (587). Her essay also emphasises the 'performative' poetics of secular, vernacular poetry: she reminds us that 'the Anglo-Saxon elegy is the product of a vernacular culture that privileged the performative qualities of the text' (583). The Porter/Griffiths translation is also in line with this emphasis on the performative.

Griffiths's own work might, in some ways, have found an equivalent of the *comitatus* in biker gangs, but it is also clear, from the concern in the early poems with borstals, prisons, and East London urban poverty, that these are poems which, while drawing on deep cultural and historical knowledge, are coming from a position of social marginality. I have tried to suggest something of the poems' engagement with an authoritarian state and its agencies—police and courts and prisons; with issues of law and justice; and their sensitivity to, as Mottram puts it, 'the precise points at which social pressure is exerted against the individual' (47)—which come out of this marginalised position. The poems' engagement with language—with syntax, vocabulary and orthography—should also be seen in this context of control and authority: they both enact a position of marginality and offer a demonstration of the arbitrariness of official order.

Appendix

WULF AND EADWACER

To my people it will be like a gift—
how they'll welcome him if he comes in their midst!
Our lots are different.

Wulf is on one island, I on another,
the island a fastness, surrounded by fens.
They are bloodthirsty men on that island—
how they'll welcome him if he comes in their midst!
Our lots are different.

I longed for my Wulf in his wide wanderings,
when the rains came, and I sat loud in lamentation;
then the bold warrior would take me in his arms,

I found joy in it up to that point—but trouble too.

Wulf, my Wulf, I am sick with longing
for you, the rareness of your comings,
with the grief of my heart, not the want of food.

Do you hear, Eadwacer. Wulf is carrying
our pitiful cub to the woods!
How easy to sunder what never was joined—
the story of us two together!

From Black Cocoa Out

TONY BAKER

Sometime in the mid-'80s I asked Bill for some work for the magazine I was then editing. He replied promptly with three pages from what always seemed an inexhaustible stock. The piece was entitled, I think, Sea *Shanties* and has recently been reprinted as *Shanties (through London to Essex)* in *The Mud Fort*. It's a sequence of three-lined strophes that begins:

> Locked in in the beauty
> locked into the beauty
> locked in in the beauty

These lines grabbed me when I first read them and have remained with me ever since.

In itself this is a remarkable if trivial fact. I remember puzzling through a conversation with the late Eric Mottram on why so much 20C poetry refuses to rest in the memory; there was it seemed an apparent contradiction between the great range of poetries from recent times that had engaged me as closely as any from any time or place, and my inability actually to quote more than a word or two from them. The tone and impact of a piece of writing might be memorable—how it reads and the shape it leaves behind in the mind—but I could rarely cite it as readily or as accurately as other poetries from other eras that I didn't even necessarily like. If the poetry was genuinely engaging, why should this be? I don't remember how the conversation ended though we surely reached one of the obvious conclusions, that many of the mnemonic devices that print a line on the memory have tended over the last century to be abandoned in favour of more particular and idiosyncratic musics whose methods can't be transferred from one occasion to another; poets have deliberately sought to make an *occasional* music to set against—or bury within—the tendency of familiar cadences to universalise words. The only generalities possible occur *in the event*, and no events repeat themselves. Memory, on the other hand, requires a kind of repetition, even if it's partial or misleading.

In this respect Bill's lines are, like everything he does, an exception to a rule: for *Shanties*, being a consistently alliterative poem, *is* constructed on a mnemonic method—and so innately more likely to be memorable— that I doubt anyone has explored so deliberately in recent times, unless it's Colin Simms. The resources the poem draws from Anglo-Saxon practice are so evident that it wouldn't surprise me to discover that it's written with a specific formal precedent in mind*; its insistent gerunds at the beginning of strophes and its heavy caesurae, allied to its alliteration, make it curiously ahistorical—an anachronistic gathering-up of wordings cast into a contemporary architecture. But this doesn't begin to explain why, for twenty years, 'locked in in the beauty...' has taken up lodgings in my memory as securely as a Beatles refrain or Humpty Dumpty.

Eric might have pointed out, had I quoted this particular instance, that the task shouldn't be too taxing, for there are in any case only five words to memorise in the three lines. If he had I imagine I'd have replied that Bill's lines have a tenacity in the memory that goes beyond mere memorisation. The words themselves have locked in in the mind like barnacles on a keel—unnoticed most of the time but belonging there as a native habitat: I'd need to scrape them off chemically to get rid of them. There's a kind of magic involved when words can work themselves so thoroughly into a personal mental landscape, invited or not, which is no doubt the skill of those who know how to spell them truly. Indeed, in so far as these lines are magical, while I may wonder how it's done I don't really want to know: demystify their magic and they would no doubt (and quite properly) withdraw their company.

---

* Bill has pointed out to me that Shanties is really a set of haiku in which alliteration replaces syllable count, which doesn't work in English, as a binding device; so the Anglo-Saxon source is 'valid but indirect'. This will probably strike some readers as self-evident. Since my concern here is with how the poem sounds—and I hear Anglo-Saxon more clearly than haiku—the question of a formal precedent isn't in any case critical. I think I'd wondered if there might not have been a riddle-form or some spell-like words for gathering plants at night that had first suggested the shape of *Shanties*.

Of course this says nothing about the virtues or otherwise of the words: I'm simply trying to describe a phenomenon—to say that it happens. I could say much the same about other sequences of words (most, it's true, being words for singing, though not all), and out of context they would seem largely stripped of significance. These for instance: "...but I call him Joe..."— "...the very Veery..."— "...unlikeliest hearts..."— "...an hendy hap..."— "...without a city wall..." &c. Everyone must have their own lexicon of such detached attachments. That "locked in in the beauty" belongs in my personal heap is of no consequence except that I think it may reflect on the way Bill's writing often works on me: common or garden words show up all over his work, spruced and fresh, bright as day, inherently unmemorable or puzzling, and yet striking and compelling, revamped in ways that instantly alert the ears. Open *The Mud Fort* at random and I know I'll find it: page 154, of Quaker-made biscuits, we get "neat fashions of crunch". It's a little inconsequential jig of words, yet versatile and original with its verb-noun and its consonants, busy as ants transporting booty. It opens up an improbable world which nonetheless is right under the nose, like looking down a microscope for the first time at a strand of your own hair.

So here I intend to try to conduct an enquiry—to find out what I can about "locked in..." and to ponder on what makes it, and Bill's work in general—if not always in detail at least in its effects—cling to the memory. In the tradition of television detectives, I'll pile up a few of the evidences that suggest themselves, throw in what may be red herrings, and imagine that a pattern will eventually emerge. It always does, even if it's entirely artifice. The cases of Sherlock Holmes were amongst the first reading that got under my skin and I think it was because the artifice was so obvious that it released the real: no-one ever decided that a person they'd never met before had recently arrived in London on the 6.30 train from Horsham just because there was chalk on the toecaps of his shoes. But the detail seemed real because the artifice, so completely framing it, freed it.

And in order not to mislead deliberately, I ought to add that I know the comparison is limited. I'm not in truth at all sure that any pattern will emerge and couldn't invent the sort of artifice that might permit it to. But it does interest me to search around for clues, as if they can be their own witness. A few years ago Bill circulated an electronic invititation to participate in an Xmas story-game which he introduced like this:

What sort of tale is being telled?....
Supernatural and fantastic elements abound, but there is also a hard

moral core deriving from generations of cultural warfare and a refreshing honesty about the shortcomings of local government under a one-party system. Are strange paranormal forces really seeking to redress the balance between good and evil, smiting down the mighty at the unexpected hour and leaving them cold crowdie to eat? Well, anything is possible if the storyteller is capable of *acting as a true mouthpiece of the folk. Theirs is the ultimately radical voice, turning tradition imperceptibly into invention* (my italics).

Serious stuff. Especially those words about the imperceptible sources of invention.

∼

Bill's mother was a capable pianist and Bill himself, equally capable, is a piano-lover. Only a lover would write of a recently purchased piano this way: 'The action is light but very responsive; the instrument has perhaps been little used, it has no sense of wear or dullness. The base is a growl, the treble rather ghostly and pale, though suddenly brightening when the dampers leave off. In short, a very neat acquisition.' His tastes in pianos are quite distinct—the earlier, it appears, the better. He will reorganise his house to receive a piano, he will spend money he hasn't got buying one and he will travel to piano auctions or Hungarian museums to fool with pianos that he will never be able to afford. To the suggestion that Yamaha's modest half-grands with their chamber-mellowness would suit me fine, he replied 'now, if I were of a Mottramesque disposition, I would respond YAMAHA MAKE MOTORBIKES and slam down the 'send' key'. A list of adjectives from his recent correspondence describing pianos might serve as an approach to his writing: '…light, tinkly, detached, jaunty, strikingly elegant, simple, robust, bright, luscious, tinny, warm, thick, cuddly, semioperational…'[1]

It's striking that he not only has a very precise ear for the sort of sounds that interest him but also that he likes to pass music through a historical filtre. This has nothing (or not much) to do with the arguments about 'authentic' instruments and performance. He knows about these as a matter of historical research. What appears to fascinate him is to hear Haydn, say, transformed in his front room by a historical instrument that metamorphoses how we might *expect* a piano to sound; that is, he's concerned, I think, not to re-create a historical sound so much as to work through history to subvert a contemporary one.

[1] All quotations from e-mails to TB.

He writes in *Shanties* of his boat on its journey through the Thames flood barrier:

> Parading, thru the pride of Greenwich
> choosing a gate thru the Barrier, how grand a gateway, and
> stunningly, no one stops us.

'...How grand a gateway...' might sound oddly rhetorical and anachronistic in anyone else's hands: the alliteration might be taken from Psalms or from a modern verse working of Gawayne. It could be a calculated refusal of contemporary language. But I don't hear it that way because the next line's alliterations, which might come from a letter or an anecdote in the pub, refuse to let me read as if there were historical dislocations. This is now-language rejigged through a historical glass. Which too of course is why 'thru' is written the way it's said, to encourage us to hear it—voice it—as immediate speech. It's as if the words were like the sounds of Haydn as reconstructed by his 1850 Broadwood piano; you might recognise the components but in this register they resonate differently. They arrive in your living space (Bill writes of playing his piano at home, not of concerts or cds) and you wonder—exactly that, you *wonder*—where they're coming from.

∼

Another story about music: we were talking about likes and dislikes. I spoke of Bill Evans and jazz, and he spoke of Brahms and not much caring for jazz. I think I was a little surprised that a poet and musician whom I knew as a committed performer and improviser (this would have been in the late '80s) wasn't especially interested in a music which, in my sense of it, had redeemed the art of improvisation: Bill evidently cared more for the music of an era that had largely buried it. He said, did I know Mussorgsky's *Kovantschina*? I didn't. A few days later by post I got a letter of four pages giving a detailed outline of the opera's plot and a suggestion as to how he thought Mussorgsky dramatised the political tensions in mid-19C Russia. From which I learnt not just about history as the context, by implication, for any work, but that Bill is scrupulous and methodical about detail. His synopsis of *Kovantschina*'s tortuous plot was written out, I feel sure, off the top of his head.

∼

A couple of citations from *The Mud Fort* that may have a bearing on the case:

Making things co-operate

Now I have come to the point

MAKING things co-operate—

is that how it seems to work? (38)

.

Once
in the plural world
there was abuttal—
hand/band/sky/eye
here were grammars of colour
I knew, adhered ... (202)

How do things connect? By adherence, abuttal, designed co-operation. There's no impressionistic infusion or osmotic transition: one thing, another thing, in a plural world, distinct and sharp-edged, pushed up against each other and made to work, sometimes awkwardly, by proximity and consideration of their separate grammars. This suggests the French word *bricolage* whose meanings include either home-made repair work done with whatever is close at hand (and may be both skilfully done by someone who is a gifted *bricoleur* or botched together—*bricolé*— with a hope and a prayer), or a sort of domestic equivalent for what would be called collage in artschool. *Mr Bricolage* is a DIY chain of stores that sells everything to enable the handyman (sic) to make things co-operate and adhere. Which is fine if you want to cut out the middle ground of invention by rummaging around in the cellar at home to see what unused item might be made to serve.

~

Pierre Joris, an immensely gifted translator, has long insisted that translation is the closest kind of reading we can do. A translator has to scrutinise his or her responses to a text so closely that someone else's words can get under the skin and occur, via a sort of biological absorption, in another language; to which there's a necessary admixture of new material that advances the translation into an original domain, placing it at a unique point on an evolving energy-spiral. In Joris' metaphor, translation appears to work like a motor's transmission:

> The pleasure of reading combines with the desire to write to engender a third, the work of translation. A sort of energy-recycling Wankel-engine with its eccentric shaft and its peritrochoid curve from which also at (the best of) times shoot the tangents that are the writing of new poems, the latter feeding on and growing out of the energy generated by the reading/writing translation-engine mixed with what they can adduce from the ambient air, i.e. Her Dailyness.[2]

Music, I think, works in a similar way. How do you create a musical form? By responding to sounds already given—by *translating* the already-heard. I imagine this might well be true of any music though it occurred to me specifically after playing a freely improvised trio-piece. You listen to rhythms, colours, motivic fragments and look for what you can do with them via your own instrument—how you can place them, not as echoes or reworkings (which they may be), but as new conditions within the ensemble of a music that's evolving (or labouring to evolve). You translate the sounds you hear and they are, hopefully, in turn translated.

The seeming anachronisms and calculated formalisms in Bill's writing, like "how grand a gateway", appear natural because they're translations that turn such phrases into synchronisms—that is, they take words from one place and ingest them deliberately within another, evolving context. They become a matter of simultaneities; they occur at a particular point on an energy-spiral from where they will be flung, if read at all, into new configurations by later reader-writer-translators. Bill surely wants this to happen(?). When he writes on a publication that it's *not* subject to copyright, he's not inviting you to copy it so much as declaring that you can't really copy it anyway. All you can do is come along after he's written it and, if so inclined, make your own translation of it— use it as you will; that is, its music will have moved on each time you hear it—each reader will visit at a different point and recognise a different energy-spiral, will 'take for themselves'.

Which is maybe why, Bill's lines

---

[2] Introduction to *4 × 1*, translated by Pierre Joris, Inconundrum Press, Albany, NY, 2002, p.5.

Swelling, the sea-swell
at the tape of the boat, tapping
and turning, a tower of noise

aren't like, say, Pound's translation of the *Seafarer* to which they might
be compared

...known on my keel many a care's hold
And dire sea-surge, and there I oft spent
Narrow nightwatch nigh the ship's head...

Pound's version sounds like Anglo-Saxon poured into a contemporary
mould; it works as a translation (which I'll risk even though I can't
sound the 'original') because Pound is a master-craftsman with an
incomparable ear. Bill's lines sound like Bill because their only moment
is contemporary however it's resourced. Hence he's free to give us thoroughly homemade and commonplace detail and it doesn't sound for an
instant incongruous

Shouting, when I show the map
because of the routes you can take out, the choice of out-routes
vowing that it has to be Bow Locks.

This of course is a circumstance an improvising musician knows well.
Every improvisation has its 'choice of out-routes' and if you choose to go
upstream via Teddington as the drummer is heading for the open sea
beyond Tilbury you may as well try looking for a paddle in a creek. Any
map is provisional and open to interpretation.

~

All of which Bill puts succinctly

But no more
shaping cups
an' pouring myself in them.

Self-generating growth but no purpose
breathless wonder the success is
and we are anywhere... (120)

If Bill's writing sounds like it's all over the place that's because it is and he's miraculously good at it. He remains as beguilingly wide-eyed as a child to whom every experience is new. He's able to toy with any material and let us register 'wonder'.

'Toy' is a pertinent word. We 'play' instruments because putting sounds together is a game in which the thing we draw sounds from is our toy. If we don't read play in Bill's work—the sort of play you find in a playground, spontaneous recreation, or re-creation, of games you can see children playing in Breughel's pictures—then we're going to misread him. We have to pick up his poems like toys and try to figure out how they work, what the game is; and we do it because it's fun, enjoyable as a skipping rhyme that no five year-old bothers to question the meaning of. As Bill says in *Toy World* 'All things that work/ are fun. /There is incipient magic' (143). Like the clattering of a Tinguely *sculpture méchanique*.

∾

There's a story that has Carl Ruggles sitting at a piano and playing a chord of 'C' incessantly. Henry Cowells finds him and says 'what on earth are you doing to that chord? You've been playing it for over an hour'. Ruggles barks back as if nothing could be more obvious, 'I'm giving it the test of time'.

∾

Repetition of a sound translates it. Schoenberg says somewhere, I think in his book on composition, that repeating a sound creates an anticipation of change that the ear will find compelling up to the point that we think that change will occur. If, however, no change occurs after a time the ear gets disappointed and the tension of anticipation is dissipated. This seems broadly true to me though I'd say there are at least these limiting factors: one, that it's very hard without artificial means, to repeat a sound that's completely identical to a preceding one (even if the ambient space in which it resonates is truly unchanged); two, that it's nearly impossible to repeat a sound within an absolutely regular rhythmic pattern (which, unless I've misremembered Schoenberg's commentary, is what he implies); and three, that it *is* impossible if the time-lapse between the sounds is long enough. The church-clock outside the window for instance strikes (mechanically, so the sound is produced more or less identically) every half hour but I can't hear this as a strictly musical rhythmic pattern, though it remains resonate of a kind of social rhythm.

It may be evidence of a particular kind of sensibility but I think the anticipation of which Schoenberg writes is equivalent to wonder: you wonder what will happen to the sound. And if you're the sort of person who can put all those adjectives that Bill finds before different types of piano-sound, you may well wonder *at* the transitions within the quality of the sound itself.

> Locked in in the beauty
> locked into the beauty
> locked in in the beauty

~

We parked in the car park, it must have been near 8 pm. The only people still around were a couple who had a camper-van and were obviously installed for the night. They had put some food on a picnic-bench, placed a rug on it and were singing, she seated and he standing, one foot on the bench with a guitar resting on his knee. They sang, both of them, loudly and with the same gusto and intensity to each song. They seemed heartily glad to sing though neither betrayed much emotion, indeed sang in a fashion that seemed half-routine. At the end of each song they looked at each other, exchanged a few words, and started up the next, the same volume, the same key. There was absolutely nobody listening to them other than us and it would surely have been a matter of indifference to them if there had been. We were twenty metres away and they never gave a sign of having noticed us.

No attempt had been made to tune the guitar; I'm not sure it had more than four strings. For each song the man played it in exactly the same way, strumming an unchanging, unaccented crochet beat, running his hand down the strings from top to bottom. Each song they sang at the same speed, their voices imposed over the guitar's same reiterated clang, the instrument serving as a tuneless percussion. Their music was as matter of fact as boiling an egg. Their voices went free as a yawn or a kettle's whistle. It seemed as automatic as it was necessary.

The sound of the guitar could not have been more raw nor the playing less practiced and yet it was extraordinary: I'd never heard the instrument played like that. I'd never heard anyone dare *play it like that, though I've seen beggars use instruments similarly; with the difference that the beggar would have had the instrument as an accessory that he made no pretence of playing. This man's strumming was committed: he meant the sounds he made. We listened for a while from behind a hedge but moved off as our presence began to seem intrusive and furtive, though I doubt whether either the man or the woman would have cared less whether we stayed or went.*

~

We're never really familiar with a thing. I've lived with 'Locked in in the beauty' for two decades and have only recently realised that 'locked' is a pun. The poem's houseboat(?) making for the open sea has to negotiate canal-locks: it must unlock its path to that open place beyond them. I overlooked the pun I think because mesmerised by the pattern of repetitions and curious about the refusal of my ear to hear the first and third lines as identical.

Locked in in the beauty
locked into the beauty
locked in in the beauty

The ear's right; the repetitions engender, in Schoenberg's sense, anticipations which make the third line sound distinct. That duplicated 'in' creates an obligatory caesura in the mouth, which 'into' in the second line runs on through—the slightest of alterations within a repetition that heightens the ear's interest in the third line. 'In' has been made to sound ambiguous by the second line; it's the focus for a minimal transition which carries over into the third so that the ear jigs around the renewed 'in in' unsure now whether it is or isn't a repetition, but anticipating that the line may change. The anticipation is enough to make the line unidentical even if it's written the same way on the page. Depending how I read the first line (and I think my ear tends to go forward from the caesura to register 'beauty' most emphatically), so the ear re-reads—reinterprets, *translates*—the pause in the third and bounces back this time to register 'locked' more distinctly. Or I think this is so. In any case, the ear rejects the possibility that what it hears is static, as it wouldn't if the lines were repeated continually. They have 'incipient magic' as a result it seems of a combination of acoustics and biology.

And as I write this, my daughter has entered, left and re-entered the bathroom singing 'we all live in a yellow submarine', repeating the line four times to the same melody. Sound is a lovely toy.

~

Which may partly account for how I overlooked the pun buried in 'locked'. You might read *Shanties* as a journey from a locked condition (London, the meanings of its largely lost waterways) towards the open state of the sea's unbridled tides (deep purposelessness, unchannelled energy) as if this were a progress towards a freedom of some kind; and you might go on to read this as somehow representative of what Bill's writing does—seizing on history's social, often neglected evidences and pouring them from 'the estuary out, out to the wider water' where the mere fact of their exposure to wild turbulences and currents leads the imagination to toss them around in a fête of self-generating energies. But in fact the open sea in the poem seems a thoroughly hostile region of 'smashed wreck(s)... blaring blasting tankers and mountainous wake', of waters that 'tumble' and 'race' and 'cascade' and 'rush', of 'mammoth' ships that leave the poet 'aghast'. If this is freedom it's a place to escape from to the 'safer' waters round Maplin, or the haven of the 'fine-sunned field of/Brightlingsea'. The boat's motor only sounds 'lovely' once it turns into the marked channels of the Colne. If the open sea is freedom, it's far less inviting than the controlled routes of the river-mouth.

So a symbolic reading of the poem seems unsatisfactory, even misleading: 'locked' may incidentally be a pun but it doesn't ask, I think, primarily to be understood as an antithesis to 'released'. Its punning truth is less fierce than its direct gaze: 'locked' stares down the line at 'beauty' and the 'beauty' in the poem is the way it sights its details.

Sites them.

The way it paces them.

That pace is what the ear locks on to and which endorses the first line's proposition: reading, we're locked in in the poem's own beauties.

~

You know when you have a skilled writer because he or she will make sounds that are unlike anybody else's. I think if you were to put something of Bill's into a heap of a hundred anonymous texts I'd have a fair chance of finding his. That scrunched Anglo-Saxonishness trundled across a floor of cobbled rhythms, broken gists and lacunae, allied to his scholar-careful intelligence and the sheer fun he has, allows Bill to invent word-salads of an originality and inventiveness you wouldn't mistake for another's. And—an evidence of true authenticity—like any really individual voice, it's extremely hard to fake. I've tried. You can devise approximations of the noises his writing makes but it's very hard to camouflage them convincingly.

You may not have a clue what's going on in a poem but if you can identify its sounds and differentiate them in the hubbub of everything else that sees the daylight in the name of poetry, you have a rare poet. It's like a blindfold test for musicians: if you can recognise a musician by his touch, or her phrasing, or that accent—by any of the elements that give a music its distinctive colour—without further clues to identity, you're listening to those with the most to say. Because they've gone beyond precedent to create something that didn't previously exist.

≈

For example, here's a short poem:

Boat Telly

In the dirty dark
Tug-boat Annie
roaring to kick the other boats off course.
Still, they all end up, only pretty grubby, kid,
in the same park.
Also I am kicking and swearing and cussing
in my sleep, dead and black
a lot of thick plastic star-blocks. (49)

Can I say what this is about?* Not very clearly though I can describe broadly some of the poem's elements. But I'm not sure there's any evidence that the author wants us to be too troubled with what it's *about*. We're engaged to it (or not) by what it *is*.

First, the vocabulary: there's almost nothing here that is Latin-derived—one of the principle sources of the English language is absent. Latin allows us mostly to consider abstractions. Bill's work deals in local, concrete, unabstracted (sometimes indecipherable) detail; it faces the opposite way to abstraction. The vocabulary is also that of speech: 'telly'

---

* When I wrote this I was unaware that Tug-boat Annie was an American-style TV comedy show back in the 50s in which the main characters were competing tugboat owners. Equally I didn't know, as Bill has recently informed me, that he can apparently be very talkative in his sleep. This obviously clarifies the detail of the poem but I haven't changed what I wrote. Any reading is only as good as what you can bring to it at a given moment.

not television, 'cussing' not cursing, 'pretty' is oral meaning 'fairly' not 'attractive'. Equally the order of the words is determined by speech-usage not by literary practice: the gerunds of the sixth line are vocal reinforcements. They struggle, I think, to pass Pound's test: use only those words essential to the presentation. Any one gerund alone would have done. Except, this is how stories are told. Literary usage, of the kind Pound has in mind, requires economy; Bill's medium is speech, or *non-literary* usage written down, which can be gloriously uneconomic. Rabelais, for instance.

Second, the structure: lines one and five are, rhythmically, near-duplicates. If the poem were in two strophes these would launch the two parts of the poem and make an obvious pattern. Every other line is rhythmically very different: the stresses vary in number and fall in different spots; the phrases run at different speeds, either held back by commas or slow vowels or pulled forward by liaisons. Any page of Bill's work will witness this: he's a master of rhythmic variety. Line will follow line, and no two will run at the same speed or follow the same pattern unless, as here, at a given moment he chooses it. (An example at random: the pages of *The Mud Fort* fall open and they offer 'or/ euphoric/ deep-root/ plum/ a-rotted snort pip' (58)—'or' and 'plum' are the only lines with the same number of syllables and these are *paced* differently. By contrast, the lines are stitched around the repeated 'or' and 'ro' sounds which don't vary. This is elaborate artifice.) No poet I know of has so deliberately reversed the methods that Bunting argued were imposed in the Renaissance on native British poetry by the importation of continental models.[3]

Third, the sound: the first two lines contain six words and nine syllables (the proportion is significant: Bill favours saying it in words of one syllable). If we count nine vowel sounds, only 'the' (said as a schwa) and 'dir', and 'ty' and 'nie', have the same sound. The last two lines contain twelve words (only one of which has more than one syllable if we discount the compound 'star-blocks'). Amongst the consonants there are four repetitions of a 'ck'-sound and five of 'l/bl/sl/pl'-sounds. This skill in controlling the density, dilution and diversity of the noises and rhythms words generate together, is the skill of an acute musician. It makes

---

[3] See, *Basil Bunting on Poetry*, ed. P.Makin, John Hopkins UP, Maryland, 1999, where the argument is implicit throughout though perhaps most clearly stated in the lecture entitled 'Thumps' where Bunting distinguishes between the way stressed and quantified languages work.

lengthy passages of Bill's writing relishable even when the sense defeats the ear.

I come back to thinking about Breughel's pictures of children's games. Bill's lines occupy the page like kids at recreation time in a playground: they rush all over the place, they stand around, they disagree, they rhyme, they try to imagine what to do next, they skip, jump, kick, fall over, they shout and repeat themselves, they reinvent history (Breughel's games are our children's games).

They play ball.

It's noisy, it's active, it's near anarchy (how many simultaneous football matches can you pack in a space)

(and still avoid the hop-scotch).

≈

A bit of etymology: 'shanty' is a corruption of the French 'chantez', recorded from the second half of the nineteenth century (so more recent than the pianos Bill likes to play, and not 'traditional'), specifically used of a sailor's song, notably one sung during hard work. A shanty is a worksong, one sung to lighten the burden of a labour, and one that operates collectively. It's opposed to artsong. It has a definite purpose and is social in its action. It incites comradeship and unifies gestures (you sing 'haul away' in order to get everyone tugging at a rope at the same time). It belongs to the people choosing to sing it; to an extent it's invented by them—to the same extent that 'It's a long way to Tipperary' was invented by soldiers as a marching song.

Bill's writing is deeply social: it's about people—about the way we speak, about how phrases form in our mouths (speech has distinct and local grammars), about things, creatures, habits, about objects we buy and play with in our day-to-day lives. It's political in a way that precedes politics; its stuff is the polis in its quirky raw state. When he writes 'we' in *Shanties* it isn't a displaced first person singular hoping for common ground with a reader; he means that he isn't alone on the boat in the poem. Of the 'four mammothian tankers' lying in his boat's road, he writes 'I see them riding to the tide, like us, anchored up.' 'I' is clearly defined within 'us'. One of the lovely directions the poem takes is to berth finally at a moment when the ship's company is named:

Alf and boat, proud as apples
on the fine-sunned field of
Brightlingsea, boat-starred

A shanty needs people to pull in unison.

~

Again, the game of detail: 'Proud as apples' is a vivid figure, and I see Alf on the *prow*.

The lines above I miscopied first, quoting 'the fine-sunned fields' with no doubt the sort of fields that Flanders or Constable's East Anglia bring to mind. It isn't: the word is singular—turning the town of Brightlingsea to a pastoral image like Langland's 'fair field of folk'. In saying Bill's work is political, I meant that it's about *folk*.

~

When I was first learning music I had no idea of what now seems a very odd approach to rhythm. Rhythm, it seemed, emerged as a result of music being written down. I'm not sure it would even have been a concern before being faced with the need to know what a particular way of writing music meant; rhythm arose initially as a thing interpreted from a page, not as a directly felt energy articulating time and occupy-ing the body. The nearest I got to rhythm as a physical entity was trying to copy my teacher's hand-claps. If asked for a definition of rhythm as it then appeared to me I would probably have said it had something to do with the amount of time that elapsed between the notes of a melody within a given measure—the measure being the time signature that appeared at the head of a score ie. rhythm was nearly a *consequence* of melody.

I can't imagine my experience was any different to thousands of others learning music at that time in Britain though it appears to reverse what now seems an obvious order of priorities. Rhythm is the foundation and building matter of any sound-structure: musicians can play together because their perception of how time is articulated coin-cides. Unless the music is designed to lack pulse, it's a shared sense of how time is traversed that creates an ensemble much more than the contours of a linear melody or vertical harmony. As it may have been Wynton Marsalis once said: 'you can play a wrong note and the music continues—if you play the wrong rhythm the music stops'.

In measured music that turns around a pulse, different musics place sounds differently in time. Rock is played on top of the beat; Latin music moves within it; classical Indian music (I'm told and it sounds so) improvises divisions of the pulse according to rhythmic modes; classical, European music, a very vague label it's true—one of the few musics to be written down—tends to limit itself to divisions of the pulse into 3 or 4 main grouped elements and to play strictly 'in time' with these and their subdivisions.

Jazz, another vague term which will have to do, moves *around* the pulse; the musician knows where the pulse is and plays ahead, behind or across it according to the phrase improvised. Jazz singers do this most obviously: Billie Holiday sings so far behind the beat sometimes you think she'll never arrive. In early jazz, up to '50s be-bop say, it's generally the 'soloist' who is permitted the freedom to treat the timing of a phrase most elasticly. In more recent measured 'jazz' the idea of a soloist with a backing has been subsumed in a more complete sense of an ensemble at work in which everyone at the same time, or nobody, is a soloist, so that all the musicians have freedom to phrase in relation to the pulse as they feel it, under the constraint only of what they hear others play and the need to recognise the pulse in an identical fashion. You could probably chart this progression in the evolution of the drumkit, from the low sound of the bass drums of the New Orleans marching bands, hammering the pulse *beneath* the music, to the 'high' sound of someone like Jack de Johnette, skimming with constant invention across the cymbals *above* the music; the point being that the pulse is as clearly felt but not necessarily stated—it's made present by the sculpting of a phrase in time. Rhythmic freedom is released by an instinctive and shared understanding of how the music's pulse works through time. Without that mutual understanding of the foundation there would be nothing to build on.

≈

I come back to Bill's 'Locked in in the beauty', which does in microcosm what so much of his writing manages: it holds me by the way it places sound in time. It's not just that he has an enormous and subtle vocabulary of verbal rhythms, nor that he has the inventiveness to string them together in ways that make his accentuations seem a source of constantly renewable energy wherever the—or a—sense is taking him. It's also that he articulates a pulse so clearly that the reader gets the licence to do the phrasing; like a good rhythm section, we're nurtured as we make our own reading. And if you *say* what Bill writes, I think you'll be naturally drawn into an elastic treatment of time—how long you give each word—around the pulse, which makes you—indeed obliges you—to be part of the invention. It's an approach to rhythm that's exactly opposite to parsing: you don't count the syllables or try to apportion a value to them in short and long sounds so they fit a given measure. You devise their weight and colour in the reading by how you feel the beat—which is dynamic, variable, impossible to define entirely in advance. You can recognise a waltz, say, because the rhythmic pattern is already defined—dum, dee, dee, dum dee, dee &c.; you can recognise a poem by Bill because the rhythmic patterns in his jumbly, gay, 'semi-operational', rivetting word-hoards emerge along the way, and you will have been nursed into finding them for yourself.

∽

Whatever else it is, poetry is a way of saying you're in love with words, just as music is a way of saying you're in love with sounds. Listen to what Fred Frith can do with a homemade dulcimer, some bowls of seeds and some bits of plastic wrapping: unless you enjoy sounds you may find the music hard to locate.[4] Unless you start from the premise that Bill uses words the way he does because he loves them, you may not enjoy the poetry, but he gives us fair indication:

> Everyone takes for themselves, makes what they can. so why
> need for explanation? (47)

Take for yourself, make what you can. Or, as his capitals put it, MAKE what you can.

∽

It would be misleading to make too direct a comparison between the kind of beat Jack de Johnette works with and the sort of beat that occurs in *Shanties*. Bill's beat is more a question of weighting of words around a pause which intervenes with less regularity than a pulse in music; it

---

[4] This example comes from the extraordinary film—an 'improvisation in celluloid'—about Frith's work, *Step Across the Border*, made in 1990, and now available on DVD, Winter & Winter Film Edition, No. 915 001–7.

might be better compared to treating a musical phrase to rubato. The beat nonetheless works as an organiser of a poem's occupation of time. Which is close to Pound's argument about harmony:

> A SOUND OF ANY PITCH, OR ANY COMBINATION OF SUCH SOUNDS, MAY BE FOLLOWED BY A SOUND OF ANY OTHER PITCH, OR ANY OTHER COMBINATION OF SUCH SOUNDS, providing the time interval between them is properly gauged; and this is true for ANY SERIES OF SOUNDS, CHORDS OR ARPEGGIOS.[5]

What Pound appears to be describing is really I think a rhythmic pattern—"the time interval" between sounds—which, when "properly gauged", determines the force of a sound or word: Billie Holiday is compelling because her ability to properly gauge a time interval is unrivalled.

If we read it—place it—at the right moment in time, a word may sound right, or at least convincing, beyond—or in spite of—questions of meaning. The rhythmic dance *is* the meaning to which a poem's other attributes, including its 'sense', accrete.

This isn't a very profound or difficult conclusion. Nursery rhymes work the same way, even if rhythmically less flexible. And in *Shanties* a beat is generally self-evident, so the game of phrasing is easy to play. I can happily fool with these words over and over because they so thoroughly marry sensuous, eye-cocked, quirky detail to a rich patterning of syllables

> In the black cocoa of Bow Creek
> the pudding-masters take a thick streak
> striping, and brand the bow

and still you could ask me who the 'pudding-masters' are and I wouldn't know, nor could I be sure that the 'streak' wasn't a mis-spelling of a 'steak' that the culinary champions had been preparing and which backed its way into the poem and grabbed its intent by way of an unintended rhyme. It's not that these details don't matter—they do and I'd gladly have them clarified. But I can't get further with them myself, so take what I *can* find.

≈

---

[5] 'Antheil and the Treatise on Harmony', in *Ezra Pound and Music: the Complete Criticism*, ed. R.Murray Schafer, Faber, London, 1978, p.296.

Which is all the evidence I want to bring at the moment.

Why has 'locked in in the beauty' stuck in my mind so adhesively? because of what happens between 'in' and 'in' when the line is repeated, because the line invites you to rephrase it—extend the caesura, prolong the 'n' or clip it shorter—when it recurs. Because it says that we have to reinvent ourselves, not as a Thought for the Day but within the terms that are under our noses, and opens to me, as a reader, the occasion. Because the line speaks of 'beauty' so simply in a world where unbeauties are latched on to so much more easily. Because the author has had fun inventing it. Because after twenty years, I still find the words operate a kind of magic.

   And if a Watson were to sort all this out and make a coherent case of it, I'd be curious to know what he'd make of all those uses of the word 'because'. They look untrustworthy to me. Unless they're said with the ironic tone of a child refusing to identify causal connections in response to a question: why...? *Because.*

'In music far mair sweet':
Bill Griffiths in Durham

JOHN SEED

First, the most ordinary situation: a man, a specific and actual man, Dick, playing a fruit-machine:

> Dick on the fruit-machine.
> Money in.
> For lights, and chances, and decisions,
> Some extra spins—guess 'n' gamble
> 'n' lose.
> Why it's like askin' aught of them,
> 'n' they sit in desks.
> Na-win reptiles.
> Sons of Sephim.
> Sackless, pereant
> Et in exterioribus partibus extravagabunt

This is a poem about money from a 1999 sequence of poems about money, 'The Seven Flutes of John Jacob Astor'.[1] Facing the flashing lights and the spinning symbols, quickly calculating odds and decisions, winning some extra spins, until finally—and note the pause produced by the line-break at the end of the fourth line—he loses his stake. All that busy excitement of the first four lines brought to a disappointed halt. In lines 6 and 7 there seems to be a different voice speaking and reflecting. Is it Dick? It is a voice complaining about 'them'—obviously some kind of officialdom, sitting at desks. This is the voice of the powerless. Dialect words such as 'aught' and 'na-win' and 'sackless' indicate that this is the North-East, an area where long-term unemployment has become the

---

[1] Bill Griffiths, *Durham and other sequences* (Sheffield: West House Books, 2002)

norm for thousands of men (and women). These have regularly, (base-ball) cap in hand, to confront the desk-bound guardians of the public purse, the buroo. Asking for anything from these 'na-win reptiles' is like playing a fruit machine—ultimately a game of chance in which the odds are stacked heavily against the punter. Who are the sons of Sephim? I don't know, but they sound as if they have stepped out of the Old Testament. My long forgotten 'O-level' didn't help me to translate the Latin phrase in the final lines much beyond guessing that the nah-win reptiles, those that sit in desks, are cursed and excluded for a long time. But I am advised that this is authentic church Latin, from the service of exorcism: the Sons of Sephim, let them perish (or go away?) and in the outer zones wander (for ever). So this is a curse as well as a poem. Part of the point is precisely that these Latin phrases *are* obscure—that, like the fruit machine, the procedures of law and bureaucracy are obscure, belonging to an incomprehensible language which Dick and his kind (including me) do not quite understand. And yet they (we) somehow participate in their own mystification, cooperate in their systematic duping by those who *do* understand how the machinery works and who fix the percentage of pay-outs in the fruit machine and in the distribu-tion of social security benefits and in all the other monetary outcomes of this economic system. The next poem in the sequence opens with at least a hint that more money is going into that evil fruit machine: 'coins again/ back in the air, bright'.

Forty or so words: colloquial English, Durham dialect, Biblical nomenclature, church Latin. In his 1992 'Introduction' to the substan-tial selection of Bill Griffiths' work in *Future Exiles*, Jeff Nuttall noted the array of languages in his poetry. He detected prison talk, biker talk, dialect, literal translation and ancient English.[2] This short poem has enabled us to add a few more. Further Griffiths' poems would reveal still more—including French and German, children's talk, the argot of Durham coal-miners (Pitmatic), and not forgetting that strange dialect: the standard English of officialdom, of official forms and signs and instructions. The list could be expanded.

But this poem also has a political edge to it. And how could it not have, since poems—like novels, musical works, paintings, films—may be almost as useful to the powers that be as the products of science—even in the serious and profitable business of killing people. Bill Griffiths'

---

[2] Jeff Nuttall, 'Introduction' to *Bill Griffiths Selected Poems 1969–89* in *Future Exiles. Three London Poets* (Paladin: London 1992), 158.

writing is fully aware of the dangers of putting pen to paper, of the infinite capacity of dominant institutions of all kinds to appropriate and recycle meanings. Patriotism, racism, nationalism, militarism, imperialism, —and other isms—have to be aesthetically constructed too. For instance, a huge poetic effort in Victorian and Edwardian England went into driving hundreds of thousands of young men to their deaths on the Western Front from 1914. And when this literary machine was thrown into reverse, the poetry of Owen, Sassoon, Graves, Gurney, Jones and others powerfully shaped the anti-war attitudes of several generations (and perhaps still do).

Bill Griffiths' writing always stands in an oblique and troubled relationship to power, to officialdom, to authority—in a word, to the *state*. This takes a number of forms. One is the often rebarbative surface of his poetry—a dimension of his writing which converges to that of Jeremy Prynne. It is nadgy at times—all knobbly knees and pointy elbows refusing to fit comfortably in any apportioned space. Have another look at 'Dick on the fruit machine'. Or here is another section from 'The Seven Flutes of John Jacob Astor':

> For the flute is all that came off the boat:
> it was
> gazelles/doves/Noah-deer
> in triplicate
> leaping n hanging
> gross books derelict
> there is
> not a
> still bit about
> so much fancy
> balancing/
> dart up

This kind of crabbed and edgy clash of words and parentheses, silences and sounds, repels any kind of facile reading. Interpretation is blocked. And we are returned to the very peculiarities of these visible words on the white page—to their weight and sound and shape—and to the oddness of any grammar and syntax. This opens onto poetry as sound, as the music of words and the human voice. If sometimes the texture of his poetry is crabbed and jerky and difficult, at other times it is smooth and mellifluous; it dances and sings. In the 1970s Bill Griffiths was, with Bob Cobbing and Paula Claire, a member of a sound poetry group and some of his writings from that period, much of it collected in *A Tract Against the Giants* (1984), was written for group performance. Much of his later poetry, whether or not performable by a choir, is also multi-vocal—a chorus of different voices. It is a poetry which takes delight in the sound patterns of words and sentences, which celebrates the sensuous pleasures—and displeasures—of the noise of human language.

More is at stake here than sound and music. This multiplicity of languages and voices pulled together into a poem, is often situated in an everyday moment, in the commonplace. Bill Griffiths' poetry is full of the small ordinary events of the day. The people he encounters, like Dick glued to his fruit-machine, pass through the poem as a name, a phrase, an experience. But they figure in the poem as voices too. They have a say! These voices are not the great and the powerful that fill, say, the pages of Pound's *Cantos*, but they too are capable of epic roles:

> All turned as we walked round the wire,
> they swivelled like one
> considering a smell like of fresh meat.
> 'Now Bill', sez my Vergil,
> 'You oughta be careful here,
> 'We're all level, you know,
> 'But these are semi-wild.

This is from a poem about a visit to Durham Gaol which I want to explore in more detail. The political edge of Bill Griffiths' poetry is not just a matter of formal innovation. You just have to look at the targets of his satire in the *Ghost Tales*. Local aristocratic landlords and coalowners, N.U.M. officials, the local constabulary, Labour councillors, churchwardens, bureaucrats and officials in every form are subjected to a variety of painful and undignified experiences.[3] One branch of the state in particular is excoriated throughout his writings—the prison and its attendant agencies. There are instances where his writing is overtly political and campaigning, such as the long Liverpool poem *Mr Tapscott* (1999), one of the outcomes of his involvement in the campaign for the Toxteth Two, Ray Gilbert and John Kamara.[4] Here we have a bitter political history of Liverpool interwoven with fragments of the autobiography of Ray Gilbert and extracts from his trial and from official and press

---

3   Bill Griffiths, *Ghost Tales of Seaville* (Seaham: Amra Imprint, 1999)

4   Bill Griffiths, *Mr Tapscott: a poem in nine sections with inserts & list of resources* (Seaham: Amra Imprint, 1999)

sources on the Toxteth Riots of 1981. This is uncompromising and angry writing:

> As to settling any minor injustices
> Finally, whoever's charged gets all the blame

Or again:

> the punishment demonstrates the guilt
> so bad or it wouldn't be

Ray Gilbert was in Durham Prison for a while and as Bill Griffiths told Jane Marsh:

> I visited him twice there before he was moved away and was impressed by his resilience and commonsense in an environment a degree hotter than Hell. His claim to innocence is not easily summarised: there is a website www.ray-gilbert.co.uk, with notes on his case by Bruce Kent, if you want more.[5]

Another lengthy poem, *Durham: a visit to Durham Gaol*, came out of these visits. There is much anger here but also much laughter, as in this succinct five-line section on visitors being searched for concealed drugs:

> 10. *The Disposal of the Chewing Gum*
>
> Chewing?
>
> you chewing?
> put the gum in here.
>
> How Tom loss his gum.
>
> Well, who would kiss who?

Here are the closing lines of the whole 23-part poem:

> I don't think
> I don't think so much of this idea

Which idea? Visiting Durham gaol perhaps? It was obviously a painful experience—not least because thirty pounds of Bill's hard-earned money

<hr />

[5] Interview in *Neon Highway* 10, July 2005, at http://www.poetrymagazines.org.uk/magazine/record.asp?id=15617, 21 Nov.2005

was purloined from his locked locker in the Durham Prison Visitors' Centre. In the words of Tommy Armstrong, himself a former inmate: 'There's nee gud luck in Dorham Jail/ There's nee gud luck at awl.' Or perhaps the bad idea is that of the prison itself as an institution? And this returns us to the opening line: 'A vast speculation'—speculation both in the sense of a vast gamble, a huge insecure investment, and in the sense of an idea, the vast abstract idea of incarceration.

There is much more to be said about Bill Griffiths and the contrary relationship of his writing to power, about his representations of borstals and prisons, about his affinities to Michel Foucault, the only theorist I have heard him speak of with admiration.[6] But there is a section of *Durham* which points us back to the question of languages, dialects and power. In *Briggflatts* Basil Bunting had burst out: 'Pens are too light. / Take a chisel to write'. Bill Griffiths prefers a quill. Section 21, 'The perception', consists of a sequence of fragments of officialese—the metallic voice of bureaucracy, peremptory, authoritarian, measuring and controlling:

> Do not attempt ...
> To get to, get through...
> Stand clear...
> The arrival at...

And so on for fifteen unfinished lines. This is the dialect of power, a minority dialect but one which is embodied and universalised in writing, and above all in print. The poem concludes with these four lines:

> From the ground the quills he gathered,
> All the little shining arrows,
> Stained them red and blue and yellow
> With the juice of roots and berries...

Can poetry, and whatever else stands against that huge disciplinary power realised in Durham Gaol, be written in standard English? Can a poem survive in the same print form as these bureaucratic edicts without being implicated in its normalising effects? Take a quill dipped in the juice of roots and berries to write! Note that here the quills are found and gathered, not stolen from the hedgehog's back. And note also that quills gathered together in sufficient numbers are an impressive defence against predators. The fox as they say, knows many things; but

6   See in particular Michel Foucault, *Discipline and Punish. The Birth of the Prison*, trans. A. Sheridan (Harmondsworth: Penguin, 1979).

the hedgehog knows one big thing. Quills can become offensive weapons too—'little shining arrows'. (Another theme that could be pursued further is the role of animals in the poetry of Bill Griffiths: 'And our bodies are mad with the forgotten memory that we are creatures' (Michael McClure, *Poisoned Wheat*, 1965). There are mad bodies and tortured animals in and around Bill Griffiths' Durham gaol—including a peacock, a pony, a tiger, frogs, ants, worms, antelopes, cows, Sonic the hedgehog, a badger's arse, a vixen, a bear's head, a dragonfly, birds, owls, spiders, and dogs, lots of dogs. Animals are everywhere in Bill Griffith's poems—and sometimes they speak! (Food is another Griffiths topic which would keep you busy for a long while.))

Counterposed to standard English, the written language of power and authority, is spoken English—dialect, in all its multiplicity and fluidity. And this brings us back not just to the miscellaneous voices and dialects of his poetry but to Dick standing at the fruit machine and *his* troubled voice: 'Why it's like askin' aught of them, / 'n' they sit in desks.' As I have said, Bill Griffiths' poetry is full of the voices and names and experiences, the pains and the pleasures, of the ordinary people he encounters, especially in the local setting of Seaham and, more broadly the North-East of England. In *Durham*, for instance, there is Tom who accompanies him on his grim visits to the prison, Neil, Ben, James and Lisa, John (and his uncle). Part of the bitter complaint of losing thirty pounds, stolen from his locker, is because of its impact on James and Lisa who will be there for the delivery of a bag of wood to Alfred Street on the following Sunday afternoon: 'How tell them my pockets are empty'. And so they too, and the economy of those with 'means too careful for coal', become part of the poem. We are asked to 'picture the wood coming to the estate' and I do, picturing Lisa at the pony's head, waving out of the poem. Hello.

Bill Griffiths does not merely use this locality and its linguistic culture, and its individual people, as the rich soil in which his poetry can take root. He also works to *produce* this locality, its culture and its dialects. Poetry does this too. But since his sudden and unexpected arrival in the North-East in 1990, he has been involved in a prodigious amount of mostly unpaid labour—as writer, editor, publisher, teacher and organiser—to preserve, support and develop different elements of the language, culture, history and environment of the region. He has engaged in a considerable amount of local history and has written and published various pamphlets and books on the Seaham district. He had hardly lived there for a year when he drafted and published *A Seaham*

Reader. By 1993 he had published *Seaham: A provisional bibliography*. And over the next few years there appeared studies of the Seaham fishing fleet, of smuggling along the coast, and of Seaham Hall.[7] And he has produced several websites to serve the local history community on the Durham coast: see especially *The Story of Seaham* (Local Heritage Group)[8] and *SR7 Seaham & Region* (East Durham Online News Journal)[9]. He also got involved in moves to preserve aspects of the local environment and has been a thorn in the side of the local Council on several occasions.[10]

The area of his work I particularly want to emphasise here—and it is a thread which runs through everything he writes in recent years—is his concern with dialect. Rural dialects have always been valued and thought worthy of study. Exemplifying older traditions and ways of life, they appealed to a powerful romantic strand in English intellectual culture. By contrast, there has not been much encouragement for the study and the celebration of the impure and unstable speech of industrial districts like Tyneside, Wearside and Teesside. For instance, Basil Bunting's great Northumbrian epic, *Briggflatts*, made much of its roots in the language of the region. 'The Northumbrian tongue travel has not taken from me', he says in the notes to the poem. 'Southrons would maul the music of many of the lines in *Briggflatts*'. We find the occasional dialect words—'spuggies', for instance, or 'oxter'— and instructions on how to pronounce a word like 'scone': 'rhyme it with 'on', not, for heaven's sake, 'own'.' Bunting grumbles about the ignorance of their own history among Northumbrians—'all the school histories are written by or for southrons'.[11]

---

7   Bill Griffiths (ed.) *A Seaham Reader parts 1–6* (Seaham: Amra Imprint, 1991); (ed.) *Seaham: A provisional bibliography* (Seaham: Amra Imprint, 1993); *In Praise of Church Street, Seaham* (Seaham: Amra Imprint, 1993); *The Mythology of Seaham: A review of Tom McNee's local history publications* (Seaham: Amra Imprint, 1994); *Readings in Seaham History* (Seaham: Amra Imprint, 1994); *The Seaham Fishing Fleet* (Seaham: Amra Imprint, 1999); *Smuggling in Seaham* (Seaham: Amra Imprint, 2001); *Seaham Hall & its Owners* (Seaham: Amra Imprint, 2003)

8   http://www.seaham.i12.com/sos/sos.html

9   http://www.seaham.i12.com/sr7/sr7.html

10 See for instance Trevor Charlton & Bill Griffiths: *The Denes of the Bishopric* (Seaham: Amra Imprint, 1995); Bill Griffiths, 'Coastal strategy in Co. Durham: Turning The Tide or Lossing The Beaches?' *Northern Review* 4 (1996) pp.100–104; Bill Griffiths 'More on the coastal zone of County Durham: the case of the overlooked denes' *Northern Review* 5 (1997), 47–51.

11 Basil Bunting, *Collected Poems* (London: Fulcrum, 1970, 2nd edition), 156–7.

Copper-wire moustache,
sea-reflecting eyes
and Baltic plainsong speech
declare: By such rocks
men killed Bloodaxe.

But, however beautiful its opening and closing Northumbrian sections, *Briggflatts* imagines a landscape and history which in most respects stopped a thousand years ago. It is a Northumbria without coal-mines and shipyards and trams and cinemas and without waves of migrants from nineteenth-century Ireland, Scotland and elsewhere.[12] *Briggflatts* is a poem which in key respects does not connect with the language and the history of the twentieth-century inhabitants of the North East and which pretty much subscribes to the romantic pessimism we find in a passage like the following:

> What we have lost is the organic community with the living culture it embodied. Folk-songs, folk-dances, Cotswold cottages and handicraft products are signs and expressions of something more: an art of life, a way of living, ordered and patterned, involving social arts, codes of inter-course and a responsive adjustment, growing out of immemorial experi-ence, to the natural environment and the rhythm of the year . . . Relics of the old order are still to be found in remote parts of the country, such as the Yorkshire dales, where motor-coach, wireless, cinema and education are rapidly destroying them—they will hardly last another decade. In those parts speech is still an art. And the cultivation of the art of speech was as essential to the old popular culture that in local variations existed throughout the country as song, dance and handicrafts.[13]

And yet the North-East dialect, with all its variants stretching from Teeside north across Durham to the Tyne and into Northumberland, is a rich and complex language, incorporating a range of Old English and Old Norse based words. There is also an admixture of maritime vocabu-lary, especially Dutch. New waves of migrants into the North-East—Irish and Scottish especially—made further contributions. It is also worth stressing that North-East dialect is not just a matter of *passively* absorb-ing sources, however important these are. From the eighteenth century

---

[12]   For an interesting account of the continuing pertinence of the pre-1066 history of the region see David Byrne, 'Is the North of England English?', *Northern Review*, Vol.8 (Autumn 1999), pp.18–26. See also John Seed 'An English Objectivist? Basil Bunting's Other England', *Chicago Review*, Vol.44, Nos.3/4 (1998), 114–26.

[13]   F.R. Leavis and D. Thompson, *Culture and Environment* (London: Chatto and Windus, 1933), 1–2.

this language was shaped by the experience and the conscious cultural and political activity of generations of working men and women across the region. They had produced by the late Victorian period a rich and complex regional dialect with an equally rich and complex popular culture. It was realised in literature and songs, in a powerful political tradition and in a strong sense of regional and social identity.[14]

But, like many other dialects, lacking any kind of consistent system of spelling, the speech of the North East has been at some disadvantage during the twentieth century. Inevitably, as first the education system and then radio, films and television, have influenced the speech of the inhabitants of Durham and Northumberland, much dialect has fallen out of everyday use. This is where there is a measure of convergence in Bill Griffiths to the pessimism of Leavis. In *North East Dialect* (1999) there is an emphasis on the steady erosion of dialect as the tight local, and generally work-based communities, that sustained it—coal-mining, ship-building and so on—disappeared. New occupations, new technologies, reinforced by education and the media, are key factors in the spread of standard English, or indeed something much worse:

> The 1980s have seen the spread of a slightly sub-standard English (dubbed 'Estuary English'), allied to right-wing views on every subject, which may give a turn to the decline of dialect.[15]

So-called standard English is a minority dialect spoken by as little as 5% of the population. In fact, it is not even worthy the name of dialect. Rather it is a specialised primarily written language: 'it is at root limited and inflexible, non-oral and impersonal, and it would be safer regarded and taught as a second language'.[16] Against this, what chance of long-term survival has an oral dialect, with no standard system of spelling?

Here Bill Griffiths has done pioneering work. In 1994 he published under his own Amra imprint the 70-page *Durham & Around: Dialect word list*. A much expanded version of this, with a long introductory essay

---

[14] I am summarising here, too briefly, two excellent accounts provided by Bill Griffiths: 'Last word: dialect' in *Newcastle upon Tyne: a modern history* ed. Robert Colls and Bill Lancaster (Chichester: Phillimore, 2001), 361–366; 'Historical introduction', *A Dictionary of North East Dialect* (Newcastle: Northumbria Univ Press, 2004), ix–xxi.

[15] *North East Dialect: Survey and Word-List* (Newcastle: Centre for Northern Studies, 1999), 45.

[16] *Ibid.*, 45–6.

and other useful material, was published as *North-Eastern Dialect: Survey and Word List* by the Centre for Northern Studies at the University of Northumbria in 1999. And in 2004 the University of Northumbria published the elegant *A Dictionary of North East Dialect*.[17] The cautious pessimism of the 1999 *North-Eastern Dialect* is more than counterbalanced by his upbeat message in more recent years—on the website of the Durham and Tyneside Dialect Group for instance. Here the fluidity of North-East dialect becomes a positive factor in its survival:

> In its free, imaginative and often humorous use of words, North-East dialect in particular seems to retain a creative energy that balances the static form of 'proper' English; its extra inputs from Scots and Dutch in the early 19th century give it uniqueness among English dialects and the keen vitality of urban life helped it develop an unusual flexibility and expressiveness; its vowels and intonation retain a singing quality, welcome to the ear, in admirable contrast to the raucous twang of the capital.[18]

'The status of a dialect/language depends not only on the numbers and energy of its speakers, but on the achievements of its literature.' For Bill Griffiths the preservation and development of North-East dialect literature in all its forms has been central to everything he has done in the area since 1990. The region may not have works to rank with the old Welsh or the Scots, as he is the first to admit. But it has much poetry and song of national significance, especially from the nineteenth century. And there is much twentieth century material still to retrieve and preserve. Bill Griffiths has published four editions of an expanding anthology of North-East dialect poetry and prose. The most recent is: *North East Dialect: The Texts*[19]. He has also produced editions of important dialect poems: Edward Chicken's early eighteenth century *The Collier's Wedding* and from the 1890s Alexander Barrass's *The Pitman's Social Neet*. These are each long and ambitious texts which had fallen into obscurity, a few ancient copies gathering dust in the stacks of libraries. He has also

---

[17]   Bill Griffiths (ed.) *Durham & Around: Dialect word list* (Seaham: Amra Imprint, 1994); ed. *North East Dialect: Survey and Word List* (Newcastle: Centre for Northern Studies, 1999, reprinted 2000); *A Dictionary of North East Dialect* (Newcastle: Northumbria Univ Press, 2004)

[18]   http://www.indigogroup.co.uk/durhamdialect/ddahistory.html

[19]   *North East Dialect: The Texts* (Newcastle: Centre for Northern Studies, 2nd rev. edn. 2002).

done work on the important early nineteenth-century dialect poetry of Thomas Wilson, especially his splendid long poem *The Pitman's Pay*. The website of the Durham and Tyneside Dialect Group has reprinted work by Wilson and other dialect writers and it is to hoped that full online editions of the long poems by Chicken, Wilson and Barrass can be provided in the near future.

So with these new editions Bill Griffiths has succeeded in preserving and diffusing these neglected collections of North-East poetry. But these are not just writings, they are also part of an oral culture. Thus the edition of *The Pitman's Social Neet* includes some of the original tunes of the Barrass songs where they can be traced and has added replacement tunes where they cannot. These are texts for performance and in the preface Bill Griffiths concludes with an acknowledgement and an invitation:

> I would particularly thank Benny Graham in West Stanley for his advice on the text and for helping me with his knowledge of authentic tunes—he has the invaluable experience of having performed the work live. May this edition encourage many more performers and performances.[20]

The Pitman's Social Neet is, then, to be relished and shared and enjoyed in social gatherings—it should be part of an oral culture and a living community. Its predominant voice and experience is that of the pitmen, young and old, with different jobs in the pit. The poem tells us much about relations within the pit. But other members of the community get a say too, including several women. The songs remain just about decent and respectable, though they contain much raucous humour, much fun and joy in life. Song 3, 'Sarah' for instance, tells of a young woman whose courting with a young pitman called Charlie Broon (Brown) is continually interrupted by her mother's chorus about the dangers:

> O, Sarah! Sarah! fie for shem, Sarah!
> Bringin disgrace te yor feather an' me!
> O, Sarah! Sarah! fie for shem, Sarah!
> Aw knew very weel what yor cortin wad de!

And sure enough on her wedding day, through difficult times and even now that they are comfortably settled with a steady income and a

---

20   Bill Griffiths, 'Introduction' to Alexander Barrass, *The Pitman's Social Neet* (Seaham: Amra Imprint, 1993, 2nd edition 2000)

healthy young family, her mother pops up and 'the aud body 'ill giggle an' cra her chorus'.

There is also a darker note running through *The Pitman's Social Neet*. Barrass was a pitman himself and these are 'sangs dash'd with experience'. They are also about hard and dangerous working conditions, low wages and bad housing conditions, cold and hungry nights, the death of children, regret for the past and the pain of old age. The conclusion nicely balances the careless pleasures of the young pitmen at the end of the night with the more reflective mood of the older men

> As seun as they had deun thor cheerin'
> Away they teuk thor hyemward beat,
>   The young 'uns laffin' an' careerin.
> While slae, an' far mair thowtful te,
>   The aud men tawk'd the past times ower:—
> Of what the binndins used te be,
>   An' what the strike o' forty-fower.

But the social bitterness that surfaces again and again in these poems/songs is deflected and softened in the final lines with the comforts of stoicism and good ale, too often the traditional resort of Geordie working men:

> Poor sowls! Aw whisper'd te mesel,
>   Yor's is, ne doot, a dowly lot;
> But ower a quiet pint o' yell,
>   Yor thoosand ills ar' aal forgot.

The Pitman's Social Neet is splendid stuff, a delight to read. It must be wonderful to hear it performed—preferably in a noisy smoky Durham Working Man's Club (C.I.U. of course). If sometimes Barrass's songs appear sentimental, Bill Griffiths warns a complacent reader, 'that is little more than an indication of our refusal to empathise with the feelings and fears of the old of that time'. He is referring to one specific song here but the point stands for our response to the whole collection.

Alexander Barrass alas had some kind of breakdown at 36 during the 1892 miners'strike. He spent the last 35 years of his life as an inmate in the Sedgefield Asylum, diagnosed as suffering from 'melancholia'. This asylum figures in one of Bill Griffiths' stories, 'The Walkers', as a grim grey place on the horizon of East Durham. It incarcerated all those helpless hopeless cases who were in some incomprehensible way ill and who failed to cope with the norms and pressures of everyday life:

Once admitted, there was no real chance of remedy; all came to act in the way expected of them, wholly dependent, wholly servile, as befitted damaged and improper minds, cared for by a humane but strict regime...

And finally these unpeople were buried without Christian ceremony in the asylum grounds—'laid out in rows, unheeded hillocks in a rough field that could never be developed'.[21] At the end of the story these anonymous graves are discovered to be empty. Had these bodies, even in death abandoned by their families and communities, been used for medical experiments? Or is this a metaphor? In either event we are back in Foucault territory here—the asylum, like the prison (and the hospital and the school), is part of the network of disciplinary and normalising power. But—and this is no more than an occasional flickering hope in the writing of Foucault—there is memory. The graves are empty because they hold (or held) the remains of the nameless and forgotten. The action of remembering projects back into these empty slots a body, a person, a life—and a life that is part of a wider network of lives, which is a society and a culture. One of these graves at least has a body now—that of Alexander Barrass, poet, died in the Sedgefield Asylum, 1929.

One other point about 'The Walkers'—I have never read anything which does so sensitively empathise with the feelings and fears of the old, and remarkably, gets inside the experience of an old woman suffering from senile dementia. And I think that understanding has something to do with Bill Griffith's grasp of the language that his neighbours speak—not just this sad sick old lady Ilma, but also Dick at his fruit machine, Tom having his feet examined by the guards in Durham prison, Neil at the skating rink, James and Lisa and the pony and cart delivering firewood on a Sunday afternoon—and the whole cast of 'Seaville' characters who fill the pages of his brilliant *Ghost Tales* and other stories. Bill Griffiths' writing is becoming increasingly inseparable from the living oral culture and social life of the North-East of England. And if that culture and its language survive and adapt, that will owe much to the persistence and hard work, year after year, of Bill Griffiths.

---

[21] Bill Griffiths, 'The Walkers', *Northern Review*, Vol.8 (Autumn 1999), 1–17.

'& that / that divide': poetry and social commentary in Bill Griffiths

FERNANDA TEIXEIRA DE MEDEIROS[1]

Around 1999, while beginning to do research for my PhD thesis in Comparative Literature, I became acquainted with English non-mainstream poetry—quite by chance, I should say. I was browsing the web when I came across two titles that drew my attention: the anthology OTHER[2], and the collection of essays *New British Poetries: The Scope of the Possible*[3]. I ordered the books and when they came I was surprised not to have ever heard of, or read about, names that seemed too significant to have been forgotten by handbooks and histories of English Literature or commercial anthologies: Eric Mottram, Bob Cobbing, Allen Fisher, Bill Griffiths, Thomas A. Clark among so many others. Not only did these poets produce extremely original work but also their critical pieces, in the case of Mottram, were vigorous and sophisticated. The ostracism of, for example, Basil Bunting, was rather baffling to me as well. I learned later on, in the course of my research, that the silence surrounding these names and the event with which most of them were involved—the British Poetry Revival, as Mottram called the 1960s and 70s upsurge of non-mainstream poetry—was informative enough in itself.

The reason for such censorious silence was that the poetry these authors produced, encompassing Poundian experiments, soundtext and

---

[1] Fernanda Teixeira de Medeiros is Brazilian and teaches English Literature at the Rio de Janeiro State University.

[2] CADDEL, Richard & QUATERMAIN, Peter, eds. OTHER; *British and Irish Poetry Since 1970*. Hanover and London: Wesleyan UP, 1999.

[3] HAMPSON, Robert & BARRY, Peter, eds. *New British Poetries; The Scope of the Possible*. Manchester & New York: Manchester UP, 1993.

[122]

concrete verse, differed tremendously from what had been canonized as "good" poetry or simply as "English" poetry, deviating from the prevailing model of the short lyrical piece, teachable and paraphrasable, as Mottram would put it, as well as engaging a different context of reception, strongly connected with performance and independent small-press publishing. The most emblematic example of the rejection of these innovative voices was to be found in the foreword Andrew Motion and Blake Morrison wrote for the *Penguin Book of Contemporary British Poetry* (1986), in which they claimed that two of the most effervescent decades of the 20th century, the 1960s and 1970s, had been doomed by a "spell of lethargy" as far as poetry was concerned. For anyone who has had the chance to read non-mainstream authors, this comment is a classical piece of poetic prejudice. What the two anthologists and establishment literary culture as a whole had chosen to ignore was a remarkable variety of dictions which gave up the lyrical voice of the almighty I wishing to express feelings in verse in favour of other adventures in language.

The tension resulting from different notions of poetry and the fact that one of these notions was claimed to be the "correct" and thus the "national" one immediately caught my interest. It disclosed the intricate relations between the politics of language and nationalizing policies for language under whose jurisdiction poetry was to be included. Besides my interest in the issue mainstream *versus* non-mainstream, I was also attracted to the poetry "on the other side" in that it was very challenging, original and, in a very positive way, un-English.

After this initial contact with non-mainstream poetry, I eventually went to London for five months in 2001 with a student's grant to do field research[4], visit specialized libraries and interview poets. This trip was one of the strongest intellectual and cultural experiences I have had and enabled me to write my thesis on British and Brazilian marginal poetries of the 1960s and 1970s, defended in 2002[5].

The point of mentioning this somewhat personal story is my belief that to read Bill Griffiths one needs to be aware of some contextual data:

[4] I was enormously benefited in my research by the Mottram Archive, at King's College, organized by Bill Griffiths.

[5] I had the honour of having Professor Clive Bush, from King's College, London, as my supervisor in England. I am deeply grateful to him, not only for his personal and academic support, but also for having supplied me with his excellent anthology and collection of essays on contemporary British poetry (*Worlds of New Measure—An anthology of five contemporary British poets* and *Out of Dissent. A study of five contemporary British poets*, respectively, both from Talus Editions, London, 1997) even before we had met.

the fact that non-mainstream poetry is rarely reviewed; the fact that there are deep tensions cutting across the apparently quiet landscape of contemporary English literature which mainstream culture makes an effort to ignore; the fact that the 1970s witnessed a very lively moment for poetry, when, for example, the Poetry Society was directed by alternative poets who opened its doors for foreign authors and for experimentalism and had Eric Mottram as the editor of *Poetry Review*. Bill Griffiths took part in that, operating the machines in the Society's print shop with Bob Cobbing.

Moreover, it is worth mentioning that to a culture which has had language as one of its main tools of empire it is no wonder that there are mechanisms to protect an "ideal functioning" of that language, and that in English terms it is noticeable that this ideal functioning has to do with communicability. Language has to communicate effectively and if it fails to do so there is something wrong with it. The same applies to poetry. The communicational model of *A* sending a message to *B* has to be respected by poets. This imposes enormous constraints, the most serious of all being the very notion of language underlying this model, namely, that language is a transferable commodity. *A* possesses a meaning which he/she will transfer to *B*, who will, in his/her turn, take possession of it. It is exactly this model which non-mainstream poetry shatters. If discourse does not have a clear owner, a defined addressee or a well organized message, and, moreover, if it indulges itself in being transmitted orally and outside the official market, language becomes a no man's land, with unguarded entrances and exits. To some, this means freedom to experiment; to others it means violation of the sacred principle of property.

Interestingly enough, though, the poem's distancing from the standard communicational model does not mean that poetry has distanced itself from people or their lives; quite the contrary. On the occasions I met and talked to Bill Griffiths it became very clear to me that as far as non-mainstream poets are concerned their ethical and aesthetic projects are deeply intertwined[6]. The option not to compromise aesthetically usually affects the poet's mode of living and vice-versa. In other

---

[6] Obvious though it may seem, I would like to stress the fact that the opportunity to interview Bill Griffiths or talk to him informally was very enlightening to me. It helped me to understand his poetry better and to have a more mature view of English culture and literature as a whole. Griffiths was kind enough to let me videotape him reading his poetry, which he chose to do outdoors, in the streets. It turned out to be a very good material (we had the help of a professional film-maker), which still needs editing, though. Bill has a copy of it.

words, there is an existential dimension to the writing which goes far beyond the accounts of one's memories or one's "feelings". The association of this poetry to performance is evidence of its connection to life. As performance, to most non-mainstream poets, represents an engagement of the poet's body and history with writing, it is the very mark of the indisociability between poetry and breathing, between the text and its concrete existence within a defined social context.[7]

In Griffiths's case the inseparability of life and art is quite evident precisely because there is a high level of experimentation in his production. At a first bite (and second and third), his poetry is much more than a non-native English speaker could chew; it is often difficult work, as he himself acknowledges, with a large range of references, found texts, foreign languages and dialect materials, besides a fondness for non-linearity of thought and its visual embodiment in line rupture. It does not seem to me, though, that it is a typical postmodern case of investment in fragmentation and collage, parody and pastiche, from a cynical perspective. Experimental risk in Griffiths is always critical and never gratuitous. His formal restlessness is rather an "objective correlative" for a deeply-felt discomfort with the world he lives in and a sign of his permanent quest for the new: "people were looking for new things in the 1970s, yes, in a sense that was part of a new movement, a new exploration, but that fits just as much now, yes you can carry on, you can look for everything that's new, you don't have to be within a predicted framework or group,"[8] he asserted when he noticed I tended to mythify the innovative drive of the 1970s.

In addition to understanding what motivates experimentation in Griffiths, one must bear in mind, when reading his work, that he is a highly educated poet who brings into what he writes not only his values and personal experience of living on the margins in the 1970s but also his doctoral training in Old English, his musician's ear as well as his literary knowledge. Taking all this into account certainly helps us build a framework to approach his poetry.

One of the instances in which this framework proves useful is Griffiths's poetry of social commentary. It is almost redundant to say that a poem is a "social poem" or that a poet writes "social poetry" in that it is impossible to detach oneself from one's own context—to varying degrees and in different ways this context will imprint itself in an artist's work.

---

[7] As regards the intrinsic connections between poetry and performance, see, for example, MOTTRAM, Eric, "'Declaring a Behaviour': The Poetry Performance". In: *RAWZ* 1, London, 1977, s/p.

[8] Griffiths in the interview I did with him in April 2001.

However, the poet may wish to address social issues in a direct way, and in Griffiths's work this produces a very interesting result—never obvious, never propagandistic, never simplistic. Griffiths is a militant; his ceaseless and prolific writing is no doubt a form of activism, albeit a skeptical one.

"The Breed" and "Trade" are two pieces produced from the perspective of the "skeptical militant". Combining formal inventiveness with sharp social criticism, they are what I would call perfect poems, perfection here meaning not stability or univocity, but a very high success in the amalgamation of imagery and formal resources into a complex and lively whole. In these poems Griffiths does not tame his fondness for breaking up his verse:

> To me the way to get out of one of the traditions of just a continuous poem is to break it up and when I read back I prefer those pieces of mine which break up the flow of the verse by bringing in information or found text or speech or quotations or something different, a different rhythm, a change in the rhythm of some sort.[9]

Yet, in the act of reading a coherence emerges at the level of construction. These two pieces, like others by Griffiths, do not "talk about" but rather materialize visually and rhythmically the clashes he is interested in exploring. Sensuous thought works in favour not of metaphors or conceits but of an embodiment of tensions in language.

Let us start with "The Breed", which, I believe, contains the core of Griffiths's social theory. It is part of a sequence called *Darwin's Dialogues*, from 1991.

The Breed

The gull pecks at the stone
yelling like a
hammer.

Things that snarl and beg:
the elimination
of dogs.

Unable to guard the world-egg properly
they break again into
argument, fight.

⁹ Idem.

The thing that doesn't work,
won't match, he
hurls it away.

How can a lady be touched
by the hand of
a labourer?

All the exhibits are cased,
glassed in, to
kill them.

Alert at his rifle for people
not to breed with, the soldier
draws a bead.

A plate, a shoe, a worker, a pavement,
a parcel, a child, a can—
sterile images.

The monster jaws appear over the grass
snatch with ridicule at
what it won't love.

The necessity is to know
the distinction
to be drawn.

The colourful ones are officers:
they do not mate with
the men, who die.

The crowds cannot tolerate one or two
not in touch: set
fire to them.

Angels sit in the boat
as sniffers—
out.

Too old to bear children
she trembles like
a witch.

And the couples discover how distasteful
their bodies are to each
other, apart.

See their deformities: huge colours,
wrong tastes & smells & that
that divide.

Unable to discover a way in to the football,
the disgruntled player
just kicks it.

The poem is built on the basis of the ambivalence of the word *breed*.
As a verb *breed* means, on the one hand, *to produce offspring, to give birth,
to beget, to engender, to reproduce* and, on the other hand, *to develop by tradition or education, to train, to nurture*. As a noun, *breed* refers to a class, a
kind, a sort.[10] Interestingly, the term evokes at once procreation and
class division, suggesting that segregation engenders itself in the very
act of "breeding". The idea is rather cruel and fatalistic, and yet the
treatment given to it is economical to the point of dryness, no space
being left for lamentation or promises of change. There is restrained
eloquence and crude violence in the images and in the very organiza-
tion of the poem: stanzas of three short lines, following a rigid pattern
of the third line being shorter than the first two. This pattern under-
scores the paradox implied in breeding: when two meet, the result is
retraction, shrinkage, diminution.

There is a sterilizing force in operation—in society? in the world?—
which makes itself perceptible rhythmically, as we have just seen, and
semantically. Ironically enough, in a poem entitled "The Breed", a sense
of separation and intolerance prevails. In the opening scene a solitary
gull by a stone promptly brings to our memories the shots we all have
seen in films about Darwin's voyage to the Galapagos islands. Yet, as
soon as the image finishes forming itself on our mental screen we real-
ize that it depicts an impossible intercourse and a painful meeting
between mutually impenetrable materials. It is another film, then, we
are to watch.

As the gull, another animal works against itself in the following
stanza. Human beings featuring in subsequent tercets—a lady, a
labourer, soldiers, officers, the crowds, a woman too old to bear children, couples—make up an aleatory assembly, bearing in common
either their violence or their impotence; they are either oppressors or
oppressed. Inanimate objects are "sterile images", and so are the child
and the worker. Angels are spies rather than guardians. Instead of an

---

[10] Cf. *Webster's Third New International Dictionary of the English Language, Unabridged*,
Merriam-Webster, 1986, p. 274.

organized progression representing "evolution", the poem presents us with a heap of beings confused in their functions and behaviours.

In other stanzas, we are confronted more directly with the Darwinian idea of the survival of the fittest in its social application: "*The thing that doesn't work, / won't match, he / hurls it away.*" (st. 4); "*How can a lady be touched / by the hand of / a labourer?*" (st. 5); "*The crowds cannot tolerate one or two / not in touch: set / fire to them.*" (12). Actions such as *hurl* and *set fire* stress the mood of intolerance the poem so aptly builds up.

In the poem's only tiny lyrical fragment—"*& that / that divide*"—the repetition of the demonstrative and the breaking of the line indicate that for a very brief moment, for a tiny little second, the poet's own subjectivity makes a sudden apparition, glimpsing melancholically the images presented, only to disappear again and leave us on our own for the final scene.

After the long sequence of snapshots rhythmically flashed before us, the final result is a chord made up of the notes of biological discourse, social intolerance, sterility and violence, notes hardly distinct from one another. In such a composition, the last scene functions as an anti-climax or at least a dissonance. The final image is quite prosaic, quite unlike the more dramatic and rhyming images preceding it: the untalented footballer, a loser, just kicks the ball, compensating for his failure with aimlessness. The strength of the evolutionary mentality, obedient to a law that determines the weak are outmoded, finds a response in the absence of logic, the casual shot of the player—an aleatory character, aloof to the arrow of progress or decadence. In the end, there is neither sympathy nor revolt, but seemingly indifference, which adds a tragic dimension to the text.

In "Trade", published in *Nomad Sense*, a book from 1998 that Griffiths considers a more international work, we see again a very intense collaboration between formal resources and a critical standpoint. In terms of form, "Trade" is more radical than "The Breed", but here again the final result points to unity and coherence.

Trade

But what is Fair Trade? I persisted.
'Monopolies that work at both ends,'
     was suggested.
'Some attempt to impute value to price?'
'Consideration for whalers?'

The white hunters are out
jab jab jab
they have seen the brown bear
becomes still

next is the pink-load mare
wood-smoke mane
no incisive outline
but smudges of colour browsing the
new brown

Ce fut le dimanche 8 septembre,
Nous etions parler faire une promenade
sur les colines environ Montignac, suivi
de nos chiens.
La decouverte fut tout a fait fortuite.
Mon chien bondi dans un fouré et ne re-
sorbliait plus,
nous decouvrimes un trou profond

the soft smoke felt of his pelt
ragged sun
dries to a toss down of pebble
there is sand handfuls lost in a century

"Les fermiers des environs et beaucoup
d'autres personnes connaissaient l'exist-
ence de ce trous mais n'e faisaient aucune
attention."

though they write words on shafts
the hunters cannot reach
there is no grip
too active in time

Accidental in length along the encased
tongue we were accompanied also large
single letters as spare time an armless
the block teeth and bones of lime
through the cave the cave Chronicle
souvenir of the Crystal Inquest Has never
been diminished dead Bears other days
thawing some days discovered in 1866
either work or letters Equally they found
with them electric the enhuged gob
embossed finished freezing was fitted
thru-out formerly were found to guide the
sounds the hotel I do not expect to be

back now before the 13th of March it
was red-full I do not have like the source
a light bone structure a mouth 3 miles of
wall never far from freezing not have
finished here and Budapest other places
postcards panoramic Rubeland a river the
sex was also the source of an aorta
Todt's we took about an hour and a half
going throughout the voice of which
when the cave was...

There is haste to get everything on board
        now.
We must have everything:
our start
our tradition
our now.
(if only we can remember it all.)
For of course there must be a product
(a Language? an idea? a poem? a
        discovery?)
to trade.
With some misadvantaging,
we all have our own level of living,
consumables, separables, and other
        competibles,
protectible with long prison sentences;
and durables;
and invisibles.[11]

"Trade" is composed in a dialogical mode. There is a question, featuring
in its first line—"*But what is Fair Trade, I persisted?*"—followed by a long and
complex answer which is the poem itself. Two comments to be made on
such a design. First, that it creates the impression that "Trade" is a fragment of something larger, possibly an ongoing conversation whose
totality we are not to grasp. The opening *in medias res* confirms this—the
conjunction *but* and the verb *persisted* are both signs that there is something previous to the poem to which it refers. The idea of fragment, of
vestige, which the poem tries to embody, is one that will be focused on
in its whole course. The second comment has to do with the fact that
the dialogue form opens the text to the presence of different voices, or

[11] There is an endnote referring to the poem "Trade" saying: "Trade includes quotes
    from Marcel Ravidat's account of the Lascaux discovery". *Nomad Sense*, p. 96.

at least makes this presence quite verisimilar, creating a context for the poet to play with the materials he likes—found texts, foreign languages, verse, prose and register mixes.

At first, three directions are proposed to the speaker's question *"What is Fair Trade?"* The first two seem to belong to a more technical domain and are dismissed in favour of the third, appearing in the guise of a hint that "fair trade" might be a subject matter for whale hunters. It is from this suggestion that a long and complex answer will unfold in the eight stanzas to follow.

In what looks like an unpretentious association—that between trade and hunting—a palimpsest can be read, revealing the relationship between the two activities. Hunting opens up the ancestry of trade. The theme of history or historicity is thus carried into the poem, broadening up its scope, inviting us to take a historical perspective in our reception.

It is the mention of Lascaux that transports history to the text. The cave of Lascaux, one of the most important archaeologic sites in Europe, turns out to be a central image in the poem, explored in its several layers: Lascaux's paintings of animals and hunting scenes; Lascaux's accidental finding by farmers; Lascaux being "ransacked" by archaeologists, Lascaux as the fragment of a past we will never get to know thoroughly. Lascaux bears the evidence of man as hunter both of material and immaterial things. Pre-historic men hunted for survival; contemporary men—including archaeologists—hunt for the sake of taking possession, and trade is suggested to be a natural consequence of that.

The passages with found texts in French, concerning the "discovery" of Lascaux by farmers with a dog are in tune with the juxtaposed scenes of hunting and flashes from Lascaux paintings. The long section in prose resembling automatic writing, in the eighth stanza, the weirdest passage in the poem, tries to represent mimetically the cave itself and the puzzle it has represented. It is possible to learn, reading about Lascaux, that besides the paintings on its walls, several other things were found there. Written signs which have never been deciphered, utensils, all sorts of vestiges. The poet takes advantage of this confusion to build in new confusions: amidst *block teeth*, *bones*, and several repetitions of the word *cave*, there are many other references in the passage inviting us to be archaeologists, or hunters, or traders of meaning! What matters, though, is that the effect obtained on the whole by the poem is that of a mosaic, or rather of a kaleidoscope, which, when turned round, transforms the fragments into frames of an animated film of man's perennial history as hunter.

In the final stanza we watch a scene in which a ship is hastily loaded—
"*There is haste to get everything on board / now.*"—which confirms the logic
of hunting/possessing/trading. The theme of commodification shows
up, everything is tradable: "*We must have everything: / our start / our tradition / our now.*" Culture is revealed as a commodity like any other: "*For of
course there must be a product / (a Language? an idea? a poem? a / discovery?) /
to trade.*" We, readers, also hunters, are ready to take possession of the
poem, too, but not without being reminded that this possession has a
limit—perhaps that is the function of the eighth stanza.

At the poem's close we may finally figure out the answer to "What is
Fair Trade?" and we understand that trade is fair not because it is
carried out with justice, but because it affects everything equally; it is
fair in its wide reach, in its comprehensiveness which leaves nothing
out, in its permanence in history. We are brothered in trade, to varying
degrees: "*With some misadvantaging, / we all have our own level of living*".
"*Living*", life or survival, is explained in a beautiful sequence of nomi-
nalized adjectives: *consumables, separables, competibles, durables, and invisibles*, terms which bring to mind different sorts of commodities defining
life itself.

∼

As, unfortunately, these pages are not able to reproduce Griffiths's live
reading, something I am sure would add more meaning to the two
pieces presented, we may try to compensate for that by remembering
the poet's gasped and cadenced elocution, which always gives a
dramatic and urgent tone to his texts, his grave voice, his casual cloth-
ing, the tattoos and the *love* and *hate* inscribed on his arms and hands. In
addition, we may remember Griffiths's history, one in which a critical
stance and aesthetic invention have always worked together.

Darwin's Dialogues as Punctuations of Equilibrium

Gilbert Adair

On November 23, 1859, the day before his revolutionary book hit the stands, Charles Darwin received an extraordinary letter from his friend Thomas Henry Huxley. It offered warm support in the coming conflict... But it also contained a warning: "You have loaded yourself with an unnecessary difficulty in adopting *Natura non facit saltum* [Nature does not make leaps] so unreservedly."

—Stephen Jay Gould, *The Panda's Thumb* (1980)

Will the climate warm up?

—Bill Griffiths, *Darwin's Dialogues* (1991)[1]

1

Jacques Barzun observed in 1958 that while 'origin of species' meant for its author "the origin of more or less fixed differences in living forms called by naturalists *species*"—species by species, each had its origin—the phrase bore for Darwin's contemporaries "an alluring ambiguity ...irresistibly suggest[ing] ... the beginning of all things" (31–2). If Alpha, then a predetermined Omega, something the theory of natural selection, however, denied; Clive Bush calls attention to Bill Griffiths titling the first poem of his 1991 chapbook *Darwin's Dialogues* "Opening,"

---

[1] *Darwin's Dialogues* is undated and unpaginated; Griffiths gave Clive Bush the date of 1991. See Bush (1997: 230–38) for a discussion of this work.

"presumably to distinguish it from the more teleologically loaded 'beginning' and perhaps to suggest the putting on of a play" (1997: 231). The curtain rises / curtains open, or we find the action already underway, as follows:

> To stir the pond—
> view now dragon-newts scurry,
> colossal action in the life.
>
> And each birth,
> rearrangement, re-patterning,
> & collapsible frame-net of calcium
>   relocated.
>
> Consuming work of the child,
> to put its mysteries out,
> while it takes and takes, collects, sorts.

The budding naturalist is suggested in the child's curiosity to arrange and display in quasi-random categories items organic or inorganic it doesn't yet understand. Meanwhile, each of Griffiths's 14 three-line stanzas here begins with an upper-case letter and ends with a full stop—until little disturbances appear toward the poem's ending, by which time we've reached:

> View of the whole product of city,
> building-turmoil,
> print of new, turning matter.
>
> where the magistrate
> stamps each seal of
> unobtainable order
>
> And
> it contiues [sic]
> to mix more
>
> make, enlong, more consume
> maximize, build, break,
> and the great fire.

The 'great fire' of London? The first mention of 'fire' in the poem is its last word, coming abruptly, casually, and terribly, connected to the preceding infinitives by 'and' and severed from them by its break of the alliterative intricacies and also by its lack of a verb, its free floating. We will come back to this much later. But note at this point that stanzas 12 ('where the magistrate') and 14 have no opening upper-case, and 12 and 13 no closing full stop (so that 'make,' the opening word of 14, is at once an infinitive and the object of 'mix more'). There is also—both strange and (given the last line) apt—the misspelling of 'continues' in 13. Deliberate? unnoticed? a typo deliberately retained—a random mutation preserved by Griffithsian selection?

Indeed, is the chapbook's entire poetic straight out of Darwin? It comprises:

> "Opening," a poem;
> "Josiah Wedgwood II & Robert Darwin," a one-page dialogue in the course of which Robert's son and Josiah's nephew is born offstage;
> "View," a 3-page poem whose stanzas range from 4 to 10 lines of irregular length;
> "Josiah Wedgwood & Charles Darwin," a dialogue in which Darwin secures his uncle's support in signing on as the *Beagle*'s naturalist;
> "Adventure," a breathless 5-page yarn told in block paragraphs each of which opens with a title in the format "*BREACH!*" "*FOUNTAIN!*" "*DRAGON!*" etc;
> "Charles Darwin & the Sea-Captain," being a verbal skirmish between Darwin and Captain Fitzroy of the *Beagle*;
> "The Breed," a 2-page poem in the 3-line stanza format of "Opening," although less varied rhythmically;
> "Darwin & the Finch," a 3-page comic dialogue on variations, island to Galapagos island, in the birds' beaks—or as the finch mischievously demurs, "I prefer [to 'beak'] the name 'bill'";
> "Steve's Garden," an 11-page poem mixing choral and lyric sections that is in many ways the work's centrepiece;
> "Darwin & Wife," a 3-page discussion between Charles and Emma Darwin concerning whether or not he should publish his theory;
> "The Relief of Aachen," a 5-page play whose main characters are the Bishop of Aachen, the Nazi commander of troops stationed in the city, and the American general to whom the latter surrenders;
> "Darwin to Marx," an imagined letter in which Darwin explains why he "decline[s] to accept the dedication of the translation of *Das Kapital*";
> "Englynion," a one-page poem of 3-line stanzas and two different left margins;[2] and finally,
> "Alternative Ending," a one-page parody apocalypse written in Latin and recited by an angel—a black-magic reversal of Genesis as a possibility on offer:

---

[2] 'Englynion' is the Welsh plural of 'englyn' or 'stanza' and names a kind of poem that first appeared, according to W.F. Skene (1868), in the 6th century C.E. The verses had initially three and later more often four lines, and a variety of meters based on syllable-count.

ut scriptum est,
terra periet

et omnes secum.
Prima die

periunt sancti et beati,
Secunda

animalia omnia,
Tertia,

sol et luna
Et astra etiam ...

[as it is written, /the earth will perish //and all with it. /The First day
//the saints and the blessed will perish. /The Second //all the
animals, /The Third, //the sun and moon /and even the stars...]

Each of these pieces, then, can be seen as an existing form adapted to
Griffiths's purpose, that is, to its new environment of Griffiths's book.
The stanza whose lines are irregular in length and often in number, and
where grammar can be short-circuited to stunningly twist meaning, is a
favourite rhythmic-semantic device of his, put to multiple uses. "Josiah
and Robert" is in the mode of Ibsenite drama, where in the course of
talking to each other 'realistically,' the characters will manage to let
drop for the audience's benefit contextualizing and thematic details (so
that Josiah is made to raise the question of heredity, observing that
great things are projected, given the Darwin/Wedgwood records of
achievement to date, for the child both of them are sure will be a son).
"Adventure" is subtitled "(Found & New Text)"; Griffiths has apparently
taken much if not all of the opening paragraphs from some story for
boys of derring-do from the 20s or 30s, and then begun to insert, in the
same apparent vein, his own decidedly more unsettling material. In a
different register, "The Relief of Aachen" opens in Brechtian style with
the Bishop levelling to the audience on the dilemma confronting him as
WW2 nears its close and his understandably scurrilous plans for
handling said dilemma (the conviction that the audience will find one's
scurrilousness entirely understandable being a hallmark of the
Brechtian villain).[3]

---

[3] See, for example, Peachum at the opening of *The Threepenny Opera* (first staged
    1928), where he explains why "[s]omething new is needed. My business is too
    hard, for my business is arousing human sympathy. There are a few things that
    stir men's souls, just a few, but the trouble is that after repeated use they lose

Let me straight away confess that I have no intention of trying to point-for-point press the creative action of *Darwin's Dialogues* into a rationale derived from natural selection.[4] I do, however, with that 'and the great fire' in mind, as well as subsequent strategies that echo it, want to gloss a little the epigraph from Stephen Jay Gould citing Huxley's reservation over Darwin's commitment to gradualism in all things. Darwin transferred this to biology, Gould observes, from Charles Lyell, "the apostle of gradualism in geology" (1980: 179); as Griffiths's Darwin tells his uncle Jos, "These views of the new age of the world, they open remarkable possibilities for the study of the animal world." In effect, Lyell's *Principles of Geology* (1833) gave Darwin the barely imaginable eons of time he needed to posit what he initially called 'descent with modification' via tiny chance mutations—of what, he did not know—that on occasion increased the organism's chances of survival and so of passing to its offspring its advantageous modifications. And yet, Gould insists, 'descent with modification' in no way depends on the gradualism that receives, in fact, little or no support from the fossil record, although it chimes with the reformist liberalism championed, in *Darwin's Dialogues*, by Josiah Wedgwood, and maintained in the face of Captain Fitzroy's creationist authoritarianism by the hero, even if it seems to him no avenue for his own ambition. Gould posits a genetic mechanism whereby new species can arise via, indeed, tiny chance mutations but without passing through intermediate stages.[5] The model he developed with his co-worker Niles Eldredge is called by them *punctuated equilibria*. Lineages change little during most of their history, but events of rapid speciation occasionally punctuate this tranquillity....(In

their effect.... The Bible has four or five sayings that stir the heart; once a man has expended them, there's nothing for it but starvation" (1979: 5–6). For a fee and cut of the proceeds he will therefore teach beggars "the five basic types of misery, those most likely to touch the human heart. The sight of such will put a man into the unnatural state where he is willing to part with money" (8).

4   Human creativity, both artistic and scientific, receives Darwinian consideration in Simonton (1999), where the chemist Linus Pauling is cited memorably stating a notion variously expressed also by Valéry, Dryden, and Faraday: "[Y]ou aren't going to have good ideas unless you have lots of ideas and some sort of principle of selection" (28).

5   The key to this would be 'rate genes,' first codified by Richard Goldschmidt in 1918 as affecting the timing of embryonic development. "Prolong the high prenatal rate of brain growth," writes Gould, "into early childhood and a monkey's brain moves toward human size" (192).

describing [this] as very rapid, I speak as a geologist. The process may take hundreds, even thousands of years ...) (184)

Again, I am not saying that Griffiths is (or is not) responding to these lines of Gould. I am saying, however, that someone mulling over natural selection as at least a partial guide to a poetic may in any case take on the question of the *rate* of change in terms of the experience of a human generation or two—even if, from a geologist's perspective, a species change requiring 'hundreds, even thousands of years' to sufficiently spread the decisive mutation is seen not as a gradual modifying process but rather as a discontinuity. In this light, the poems and other pieces of *Darwin's Dialogues* may be seen not only as swift dances of language but also as moments of aesthetic homeostasis acknowledging and punctuating the often verb-annihilating rush in the world at large that traverses them.

2

The spirit of evolution hovered over the cradle of the new [19th] century. So far it was not tied to any underlying philosophy. It followed its subject matter: mechanical action in astronomy and geology; unconscious will and purpose, or use and disuse, in biology; climate and the conscious aims of men in the social progress revealed by history.

—Barzun, *Darwin, Marx, Wagner*

Griffiths's "View," concerned with the attempt (initially the child's attempt, in post-WW2 austerity Britain) to survey the components of one's world—eventually, to make a home for the author and "the elderly one," his mother—notes at one point an enclosing "fog" where "outbeasts appear /their long coats quiet /& they chew." "The Breed" opens with the image of a scavenger bird on the wrong track:

> The gull pecks at the stone
> yelling like a
> hammer.
>
> Things that snarl and beg:
> the elimination
> of dogs.

In the gull, the circularity of instinct; in the human, perhaps, designating as 'dogs' the 'things that snarl and beg,' the irritated impulse to genocide. The poem is a brutal setting-out of racism and classism as modes of apartheid pleading for natural alibis:

> Alert at his rifle for people
> not to breed with, the sold-
> ier draws a bead.
>
> …
>
> The colourful ones are officers:
> they do not mate with
> the men, who die.
>
> …
>
> See their deformities: huge colours,
> wrong tastes & smells & that
> that divide.
>
> Unable to discover a way in to the football,
> the disgruntled player
> just kicks it

—a clear echo of the thwarted gull in the opening stanza. The final three words of the third stanza cited here shape up to say 'that /which divides,' and instead produce '*that divide*,' an uncrossable noun, again subtracted of a verb. When another stanza announces, however, "The necessity is to know /the distinction /to be drawn," we might in the context add 'the distinction' between human and (non-metaphorical) animal, that can never be definitive, for it must pass first through the human (Agamben 2004, 15–16). This thematic necessarily threads *Darwin's Dialogues*.

"Adventure (Found & New Text)," for example, foregrounds a number of motifs found in adventure stories written in the wake of Darwin and in a spirit of human-to-beast regression-anxiety when it came to penetration by colonizing forces into what Conrad called in 1902 the 'heart of darkness.' Reaching a sulphur-walled plateau, Griffiths's "adventurers" find in a cave apparent maps of the area (the map is always a cruel mockery in such narratives) and "various humanoid skulls, most with horns." They emerge from the cave and are pelted with rocks from the cliff-tops by monkeys. Dispersing the "animal army" by firing their rifles in the air, they presently notice "a grotesque head carved out of the rock. As in the cave, these were like human heads, but strangely deformed with long horns, twirled and ribbed as tho' merged with an ibex." An uncanny mist now settles over "the images of some long-lost empire"—the long-lost empire being a stock feature of Edgar Rice Burroughs's Tarzan novels, among others—but a passage follows that never appeared in a story for boys of any age:

> WHISPER! Each began to hear like his own voice, like when the ungodly curse Satan, and but curse their own souls, as if our own imagination around us can make all evil unaided. Startled, they called, yelled even, to keep contact.

The mist rises to show "tall speechless bipeds," dragon-like, "scaled and fierce-headed, but curiously human too, in their assumptions of home and art." After further uncanny and painful vicissitudes, the adventurers make it back home, only to face, Gulliver-like, the disbelief of their fellows and their own alienation:

> [T]heir memories were incoherent, each animal they met strangely hostile for all their future, while their wild claims were never credited, and people only thought it obscene to imagine that animals had ever dominated the world, creative beings living outside God's rails.

What the civilized world is effectively rejecting here, as in Conrad's 1902 novella and other texts, is "the implication," in Graham Huggan's words, "that a return to the origin reverses the process of civilization to reveal the essential bestiality of man" (1989: 34). And yet the civilized world was at the same time embracing enthusiastically its own 'essential bestiality,' as anticipated by Griffiths's Emma Darwin, who tells her husband that if he goes ahead with his decision to publish his theory, who knows what will result: "A pure faith in war and victory? In nothing but struggle and competition, cheating and worsting? The world will be at each other's throats if there is no morality but success.... Unity, if we only accept the lewdness of animals?"

Darwin has a number of responses, not entirely consistent. He doubts that God or anyone else will be much influenced by what he writes. He declares, conversely, that he "will put mankind in the Sun at last. Let him see what power he has. He is no puppet to this or that version of this or that revelatory religion, he is a free agent ..." He insists that "it is only fact and observation and conclusion I really deal with ... Co-operation I can guess at, but competition I can prove"—although in the letter to Marx he allows that he "may to some extent have been influenced indirectly by the imperial competitiveness that is such an obvious factor in our own century." Perhaps most accurately, but still somewhat disingenuously, he tells Emma that "everyone will be just the same, you'll see. Hostility at first. Then they'll all imagine that my theory predicts the triumph of their own ideology, and the extinction of all their opponents, just as they always have." That was not long in coming, certainly, in the century's closing, strife-besotted decades that saw widespread conceptual self-delivery into the mechanistic helplessness of instinctual action. The grotesqueries of social Darwinists cited by Barzun include the remark of the historian Renan, "smarting under the defeat of his country in the Franco-Prussian War of 1870… that 'war is in a way one of the conditions of progress, the cut of the whip which prevents a country from going to sleep'"—Barzun comments, "If the vanquished said it, what else could the victors say?"—and the 1895 dispatching to a Chicago journal of articles by the scientist Topinard "advocating a social free-for-all, *without* education, which might interfere with natural competition" (1958: 101–2). Darwin "imbibed" his philosophy, Barzun writes, "from the economic, social, and metaphysical speculations of his time …. What brought him rapid victory and prolonged sway over his age was thus the ability of the age to recognize itself in him" (87). Marx, after initial enthusiasm, had sketched this about a century earlier, writing to Engels in 1860:

> I am amused by the statement of Darwin… that he applies the "Malthusian" theory to plants and animals also, whereas the whole point of Mr. Malthus lies in the fact that he does *not* apply his theory to plants and animals… It is splendid that Darwin again discovers among plants and animals his English society with its division of labour, competition, opening up of new markets, "inventions" and Malthusian "struggle for existence". (Cited in Bukharin *et al.*, 1935: 193)[6]

In a manner characteristic of *Darwin's Dialogues*—where, for example, "The Breed" follows a discussion of class hierarchy between the protagonists of "Charles Darwin & the Sea-Captain"—"The Relief of Aachen" offers both a thematic riposte to Emma's belief that "With

---

6 With perhaps, again, disingenuous honesty, Darwin—both in the Introduction to *On the Origin of Species* and also in Chapter III, "Struggle for Existence"—credits Malthus's *Essay on the Principle of Population* (1798) as a major influence on his thinking. For the record, it seems unlikely that the brief letter found among Marx's papers in which Darwin declines to accept a too-political dedication was actually addressed to Marx; see Feuer (1975) and Fay (1978).

God's creation of life and the Bible challenged, the whole fabric of society weakens," and an implicit dialogue between the absent naturalist, the Europe that had sworn off social Darwinism following the mass slaughter of 1914–1918, and the representative of an America that in the words of a Thomas Pynchon character, "has learned empire from its old metropolis" (1974: 722). Griffiths's Bishop of Aachen, observing that a thousand years of Church anti-semitism and authoritarianism helped pave the Nazi route to power, decides that if he obeys the order for all civilians to evacuate the city, "the Church will be seen as acquiescing in Hitler's arrangements once again." He decides to hide in the cathedral's "hollow throne of Charlemagne," further casting the action in the shadow of religio-military ('Holy Roman') empire. The American General and the Nazi Commander now come onstage and report on the progress of the siege from their respective points of view. The city falls fairly briskly and the General and his Lieutenant go exploring in "the famous Cathedral of Aachen." From the throne the Bishop calls, "Hello, hello? Who is there?" and a rather comic scenario follows of the General forced to directly address his interlocutor's commode-like hiding-place. Before he will emerge, the Bishop wants to get some things straight: "Alright, we haven't been exactly uncommitted, but only the Church can rebuild Germany now ... The only alternative is Communism sweeping the country." The General can see the point of 'Christian democracy,' and declares that for this cooperation "the world will be infernally grateful" (as opposed to 'eternally grateful'—another small mutation, perhaps).

From even so brief a summary of Griffiths's vignette, one can register a complete lack of the elements that in Part XI of the *Poetics*, Aristotle establishes as essential to tragedy: a *peripeteia* or reversal of things combined with a recognition, a change from ignorance to knowledge, which together produce the cathartic emotions of pity and terror. On first reading "The Relief of Aachen," one begins to feel, nearing the end, Why, there's no drama here! The Bishop and General, with whom we feel no impulse to identify, are simply getting what they want. It is Brechtian non-tragic lack of sensationalism (meant to encourage a critically thoughtful audience) minus any sense of large dialectics. Its bleakly deadpan presentation of *realpolitik* in the wake of genocide forestalls the alibi of outrage, but also any optimism of challenging this political order in arenas outside the theatre (Brecht's rationale for stymieing the using-up of emotion in catharsis). One response would be to try to imagine into these undated lines from Benjamin's "What is Epic Theatre?

[First Version]" some sense of the conditions of our own time (or of the long-ago early 90s, when *Darwin's Dialogues* first saw the light):

> The more far-reaching the devastations of our social order (the more these devastations undermine ourselves and our capacity to remain aware of them), the more marked must be the distance between the [audience] and the events portrayed. (1973: 5)

3

> There is a mode of individuation very different from that of a person, subject, thing, or substance. We reserve the name *haecceity* for it .... Lorca's "five in the evening," when love falls and fascism rises. That awful five in the evening![7] ... A degree of heat, an intensity of white, are perfect individualities... A degree of heat can combine with an intensity of white, as in certain white skies of a hot summer.
>
> —Gilles Deleuze, "Individuation" (1993)

Deleuze usefully brings into play, but makes no pretence of being the first to conceive of, a haecceity, a 'here-this-collectively-is, identifiable in the things it brings together.'[8] His last instance cited above finds coincidental echo when "Steve's Garden," at something like the centre of *Darwin's Dialogues*,[9] evokes "The absolute glaze of a tile-day." The sun smashes off this surface, makes it hard to see anything.[10] To get some

---

[7] "A las cinco de la tarde" (*tarde*: 'evening' or 'afternoon') in "Lament for Ignacio Sanchez Mejías" (1935). The phrase was translated "At five in the afternoon" by Spender and Gili for an equivalent rhythmic hammer.

[8] I cite the footnote to the word given in *The Deleuze Reader*: "This is sometimes written 'ecceity,' deriving the word from *ecce*, 'here is.' This is an error, since Duns Scotus created the word and the concept from *haec*, 'this thing.' But it is a fruitful error because it suggests a mode of individuation that is distinct from that of a thing or a subject" (263).

[9] To be exact: *Darwin's Dialogues* has 44 pages; if they were numbered, "Steve's Garden" would be on 22-32. 'Steve' is a quasi-public reference only to those familiar with librarian Steve Clews.

[10] Griffiths's fondness for hyphenated compounds, evident throughout *Darwin's Dialogues* and his work in general, perhaps derives in the first instance from (unhyphenated) compound words in Old English poetry, described by Daniel Calder as "mere juxtaposition without elements of juncture," which in "correspond[ing] to the paratactic sentence structure" present "a significant instance of parallelism between lexical formation and syntax" (1979, 21).

sense of the complex role of haecceity in "Steve's Garden," which as already mentioned mixes choral and lyric sections, we need to see the immediate 'tile-day' context:

```
(chorus)
     White milk        White frost
                 .        .

     The absolute glaze of a tile-day
                 A woman
                 .        .

         opaque          soft
         continuous      dissolvent
         form            textures

     The tabular face of the scene-lay
              a walk-window
              a profectual text
```

In its formal symmetries, this is a threshing of unions and disjunctures. 'White' and 'White' are synonymous, but 'milk' and 'frost' oppose each other not only in their associated temperatures but also in the liquid volume of the one, the hard surface of the other. Both phrases thus lead down to a couplet combining surface (white glare) and—taking up the maternal associations of 'milk'—female body; the couplet branches into two haecceities (although perhaps only one woman), and the passage concludes with a triplet where surface looks to oust volume. 'Profectual' ('a profectual text') is a coining that's itself a nexus of meanings apt to Darwinism: 'profect,' according to the OED, is an "obsolete by-form of PROFIT"; 'profection' means "the action or fact of going forward; progression, advance"; and 'profectitious' refers to something "that proceeds or is derived from a parent or ancestor."

To branching (presumably a figure for, among other things, evolution) and haecceity, we need to add the motif of a wrenching contortion of body, as when the children of "the first God," in a conflicted search for origin,

```
     turn their tummy to the sky
     /their breast to earth
```

This moves into another choral section, whose branchings are four:

```
         The strange
         INTIMATE
         grace of the
```

```
     nose-thyril           nosethrill
         .                      .
         .                      .
     the                   as it
     bodies                scoops
     roughly               your body-
     knit                  scenting
       .    .   .              .       .     .
     .            .          .           .
     FRICTING  GLOWING  SOUL       MOOD
```

The OED lists no 'thyril,' but 'thirl,' 'thyrle,' 'thirell,' and 'thirlage' all circu-
late round the notion of reducing to bondage or servitude, not far from
'thrill' (from Old English 'thyrlian,' to pierce). There's also something irre-
sistibly flowerlike, I find, about 'nose-thyril' (the 'y'-effect of 'thyril' seems
to swirl in Elizabethan associations of nosegay or garland). 'FRICTING' is a
Griffithsian coining from, one imagines, 'friction,' and in context evokes
an active short-circuiting by sex. The presentation is of a sensory intensity
leading to an anxious division of body and soul and further taxonomic
niceties that wittily assign a 'mood' to soul (subjectively various, if with
overtones of 'moody') and to the fornicatory body only a 'glow.' Clearly
there is nothing exhaustive in such writing, no seizure of essence, rather
the production of apprehensible, provisional form; as he says,

> A sudden pervasion of pattern,
> …
> And everything moves into patterns
> like words in poems
> if they stay there

Following this, through choral introduction of an impulse, in plant
and human, to "jewllism," there comes a sudden boost of thematic reach:

> to feel the very strands of the arm
> bloated with strength
> circling from bank to sky
> without why
>
> So much of it, a surplus
> where pyramids come of,
> octagons, towers,
> kings, saints, snowmen
> & like immodesties

The 'snowmen' at once turn the kings and saints into statues and intro-
duce a comically perplexing discrepancy of scale. The lines remain,

however, whether by accident or design, a fairly direct transcription of Bataille's sense of 'the accursed share':

> The living organism, in a situation determined by the play of energy on the surface of the globe, ordinarily receives more energy than is necessary for maintaining life; the excess energy (wealth) can be used for the growth of a system (e.g., an organism); if the system can no longer grow, or if the excess cannot be completely absorbed in its growth, it must necessarily be lost without profit; it must be spent, willingly or not, gloriously or catastrophically. (1988: 21)

Together, Griffiths's 'snowmen' and Bataille's 'gloriously or catastrophically' raise the question of a branching, not simply binary, of creative energies. Griffiths first assimilates "flowers /battling to be first /in a muscular way" to the mythical ferocity of "orcs & dragons"; there follows a triplet that may mix wild floral tenacities, greeds for space and sunlight, and the ordered restraints of garden (or may not—and either way, the divisions are indeterminate):

> (chorus)
>   The play of glad yellow
>   the sword of great colour
>   witches of growth —

There are moral as well as sense ambiguities in the swift play of haecceities here over the world's apparent integrals. These ambiguities persist in Griffiths's evocation of "The walking Wordsworth /dodging /the cues & spikes /of super-government"—a fusion, perhaps, of the poet's 1790 walking tour through Revolutionary France, his Grasmere years before and after that, and his later Westmoreland retreat from anything like political radicalism. Wordsworth "makes," Griffiths writes,

>   a new plant
> of so many lines-length
>
> meting out five or four[11]
> polishing the bits
> that fit
> into flowerhead

[11] For the record: "The Idiot Boy" is made up of five-line stanzas, "We Are Seven" has four-line stanzas except for the last, of five. Both appeared in the first edition of *Lyrical Ballads* (1798), co-authored with Coleridge (who had experimented with metrical and stanza-length irregularities in "Christabel," 1797). Of Wordsworth's

What Wordsworth crafts and delights in fuses with the "plant" which provides "a refuge from tainted haggle & affection," but is also "a joyless life-in-death; the mouth-drum /to silently /call to grow." But this is not only assimilated to Wordsworth, for plants are indeed, one supposes, 'joyless,' and their life, if we reasonably say 'tenacious,' difficult if not impossible to imagine. We are promptly launched into an indeterminate dissolve from one haecceity into another already begun, a 'fricting' in the sense of an invite-rebuff flow where line to line, part wants to go, part to stay:

> Sometimes plastically extreme,
> or thread-fine,
> from every throat of calyx,
> all/each green increasing
> sweats into yellow making,
> fantastic beads
> of tree & black-letter,
> breathing flint,
> floss of gold,
> pumpkin-rose
> (natural ghostly everything)

'[G]reen increasing' may suggest photosynthesis, but why does it 'sweat' into yellow (flower?) making? As a surface-breath of dew? Sweat can then prompt 'beads' and fast changes of scale; trees as 'fantastic beads' on the earth make sense, perhaps, but black letters would surely constitute beads of a different kind—braille? is some blind reader intimated here?— somehow connected with 'breathing flint' (living earth) and 'floss of gold,' 'floss' linking to the earlier 'thread-fine' and the entire stanza now appearing as a gloss on the two opening lines: an inter-activation of diverse and metamorphosing forms, 'plastically extreme' indeed. We nonetheless feel a kind of existential hairiness in opting for particular interpretations, a resistance of language to be provisionally overcome from where we are as readers, but never to be annihilated.[12]

---

five "Lucy" poems of 1799, four have four-line stanzas, one ("Three Years She Grew in Sun and Shower") has six-liners. Griffiths's point seems to be that Wordsworth indulged in constrained innovation.

[12]   Again and again, from as early as *From the Handbook of That & Furriery* (1986), Maggie O'Sullivan offers her own versions of something like this.

In context, '(natural ghostly everything)' is validly mysterious, inciting of wonder.[13]

With the main thematic-formal elements of "Steve's Garden" introduced (branchings at multiple levels in interplay with frictional haecceity-dissolves over the world's apparent integrals), we can move more quickly. One conceivable outcome of multiple preparations in both poem and chapbook appears as follows:

> (chorus)
> There is a red purse   A morning sun
> of money   too red
> .
> .   .
>
> The tree has swayed too much!
> Alcoholic Queen Anne
> of a gin-raced city,
> & edged with the Hounslow gibbets,
> a sudden falcation

'Falcation' means "the condition of being falcate, bent or curved like a sickle," or in a 1656 usage, "a mowing or cutting with bill or hook" (OED); the same year that *Darwin's Dialogues* appeared, Hounslow's skyline advertisements ('tree & black-letter') for obedience to 18th-century laws of private property were discussed in Peter Linebaugh's *The London Hanged* (1991). Queen Anne, who presided over the concurrent 'fiscal-military state,' sometimes at Hampton Court took "Counsel," as Pope reported in *The Rape of the Lock* (1717), "and sometimes *Tea*," the prize of India (1963: 227); I defer to Griffiths on her fondness for the bottle also.[14] In any case, the post-Glorious Revolution 'gin-raced city' quickly extends into contemporary scenes of violence and confusion:

> one night
> the whole garden gets angry
> will not settle to direction itself

---

[13] In his discussion of "Opening," the first poem of *Darwin's Dialogues*, Bush notes that "in the image of the child which haunts this poem… the future will be characterised in terms of recapturing wonder, that state of astonishment or lostness of self-consciousness before the world and which distances itself from the mechanics of need by a kind of grace"—although "alienated labour" will also haunt the poem as a child's probable future (232).

[14] Griffiths observed in a note to me after this article was written that the Queen's "statue outside St Paul's is so positioned (and it's caused comment) with her back to the church and her face to the nearest pub."

> but turns & turns
> a magic carpet
> with a label of derision

An upshot is that "all the garden is meat," potential prey in the war of each against all with which by 1991, Thatcherism for over a decade had laboured to supplant any vision of 'society,' let alone class society. The poem nears its close with an evocation, perhaps, of the north of England's devastated industrial towns and cities:

> There is no smoke in the chimney
> no dog in the basket
> no bicycle in the drive...
> But the stars sneeze shut... [both ellipses in text]

The landscape stutters to a halt in all but name,

> capped
> with a spine-pack
> of hoe-black boxes
>
> A black calendar
> at last,
> all made of full-stops
> with everything hidden.

The 'hoe-black boxes' leeched to the spine *are* the days as meted out by the military slams of rhyme (pack—black—black) of the entropic 'black calendar,' again a wrenching contortion (hurry up and go nowhere) of the body.

Interweaving these passages, Griffiths seems to propose alternative possibilities, the first in a creaturely commonality, "A L L /in the mirror of the Sun," wherein is found

> a flowing of flesh/matter
> into appetiteless communion
> ...
> a great chorus of harmoniums
> round the borders
> : surely
> it must be an EXCHANGE

Yet how can you have exchange without appetite? Similar problems attend the later supposition of a "tremendous multi-vocal constancy" in which rats and weeds are tolerated "& the cat [was] caught playing, becos it was not cruel"—at the end, letting the mouse go, with a slap on its little back? These are at first sight not utopian proposals but parodies of such as partial and immobilized. In a further twist of the screw, the poem thereby becomes itself a precursor of the shutdown of large dialectics that will mark "The Relief of Aachen." It is not, however, a shutdown of dialectics at the level of poetic form:

> in the rare cones   in the air
>
> ARE
> spas & flakes
> platforms, links, strange
> rounding power of sound
>
> beautiful how   quite oblivious
> THEY FORM   of observers

The closing haecceity of "Steve's Garden" holds material and immaterial, up and down, things and sound. If we read the final branching couplets vertically—'beautiful how THEY FORM // quite oblivious of observers'—the non-sentient cosmos, following its own laws of morphogenesis, is wholly indifferent to the human. If we read horizontally—'beautiful how, quite oblivious, THEY FORM of observers'—then observation becomes what makes cosmos, cosmos; human otherness from and contribution to cosmos are together glimpsed for a paradoxical moment.

4

'So careful of the type?' but no.
    From scarped cliff and quarried stone
    She cries, 'A thousand types are gone:
I care for nothing, all shall go.'

—Tennyson, *In Memoriam* (1850)

The debate has been intensifying because Earth is warming much faster than some researchers had predicted.

—Juliet Eilperin,
"Debate on Climate Shifts to Issue of Irreparable Change" (2006)

In his valuable reading (236–8) of some of the closing lines of "Steve's Garden"—glossing, among other things, the stars sneezing out and the calendar of full-stops with everything hidden—Clive Bush notes their model near the end of Pope's *Dunciad* (1743), where the universal sway is established of the empire of *Dulness*:

The sick'ning stars fade off th' ethereal plain;
As Argus' eyes by Hermes' wand opprest
Clos'd one by one to everlasting rest;
Thus at her felt approach, and secret might,
Art after *Art* goes out, and all is Night. (1963: 799)

Pope implies moral apocalypse, figured above all for him in the replacement of high culture and the sciences by venal plebeian jackasseries (the
scatological Grub-Street games of Book II). His method, as Thomas
Jemielty shows in detail, includes penning a mock reversal of Genesis and
Revelation, so that the former's creative Word is undone by resumption of
the Chaos into which it first struck, and in the equivalencing of jabber
and silence, the dunces rather than the blessed are vindicated as the elect
of history. This has been consummated; Pope is out to curse, not to
reform. Apocalypse skirts immodesty, to put it mildly, and its rationale to
the doomsayer always appears irresistible. Yet the apocalyptic work that's
intuitively alert can help us think critically (dialectically) about the
present. Its time forms with the present a kind of haecceity, the difference between them real and needing to be respected, but non-absolute.

Griffiths's "Alternative Ending," his parody apocalypse in Latin, has
already been noted as itself a black-magic reversal of Genesis. The logic
is in fact teasingly uncertain, with the perishing of sun, moon, and stars
on the Third day being followed by that of the winds, heat, and light on
the Fourth, all sounds on the Fifth, and only at the Sixth, all generations
of men; while

> Ad Septam
> Transibo etiam
>
> Et tota materiam
> Universa hujus.

[At/to(?) the Seventh /Even I (presumably the "Angel" reciting the poem)
will pass across /And all the matter /of this Universe—except that the last
stanza in Latin is a chaos of grammatical agreements: literally, 'And all
the Universe' (subject), 'matter' (object minus verb), plus 'of this.']

Its companion poem, "Englynion," opens with reference not so much
to specific organisms as to natural feedback loops essential for the
creation and maintenance of life on Earth:

> This one, you see,
> breathes nitrogen, a little oxygen to breed;
> it can live on organic compounds.

> And this, this takes in carbon dioxide,
> releases oxygen, then reverses that.
> It builds the atmosphere.

Plants use root nodules to capture nitrogen as a nutrient, strengthening them for the photosynthesis that releases oxygen as a waste product, thereby permitting animal species to breathe and breed. In an intersecting cycle, the earth mantle takes in carbon dioxide and releases oxygen through plants and—through plate tectonic motion and volcanic eruptions—carbon dioxide again, as a greenhouse gas helping to keep Earth warm enough for life to subsist. Do the atmosphere-building interactions glimpsed here between, as James Lovelock might put it, "living and nonliving parts of the planet" (in Barlow, ed. 1991: 4), offer another way of interpreting Griffiths's earlier 'appetiteless ... EXCHANGE'? Lovelock's 'Gaia hypothesis'—meant not, he says, as "a teleological concept" but rather to propose planetary homeostasis as the result of a "not [consciously] purposeful [but] goal-seeking system" (15, 18)—may then be one of the concepts hovering over the following lines from "Steve's Garden":

> And there is
> a patient mewing in the night.
> What is it—lead, steel, nickel?—
> (World Soul)?
> Keeping the leopard on its back
> till it tires.

Which is to tire here, leopard or World Soul? 'Mewing' obviously suggests some kind of plaintive crying, but in a derivation from the Old French, it also means 'moulting,' losing one's covering. The stanza thereby chimes, not at all uncannily, with Lovelock's projection for 21st-century global warming in an article recently published in *The Independent*: "Much of the tropical land mass will become scrub and desert, and will no longer serve for [homeostatic] regulation; this adds to the 40 per cent of the Earth's surface we have depleted to feed ourselves" (2006).

Griffiths's 'great fire,' now in the guise of a (tangential) figure for planetary pollution, reappears as suddenly and inexorably[15] as in "Opening":

---

[15] Eilperin's article cited as epigraph to this section discusses current concerns of scientists that the climate is nearing a 'tipping point,' where a small increase in overall temperature could trigger a massive positive feedback loop.

Imagine something more complex:
burning oxygen, it lives as
fast as a fire, and grows great.

It uses up everything around it ...

In fact, however, "Englynion" does not call down apocalypse. It shifts to its second left margin and longer lines, and might indeed be picking up on an earlier Lovelock at his most euphoric. First, the scientist:

[Gaia] is now through us awake and aware of herself. She has seen the reflection of her fair face through the eyes of astronauts and the television cameras of orbiting spacecraft. Our sensations of wonder and pleasure, our capacity for conscious thought and speculation, our restless curiosity and drive are hers to share. (In Bates 1991: 19)

And then Griffiths:

One of the new formats will attain the ability to quiz
    the universe as to what it wants of us.
Whether it wishes to be packed away in its box, or ex-
    pand to an equivalent of nothing, or be stabilised.
We will no longer be concerned with solving our own
    problems, but agents in the more fundamental matrix
    of the universe.

A singing cohesion, unimagined potential!
Every last thing alive, joining in participation in
    existence!
With all Matter converted to Meaning!

I have cited the last two stanzas of "Englynion" in full in order to make apparent the subtle, rapid, and daring play on tones of voice that enables the coexistence—the simultaneous impression—of a sardonic critique of hubris, an empathy (self-implicating, therefore: see "Darwin & the Finch," neglected here) with the comedy of it, and an empathy too for the desire (on the brink, as it would turn out, of the first internet decade) to belong in a global communion. All three of these, at least, variously inflect the conversion of all matter to meaning, as does the *Dunciad*'s closing refusal to distinguish, in the world at large, between silence and jabber.

References

Agamben, G. 2004. *The Open: Man and Animal*. K. Atoll, Trans. Stanford, Calif.: Stanford University Press.

Aristotle. 1987. *The Poetics of Aristotle: Translation and Commentary*. S. Halliwell, ed. Chapel Hill: University of North Carolina Press.

Barlow, C., ed. 1991. *From Gaia to Selfish Genes: Selected Writings in the Life Sciences*. Cambridge, Mass., & London: The MIT Press.

Barzun, J. 1958. *Darwin, Marx, Wagner: Critique of a Heritage*. Garden City, N.Y.: Doubleday.

Bataille, G. *The Accursed Share*, Vol. I: Consumption. 1991. New York: Zone Books.

Benjamin, W. 1973. *Understanding Brecht* (1966). A. Bostock, Trans. London: NLB.

Brecht, B. 1979. *The Threepenny Opera* (1928). R. Manheim and J. Willett, trans. New York: Arcade Publishing.

Bukharin, N.I. *et al.*, eds. 1935. *Marxism and Modern Thought*. London: George Routledge & Sons, Ltd.

Bush, C. 1997. *Out of Dissent: A Study of Five Contemporary British Poets*. London: Talus Editions.

Calder, D.G. 1979. *Old English Poetry: Essays on Style*. Berkeley, Los Angeles, London: University of California Press, Center for Medieval and Renaissance Studies.

Conrad, J. 1995. *Heart of Darkness, with The Congo Diary*. R. Hampson, ed. London & New York: Penguin Books.

Darwin, C. 2003. *The Origin of Species by Means of Natural Selection; or, The Preservation of Favoured Races in the Struggle for Life*. New York: Signet Classics.

Deleuze, G. 1993. *The Deleuze Reader*. C.V. Boundas, ed. New York: Columbia University Press.

Eilperin, J. 2006. "Debate on Climate Shifts to Issue of Irreparable
    Change." *Washington Post*, 29 January.
    http://washingtonpost.com/wp-dyn/content/article/2006/
    01/28/AR2006012801021.html
Fay, M.A. 1978. "Did Marx Offer to Dedicate *Capital* to Darwin?" *Journal
    of the History of Ideas*, 39: 133–46.
Feuer, L.S. 1975. "Is the Darwin-Marx Correspondence Authentic?"
    Annals of Science, 32: 1–12.
Gould, S.J. 1980. *The Panda's Thumb: More Reflections in Natural History*.
    New York: Norton.
Griffiths, B. 1991. *Darwin's Dialogues*. London: Amra.
Huggan, G. 1989. "Voyages Towards an Absent Centre: Landscape
    Interpretation and Textual Strategy in Joseph Conrad's *Heart of
    Darkness* and Jules Verne's *Voyage au Centre de la Terre*." *The
    Conradian*, Vol. 14 (1–2): 19–46.
Jemielty, T. 2000. "'*Consummatum Est*': Alexander Pope's 1743 *Dunciad*
    and Mock-Apocalypse." In C. Ingrassia and C.N. Thomas, eds.
    "More Solid Learning": New Perspectives on Alexander Pope's Dunciad.
    Lewisburg & London: Buckness University Press, Associated
    University Presses, 166–89.
Linebaugh, P. 1991. *The London Hanged: Crime and Civil Society in the
    Eighteenth Century*. London & New York: Allen Lane, Penguin.
Lorca, F.G. 1998. "Lament for Ignacio Sanchez Mejías" (1935). In *In
    Search of Duende*. Various trans. New York: New Directions, 66–81.
Lovelock, J. 2006. "The Earth is About to Catch a Morbid Fever That May
    Last as Long as 100,000 Years." *The Independent*, 16 January.
    http://pjoris.blogspot.com/2006/01/gaia-in-trouble.html
O'Sullivan, M. 1986. *From the Handbook of That & Furriery (Piece for Voice &
    Slides)*. London: Writers Forum.
Pope, A. 1963. *The Poems of Alexander Pope: A One-Volume Edition of the
    Twickenham Text with Selected Annotations*. J. Butt, ed. New Haven:
    Yale University Press.
Pynchon, T. 1974. *Gravity's Rainbow* (1973). London: Picador.
Simonton, D.K. 1999. *Origins of Genius: Darwinian Perspectives on Creativity*.
    New York & Oxford: Oxford University Press.
Skene, W.F. 1858. *The Four Ancient Books of Wales Containing the Cymric
    Poems Attributed to the Bards of the Sixth Century*. Edinburgh:
    Edmonston and Douglas.

Tennyson, A. 1973. *In Memoriam*. R.H. Ross, ed. New York & London: W.W. Norton & Company.

Wordsworth, W., and S.T. Coleridge. 1976. *Lyrical ballads; The Text of the 1798 Ed. with the Additional 1800 Poems and the Prefaces*. R. L. Brett and A. R. Jones, eds. London: Methuen.

Bill Griffiths's **The Mud Fort:** *Language as vulnerability and revolt in an age of compliance.*

WILLIAM ROWE

These poems, which Bill Griffiths gathered together for the Salt Books selection of his work from the past twenty years, are full of delights for a reader: tight turns, strange overlaps, breath-taking leaps, and sudden dissolves. And that is the opposite of crunching ideas down to transferable segments in grand planning dictats: the operational language which reduces thinking to models, blueprints, projects, road-maps. The sheer liveliness of Bill Griffiths's language, its dazzling variety of forms, is in deep collision with the linguistic engineering of thatcherblairism. Its sources are astonishingly multifarious: Old Norse, Anglo-Saxon, Latin, Romany, north-eastern dialect, cockney, the speech of West-Indian migrants. The aim is neither erudite showing off nor soap populism but to find the irreducible substance of word-events, as in this scenario of addiction and institutional cure: 'Kick, kick and kick and kick / the door / as if / chemicals excite, metal moves.' There's a piece missing in the syntax: *just as* 'chemicals excite, metal moves.' The missing beat syncopates the language, the thought. This is not the smooth language of the managed word, laying out scenes and objects in convenient order (a feature of English that has been on the ascendant since John Locke). Instead, things jut into consciousness, where the formless meets shaping forces: gaol, psychiatric hospital, city; but not only those, also the force of delight in form and shape: 'So what is wrong with you? / me? / Wow / I can tell like / see Nature's new dyes and the green / water-weeds laugh outright'.

Basil Bunting and Gerard Manley Hopkins are alive in this struggle of languages that underlies Griffiths's poetry. On the one hand:

Once
in the plural world
there was abuttal
hand/band/sky/eye
here were grammars of colour
I knew, adhered,
flexed, forget, warm, collapses

And on the other:

Now prime words
re-regulate and define the cluster
I compete in.
They do not touch
much,
but from time to time I remember to snarl.

His bottom line is not nostalgia for some lost and inert authenticity but fierce refusal of subjection to actual destructions occurring now: 'to comply / equals / to vanish.' And that is much more difficult, since there is no available image of the human that can protect us. On the contrary, the idea of the human is part of the danger of subjection: 'and set up to it / again, again, again / 'n' being addicts / of being human.' What if the *of* also means because of, signaling the propensity to be addicts of our selves, through need for repetition ('again, again, again')? Another, explosive meaning dawns.

Griffiths is no believer in the value of form for its own sake. Several poems take us through machines that plan and regulate time, mortgaging the future by producing predictable order. 'Orrery' makes a link between working models of the solar system and a certain type of poetry: their makers are, in a lovely pun, 'steelers of time'. 'Without any consciousness of loss / they have synchronised / the closing of flowers / the run of the mortgage / the tidal land of permitted waking / or working / in the shell of / rhyme.' The poem presses towards truth: such models synchronise and give security, but they are not accurate, they appear to give time but they take it away. The poem exposes the workings of those alibis for order as they shape us ('all the indicatees are agreed / how we look') and urges against them ('You see the way industry us subsumed?') and towards the work of each one in the active making of whatever it is we inhabit ('Separately we work and the lathe / masters / rotates / the sun.') This is consistent intellectual anarchism and as poetry it sets the language out of order into music—or better, musics, since the measures of Griffiths's poetry are highly varied and invite us into finer perception by frequent alterations of pattern and mode.

The predictable order of the Hardyesque mainstream of English poetry offers some security against the contemporary world's destruction of environments and memories. But it's a nostalgic security: it doesn't show us how we might be responsible for the destructions. Griffiths writes, 'Nothing has prepared you | . . . for the sheer nihility of towns laid dead', refusing passivity towards 'the snippets of Darwin | that snarl and fight' and by the same token—i.e. by the analysis of those continuing intellectual programmes that underwrite contemporary society— refusing postmodernism. 'Evolving' smashes the Darwinian schema (subsumption of human future to competitive use of resources) against the more chaotic but rich movement of biological material by quoting Darwin himself: "the delicate yellow . . | and eggs of the white . . . | these spiracles . . . | gregarious . . . and disperse . . .".

The morality is in 'Not gnawing at the body store | like some machine set in bad gear | having to work backwards now', in other words not to hand over aliveness to some schema of purposiveness which feeds on the past, like the heritage amnesia so well charted by Iain Sinclair, who wrote the preface to one of Griffiths's most uncompromising books, *The Book of Spilt Cities*—one of the fifteen or so that the Salt collection draws on. Instead of merely suppressing anxiety by nostalgia, Griffiths opts for 'a like gipsy humour . . . | safe in being alive at least,' which means to 'dare at | handing the zip and hugging by chest,' his version of Conrad's 'in the destructive element immerse'.

This kind of intellectually tough humour is open to the intimacy of tender and childish feeling, in fact protects a place for it in the world: 'the twist of the cracker ex | plodes in | to model | fruit | nuts hazel 'n' beechnut | miniature house-horses | and trash-rings | with gem holly-scapes | and sea mobile | to please'. And then, with a breath-catching plunge, this child's-eye diorama of Xmas cuts to close-up with 'spindles | on the cot', the infant memory, not yet ordered into a world. 'Self-analysis' shows the child and the man:

> For several years
> I thought I might have been a mucky sort of toy
> or maybe a clumsy cat
> till I learned I was human
>
> But no more
> shaping cups
> an' pouring myself in them.

Self-generating growth but no purpose
breathless wonder the success is
and we are anywhere . . .

Anarchic humour and responsibility—that we are responsible for the way
we interpret (and thus make) the world—come together in a whole set of
poems that work with the narrative compressions of comics, like 'On the
Sun', which makes Larson *Far Side* humour into a brief epic: 'It was a cruel
fite / my ears are ribboned / Nape gooey wiv blood / But I won it / I am to
drive the Sun-Lorry all day...' The pleasure in the ungroomed spelling and
grammar of the non-educated respects their intelligence, and so has no
condescension about it. What emerges is a lovely physicality of language
and world, the segments of each rubbing and sliding against each other:
'It / iz / a / dance / (an oboe? / a dart-over / ova text / an acrobat / ova text'.
This dance with and of words comes out of Griffiths's involvement in the
1970s with concrete poetry; with Bob Cobbing and Paula Claire he was a
member of Konkrete Canticle, who performed in Europe and Canada as
well as the UK. But the transmission is far longer: behind the experience
with sound and concrete poetry there is his work with Anglo-Saxon,
Norse, and early English lyric as translator and scholar (he has a PhD in
Old English). The result is not only a sense of words as having physical
mass—and laid out in phonic abuttal rather than iambic smoothness—but
also a sharp awareness of their magic, world-producing power. That
power is constantly held up to critical scrutiny (and so the magic is not
romantic and nostalgic) as the poems expose language that orders, hier-
archizes, surveys and in so doing makes us less alive. In 'Birthday poem'
the salt at breakfast goes 'sigit-cheep, sigit-cheep', and 'words are heavy, /
with deliverable masses. / I know, for I am a word'—and, like in a fairground ride, you get ready for the next plunge, but it is still beyond anticipation: 'There are other words like me. Perhaps we are all one word. / But
it is my word, too, is me.' The particular mass is suddenly lost into the
gaze of a god—or gaol—but then, just as quickly, the grand scheme is
refused, aliveness rescued. 'Mud fort' is a metaphor for the human body,
Griffiths has pointed out.

Hence the recurrent scenario of gaols and other damaging spaces,
places which reduce the scope of the human. It has been there since his
earliest work (such as *Cycles*), informed by his own prison experience and
others' of corrective institutions. Here is the beginning of 'Liam's Song':

The room
is the reality.

Block-mouth'd
sure wall, imposing area.

The place of brick
as strong as a word.

Variety of environ
all the edge-nick combinations
in a small ring of syntax.

Who holds the value words?
The key-man,
self-appointee,
lion and devours.

This confinement is social training ('we will make youngsters more socio-acceptive / by schooling them at the majic age of three'), a mirror held up to the work of language and walls, hidden work of soul-making: 'When I first scent death / the false bla'mange face onna life-packet / then I hurt a tadge.' The poetry scents out death in the hidden intimate places of socialisation. It really does turn English Literature inside out: as Gertrude Stein said it, 'If you write the way it has already been written the way writing has already been written then you are serving mammon, because you are living by something some one has already been earning or has earned.'

Griffiths holds to a different way: 'everything seems large, local. / Perceived intimate; / as history of itself.' What is this condition? Certainly there is no acceding to it without rigorous attention to the actual composition of the real. Then what gives the strength for that? Certainly not mere mesmerised fascination with the forms of movement, like the officer watching the swaying empty mess tables in *Battleship Potemkin*: he doesn't know what's going on, he's lost the plot. And simply being vulnerable to the assault on the senses is not enough: shock, disavowal, disgust do not constitute an understanding of how we are trained to find the intolerable normal. To create an eye and an ear for the actual composition of environments, this is what the Elizabethan poets did with language, as they responded to new times, spaces, technologies, passions, and revealed in the plasticity of their language the rituals by which the social is made. Only if poetry gets that far can it take responsibility for itself.

Griffiths, like few other poets in English, has the energy and intellect to grapple with the postmodern epoch without either being a passive conduit, a nostalgia addict, or a preacher. 'Darren in the Alps' tells how the snow is 'pristine' every morning after being 'rutted' and 'doughed up' by snow-boarders: every night 'Onto the spoiled territory / the grand machines settle forth' and put 'the ALPS . . . back in place'. It's the total production of environment ('these are the Playing Fields'), scene of the postmodern, whose process extends into everything. So what is the active principle that allows a poet to take it head on, the difference between the mesmerised eye and nostalgic ear, and the sovereignty of poetry? Partly an acute awareness of the historical energies in the language, the past alive in the present, as in Griffiths's masterly use of the pastoral:

> stirring motors are like a ruminant . . .
> and horns toot, far-off, in alps . . .
> maybe it makes goats 'n' bells in a dream, to the
> 　　snow-pals fallen fast and packed asleep
> a smoothing passing night-carol of girls
> 　　before the green dawn slants
> 　　before the lamps dim
> 　　　　IT IS PRISTINE

No Movement epigones ever got near such dazzling skill, and all done with such light touch. Poets who are not interested in unhitching themselves from the past as unearned inheritance—worried about sawing off the branch they are sitting on—are not going to be able to take the present apart, find the unseen machines that clear the ground for our enjoyment, the same machines that order the possibility of meaning, the page where we read and write. Mallarmé did—and Eliot and Pound—and the work continues.

To find out how the present is put together, 'our very models of cultural shape will have to alter'; that was written by Appadurai, one of the sharpest analysts of contemporary modernity, and it fits what Griffiths is doing. So also does his proposal that 'we begin to think of the configuration of cultural forms in today's world . . . as possessing no Euclidean boundaries, structures, or regularities.' This principle can be recognised, at a micro level, in Griffiths's syntax: 'the toffee-diesel scent of arriving in Newcastle. / Its new half-new stone new castle signalbox.' Nouns become adjectives and vice versa, and elsewhere verbs too: there's an uncertainty at the core—and it makes the words work harder. 'An' the bells make a pleasing invention, / they echo people move': is *move* a noun (the moving of people) or a verb (how people move)? If the ambiguity were resolved, it would give more control: there would be a perspective, the raw elements of meaning would be overcoded. From the same poem ('Xmas 1'), there is this:

> the boy on the carousel
> rings and ring the bell.
> round & round the car goes scoot,
> he makes the horn go toot!
> His shirt is holiday blue—
> with a foot and a whirl of diff'rent patterns.
> Sometimes he sit' aside the counter his dad' stall and watch it all.
> Like learning to talk.

Here there is another—succulent—kind of intelligence which is not that of one who exercises power by the administration of things. Sound and image in movement are flush with learning language, with meaning. To read this poetry is to be in touch with a primary modelling in which words, music, image intersect, in the rhythm of basic segmentation out of which meaning emerges. There is joy and power in that—the emergence of shape out of nothingness—including the power to change oneself. In a riposte to the critics who 'find me unsympathetic', Griffiths is clear enough about the desire to control and organise that he is writing against: 'minds sharp as axe / ready to seize on any little homogeneity for fascist / like shirts.' He adds, with a nice pun on sticks as denoting both glue and the axe handles of the fascist symbol of mass power, 'I hope they will be well haunted. / I mean their own mass mind—/ the sticky columns of the smart-alike journals.'

At the macro level of power and culture, *The Mud Fort* includes scenes of the post Second World War carve-up of the world, the social violence of the Thatcher years ('The Toxteth Riots', 'Ballad of Orgreave'), and the colonial atrocities ('In Malaya', 'In Kenya') which are, as Paul Gilroy has pointed out, the repressed of British history. 'In Kenya' begins with the line 'The *Land Freedom Party* was founded in 1950' and takes us, without ideological point-scoring, through the gardens of the white estates ('magnificent red of saffron'), through facts of the violence ('British troops cut off their hands as symbols / Piles of gripped-fail to prove the point'—the word 'symbols' bursting open suddenly as you read 'gripped-fail'), to snatches of talk of the colonists ('*And what exactly are the curried*'), and the ritual oaths of the Mau Mau ('*And if I fail to go / may the he-goat that straddles the sky . . .* '). In a masterly move, the poem plunges from Kenya in the 1950s to the time-space of the UK now: 'The traffic-light has changed, / I advance three paces. Dutch-dykes of non-nourishment, negligence, non-involvement are hedges, pave, side-to side / the march of/ centuries move forward / the set of each white rule in Africa'. The present now that any relationship with history begins from is thrown against the past that made it possible, the two overlapping as ordering of movement in time and space. Here are Appadurai's 'complex, over-lapping, fractal shapes'—if we don't grasp these shapes, he writes, 'we shall remain enmired in comparative work which relies on the clear separation of the entities to be compared before serious comparison can begin.' In other words, unless there's an understanding of these new overlapping types of relationship between cultural scenarios, there will be nostalgia for an order that's gone—however postmodern and popular the language used, something common enough in current English poetry. Bill Griffiths eschews superficially postmodern vocabulary and instead goes for the schemes of power that language effectuates: 'all the signs-moves / of logic-magic.'

His writing grasps the nature of the times through white hot poetic condensations: 'upon a desk / a packet of biscuits / that are just another consumer item // as to which . . . here are whole systems of messages / looped like fruits / bob-tempest / . . . Any number of disguises. Points of admission.' These lines (still from 'In Kenya') trace continuities between the grammar of colonial atrocity and the everyday information envi-ronment, how the one can bleed into the other and be hidden (from colonialism to traffic to biscuits). The wild juxtapositions of avant-gardism have become the stock in trade of social training with its wild information clusters (*bob* means cheat as well as bunch), the condensed word-clusters of the poem holding a mirror to the logics of consumer society. The method—the overlapping of contradictory languages, the presentation of history without completion—has been learned, among other sources, from Eric Mottram, another master who Griffiths acknowledges. But he brings his own combination of tenderness, high velocity humour, and music, as in these lines from 'Hanuman', a poem about the Indian monkey-god: 'The goat with no mouth / . . . indicator... / buried rules in secret hands / . . . how maths uses to laugh at mammals / the / thought-kali.' This astounding ability to get inside 'logic-magic', as he calls it, here in maths as damage, permits him to bring out the morality of every turn of meaning without imposing any system of morality: nothing is neutral, as the purely operational language of neoliberal power wants us to believe. Griffiths's poetry gives the speed and alertness necessary to resistance: otherwise the 'IS' of established power gets there first ('we say / is / IS').

The critical alertness extends to mathematics, as in a poem called 'Zero': 'ANNIHILATION area / / what walks towards? // blank // close // at face of mirror // who meets? // to overtake // (anticipate) // before // to be before / (in advance of)...?' And in 'Hungary', 'in a zero I stand protected / it flattens the stars / is ownerless / extinct / equal / no place of solar sound / only indication of animal after animal / to a thousand and a thousand thousand.' The context is the making of the nation through imperial invasion ('the great Russians in their universe'), and the way that logic sweeps through the synergy of money and global power: operational language is damaged and damaging. Try reading 'Medical Histories' for a rapid and devastating exposure of the secret cost of the current world order: how 'uncooperative army personnel / with personal problems' had methedrin and ether administered to them 'to bring to the surface / all those awkward little expected pre-indicated traumatic diversions / that prevent the human from growing up a normal plain killer. . . / Most humans now agree it is safest to have a subconscious.' No escaping the question: what is the condition to which 'to comply / equals / to vanish'?

Scars in a haunted landscape:
Bill Griffith's *Ghost Tales of Seaville*
STEVE COX

A friend of mine once told me, and I still half-believe him, that not so long ago, Archaeologists up in the hills of West Wales thought that they'd found the skeleton of a deformed, eighty year-old Stone-Age woman ritually interred beneath a toppled Neolithic standing stone. Further tests, however, had showed that she'd only been around eighteen when she'd died—and that she'd had long, blonde hair.

However, what had really excited and puzzled the Archaeologists was the way that the body had been positioned post-mortem—flat on her face with one arm stretched out, with its hand clenched and one finger pointing straight out over the Irish Sea...Who knows.

I think, for a while, they'd thought they'd dug up a Fairy.

I'd already noticed that similar quaint folk themes crop up in some of Bill Griffith's folkloric fiction—hints of the Little People, the Hidden Ones, the People of the Hills, even if he never quite gets around to labelling them as such. In *"The Amulet"*, Bill deals with a subject that has usually been dealt with in a far more euphemistic way by the more popular writers of supernatural fiction, especially the nervous ones who happened to live alone, in remote upland locations, a hundred years ago; we're not dealing with Tinkerbell here. I think we're dealing with our ancestors. And they may need placating, occasionally.

Bill's Hidden People in *"The Amulet"*, when the bones are found, turn out to be the discarded results of failed Mary Shelley-era Lamarckian experiments by the then pit-owning gentry, who were attempting to produce a stronger, shorter-in-leg-and-brow workforce without the mind for wages. Once revivified and back up hiding on the moors, of course, they soon revert to type by creeping back into the small town at night and wreaking awful, bloody mayhem and revenge upon the hapless teenage jobseekers who'd disturbed their forgotten resting place as part of their bail conditions. But they're basically harmless, if left alone... or so tradition says.

Another thing struck me about Bill's ghost stories—their always mundane jumping-off point. People who live in ivory towers may get lots of visions, but you're far more likely to genuinely cross wires with things differently-natural when bored out of your mind on a night job or point-less daytime probation scheme. If you want to hear, as opposed to read, the real, hair-greying stories of things from not quite right to the down-right bowel-evacuating, ask any ex-demolition worker. Or night watch-man. The sort of people who *don't* go out looking for supernatural thrills tell the best ones. Ghosts always creep up on you—it's what they do best.

I had to quietly mention my earlier experience to Bill, after I'd read his *Ghost Tales*, and, *sotto voce*, ask whether he'd ever heard of somebody called Arthur Machen. Stupid question. He's also, as I soon found out, only the second person I have ever met who has read William Hope Hodgson's "Carnacki the Ghost Finder" stories, a fact that I find deeply incredible in more ways than one. Like the darker, occult-inclined masters of the Edwardian *outré*—especially Machen—Bill's writing has that hard-won connoisseur's trait of burying the deeply disturbing and unpleasant in ever-darkening layers of erudition that repay repeated reading with evermore stomach-churning revelation and insight.

"*Luke's Wake Walk*", for example, is far more inexorable and haunting in its casual walk to the sea if you about, or stumble across, its firm root-ing in pre-Christian British funerary beliefs. Even if, like me, Anglo-Saxon theology or northern Council Politics leaves you blank, there is still a naggingly familiar undercurrent to the proceedings that makes the storytelling ring true. You may not know the exact mythology, you might not catch on until later, but you *feel* something working and let it carry you on to the end of the story: the internal logic of ghosts. And, by extension in Bill's case, Northern Councillors.

The "Other People" (and hedgehogs) of Bill's tales only emerge from beneath their industrial long-barrows and abandoned mine-workings to extract the occasional savage but, to them, perfectly just revenge upon those who disturb them. They're comparatively benign: there is another strand and specie of far more virulent counter-human evil that runs through "*Ghost Tales of Seaville*" like a bleak red map-line on a Civic condemnation order—Local Councillors. Fatted blokes, with chains and

Jobs for Life to us Southerners, in Bill's Seaville Cosmology they are the opposition, the *adversary,* the deceivers; the very fallen ones themselves. I think that nicely sums up Bill's view of Councillors; seems they have the power up there. Almost like minor gods.

It was a real shock to discover that Seaville actually *existed,* even if they do spell it slightly differently up there. It was bound to have a *local council...* or plenty of abandoned earthworks. When I checked, and found it *had both,* I began to worry about Bill's physical safety.

The first time I visited him up there he seemed unconcerned; he declined my offer to prop the chesterfield against the hastily closed front door.

'Bill,' I choked, getting my breath back, 'Some of those stories are based on... the *truth,* aren't they? The Councillors—'

'Hmmmm, well...' He mumbled, benignly but evasively.

In that awful, soul-blasting instant, I *knew.* I padded into Bill's kitchen, turned the main light off, and trained the beam of a piano lamp out into the dark vastness of his back yard, all the better to show any portly, bechained figures who might be trying to creep up on us and silence us forever. You can't be too careful in these small towns. I pulled a chair into the hall, checked the door, sat down, and felt a little better. Bill still looked remarkably relaxed.

'I doubt, very much, if many of...*them* have read those stories,' said Bill, calmingly. I'm certain I caught a slight end-of-phrase tremolo of doubt in his voice. Not a very deep one, but...I checked through the curtains again, and strained my ears for the sinister, worsted-muffled chink of gold on enamel.

'Look, Bill.' I whined, 'That bit in "The Tapes", that Councillor's Grandfather...the Town Clerk—' It all came tumbling out.

'Ah,' said Bill, with a massive finality.

'But the cave, the transients, the nanny goat impersonating...' My voice was shaking. I was on the edge of truth, and it unsettled me, deeply—'My gods—offering himself...passively...to tramps...the cave...'

I stared at Bill with almost childlike eyes, silently beseeching him to tell me it was not so. Bill smiled.

'Well...' he said, 'There *is* a small track running down to the sea around here called Nanny Goat Path. And some people, back in the old Town Clerk's time, *would* have been living in those caves on the beach; and—'

'But...but...' I said.

Six hours later, Bill had managed to coax me into taking down all the barricades. We ended up sitting by the fire early into the morning, drinking tea and talking about Seaville's dark municipal history. I learned things. A lot of things.

In Bill's short tales his power-drunk Local Councillors generally share the short-term life expectancy and lurid terminal fates usually reserved for American Prom Queens in beyond-the-grave slasher movies. If they're lucky. The one time his Councillors find anything like peace and moral redemption, let alone a happy ending, is solely down to the powers of spinach and an international misunderstanding, rather than any implausible Scrooge-type change of heart or Civic policy. A very bleak view of Local Authority.

'Are these scurrilous blasts of gruesome vengeance *personal*, Bill, or just literary convention?' I asked.

Bill thought over that one for a long time.

'Well,' he said, pause over, stroking his beard, 'There *is* the old M R James tradition of supernatural intervention in the ghost story—of the ghost being the agent of morality and social retribution in the world of the living—because, let's face it, there's bugger all apparent justice down here...' After having taken aboard Bill's local history lesson and the morning news, I could hardly disagree with him. Thankfully, it would soon be time for me to catch my train and get the hell out of Seaville.

'Ahh,' I said, remembering the exception, 'But in "The Marchioness", there's no supernatural element to the come-uppance at all... in fact—ye gods—it would have been a lot less unpleasant if there *had* been one.' I shuddered. It had been horrible. 'It does *sometimes* happen that way,' said Bill, smiling the ghost of a smile to himself.

'Right!' said Bill, standing and noticing the time, 'Out you go!' He ushered me out of the front door and into the howling, rain-scoured morning.

I still had the distinct feeling that I'd learned too much; I was halfway down the street when the chocolate-brown 1970's Rover screeched to a halt in front of me and burst open its doors like something out of "The Sweeney". The overweight but still burly man taking the lead screeched too, but in a deeper, more guttural way. 'How!' he barked, most definitely meaning business, 'Wheeze warra paarsonarl waard wiz yeez!', or words similar. He was breathing heavily, and wearing a chain—a huge, rusty one, doubled crushingly round his ragged shoulders like a sentence. There were tough little bits of seaweed caught in its links, I noticed with a sudden rush of horror. His mates from the Town Council were still very much from the world of the living, though, and every bit as furious as their Predecessor was. I was Seaville History.

Interview with Will Rowe*

WR: How did you come to start writing poetry?

BG: In my teens I was equally keen writing poetry and music. But with the music there was the problem I was tied to the classical modes I had been brought up in, whereas I had had relatively little instruction in poetry, and felt freer in that form of expression. Western music ultimately depends on the key system and a scale of 7 notes; using language I have some 40,000 words to work with!

WR: You use the words 'expression'...

BG: A tune I see as a memorable arrangement of notes that conveys an interesting emotion. It is easier (for me) to put that 'emotion' or 'idea' into words than notes. These are the 'ideas' or groups of words that come most strongly at the edge of sleep; I still keep a piece of paper and a pencil at my bedside. This may be why the results are so jagged, seldom capable of being sustained for more than a few lines. Almost all my poems are made up of short images that build up into hopefully connected themes to equal one poem.

WR: Not a conscious technique?

BG: Initially it has a lot to do with sounds of words and how that makes its own syntax. Early models were Hopkins, Keats, McClure—in all of them, as I see it, sense and sound balance. As a purely half-tamed youngster, it was also a matter of experimenting with trying to find a poetry that would cover modern fairly dangerous and fraught themes.

* Thanks to Jennifer Fraser for help with transcription.

WR: What about the types of speech that you wanted to use in different ways in your writing?

BG: There isn't much of any direct speech set down anywhere; the language I use is definitely colloquial and intended to be and again… it's the idea that I had, not just my idea I'm sure, that you ought to be able to fit anything into poetry. It was deliberately trying to see if I could make something that would work as a poem come out of strange experiences and ideas. The freedom was there in Catullus and Villon; it's lost in Tennyson or Hardy.

WR: You've mentioned no modern British poetry.

BG: No…there was none…

WR: That means it simply hadn't been of any use… what you'd read up until that point.

BG: I'm not sure if I was aware of very much. Umm… if I can remember the names after all this time… Plath?

WR: Plath and Hughes and Tom Gunn and that stuff.

BG: That's it, but only marginally aware of. There wasn't anything there that was inspiring me in any sense. It was much more if anything the inventiveness of McClure that was showing me that you could use it in poetry in different ways. But… there is a big difference between optimistic California and shady Outer Middlesex.

WR: So you drew a line after the first three *Cycles* and meeting Eric Mottram?

BG: Yeah, what actually follows them are a few unnumbered poems, sets, a few magazines pieces and so on and then *Cycles* 8 to 16. The point being that what was intended as *Cycles* 4 to 7 was actually being published in *Poetry Review* or other magazines and I thought 'Well, I won't reprint that, I'll leave it to later' but when it actually came to later I wrote a different *Cycles* 4 to 7. So the actual order is *Cycles* 1 to 3, 8 to 16, 4 to 7 and the publishing order was 8 to 16 and then 1 to 7.

A bit awkward but by the time I'd struggled through that, I decided that was enough of that frame of approach.

WR: What sort of things did Mottram put in your way at that time?

BG: The first most important thing, bless him, was to offer to publish me.

WR: That was in *Poetry Review?*

BG:–which I suspect led him into quite a few difficulties. I was quite innocent really of the sort of problems that were going to turn up at The Poetry Society and assumed I would be welcome with open arms. But that was a tremendous sort of threshold because if you are struggling there writing poems with your stubby pencil and what have you in the equivalent of your undeserved garret, it is a tremendous boost to find that someone will take them seriously and take them on. So that I feel that after that there is much more confidence in the actual writing, in the poetry. Before that, I mean I enjoy them still in a way, but they are stark and slightly insecure. It seems to me that they gain a bit in... you know I feel a bit more assured or able to experiment and to work harder at it after that. And the second advantage, of course, was the contacts it brought to me. From then on it did open up a great range of contemporary poetry. American poetry through *Poetry Review* and actual contact with people like Tom Pickard, Bob Cobbing, Jeremy Adler.

WR: The gang down at the National Poetry Centre.

BG: Well, not simply them, but you know people beyond. Obviously it encouraged me to read Bunting for example and McDiarmid. Although I probably knew of McDiarmid a little before then. Basically the sort of resources that were in *Poetry Review* and it encouraged me to follow up either by reading and actually being able to talk to the people.

WR: Well that's very clear.

BG: An important stop was meeting Bob Cobbing. We were introduced at a strange gallery event. All I can remember was that it had perspex boxes full of what appeared to be coal dust shaped in them, which was deemed highly artistic. (I thought they might be mobiles and went round tapping them.)

WR: Something like the Air Gallery.

BG: Don't know. I wasn't one for going to galleries and the like. And I was very much an outer city person, an Outer Middlesex type. Anything that was Outer Middlesex: Hendon, Harrow, Uxbridge way. I hardly went into the centre except when Eric urged me to attend this gallery opening you see. And Pierre Joris of course was another person that I came into contact with. So there I was talking to Bob Cobbing and it became clear that he actually had the capacity to print. Which was, we are talking now about 1972 say, really a rarity.... My poems I'd attempted to duplicate on a pathetic ink screen thing but not very well... and here was Bob with what for the time was a quite remarkable set up, not only a Gestetner duplicator but a scanner that would make stencils from visual material, and best of all, a great deal of experience in producing small books, designing them and even marketing them. We quite hit it off and after that I began to think in terms of production as a book. For example, *War w/ Windsor*....

WR: So what you're saying is that the availability of printing in your own hands made the idea of a book kind of different. It made it more varied, it put it more in your own purview.

BG: Yeah, I mean there were several lines I could have taken. I could have followed on with magazine entries but I wasn't keen on those because they are sort of scattered all over. You haven't really got any context for a poem if you do that. Or I could have tried to get into the high class offset litho world of...

WR: Commercial publishing?

BG: ...of Iain Sinclair in effect, in the paperback tradition. But the problem there was I was thinking in fairly small units so Bob's solution was the ideal one. I was writing poems in small groups and the small press booklet seemed an ideal medium. But as a result of that it wasn't until the mid 1990s that I actually got a UK paperback offered because I was all the time committed to producing at the booklet level.

WR: I mean readers won't necessarily be able to visualise the variety of small books that you did produce. I mean in terms of format in terms of use of visual stuff.

BG: Well it's infinite isn't it. It isn't just a matter of stapling in the centre or stapling in the side, you can sew them in cotton, you can put them into little bags, boxes whatever. You can print single-sided you can print double-sided. I also had access to a silk screen workshop in Dalston. Suddenly coloured covers started appearing, you see. And then there is hand colouring which is not too bad on a small run, for 50 or less...

WR: So each book becomes a unique thing.

BG: The only thing that tied us down then was the typewriter and literally all that we had was a manual typewriter. And it had to be heavy. The heavier the better to cut a stencil.

WR: To get through the stencil.

BG: That changed slightly when the golf ball typewriter came in. It made larger texts more feasible. There was Eric Mottram's one, what was it, *About Poetry*?

WR: *Towards Design in Poetry*.

BG: *Towards Design in Poetry*. I typed that up for Bob. We couldn't have done something that length before the golfball. And you couldn't centre the poems like Michael McClure because you need old-fashioned type-setting with tin letters for that. So it influences my style. You get poems that are set left which is the typewriter return carriage...

WR: Nevertheless the variable spacing is necessary to get these short lines in the right sort of place.

BG: Well... I met the American system of 'open field'—of spreading over the page—too late really for it to make much impact on me. I'm not sure how I would have used it or understood it.

WR: Yeah, okay. Because I mean Olson talked about using the typewriter as a key part of composition.

BG: Yeah, you can do that on a fixed space typewriter—you can spread out over the page with gaps as you like and yet as you know if we translate it into another media like a website, you can't easily do that. Dom

Sylvester Houèdard's work very much depends on a fixed space type-writer methodology.

WR: And the combination of verbal texts with visuals is something that you came across in Cobbing or something that you had already been experimenting with?

BG: I don't, if you think of it, do a great deal of visual work. In *War w/ Windsor* yes, there's Sean O Huigin's visuals. They're collage. They're *Times* newspaper headline lettering and so on.

WR: The *Three Novellas* use a certain amount of overlay, visual overlay.

BG: A certain amount of visual spacing, but it's more related to multi-voice. And that again was something that Sean introduced me to. Perhaps we should explain that he was part of these workshops that Bob ran at Earl's Court. The Writer's Forum Workshops. And they included Clive Fencott, Jeremy Adler, Sean O Huigin, and many others, well, for instance, Laurence Upton.

WR: cheek?

BG: chris cheek, yes, a little later but certainly by the mid-seventies. And...he died recently—down in Devon... Alaric Sumner. Him and chris cheek and so on were there but perhaps a bit later.
    So, there was lots of inspiration to take in. On the other hand having settled and fought my way through to the strange rather jagged rhythm line I use, although I try to vary it by introducing prose or multi-voice or list poem or what have you, under the sort of Burroughs example of experimental conventions, I tend in the end to come back and stick with the sort of short line that seemed to suit the unit of sound and thought and rhythm that I...

WR: Because it is already there in *Cycles*, that line.

BG: Yes.

WR: You've mentioned sound now, unit of sound and thought, and you mention Keats in this connection... When you're dealing with small short units of sounds you're not talking about metrics I take it?

BG: By metrics I would understand the pattern.

WR: The pattern as detachable from the actual writing?

BG: I spent quite a lot of time when I was doing the first writing for *Cycles*, as it were, escaping from patterns. I mean, English has quite a strong pentameter bias somehow. We only have to stand up and speak and out come perfect five stress iambic lines. It's sad, but it can take a lot of effort, trying to escape from those cadences, which still somehow dominate English.

WR: Yes, they diminish attention I think.

BG: I mean, I remain with a sense of pattern but it's a deliberately irregular pattern, if you can have that. If you are going to try and work for a fixed pattern it just disrupts the content doesn't it? It takes precedent over the content. It's too much of a limitation.

WR: And were there any musical memories or equivalences that are, that were playing into the way you were working in the '70s. I mean, for example, given that some of the subjects were to do with biking, the question would be you know was there a rock music connection?

BG: No, I've often dreamt, you know, that my poems would be seized on and set as fantastic pop songs. But it's not to be. Even when I try to write dialect poems in neat four-line rhyming stanzas, my local guitarist says 'No, I cannot set them. They are just not regular metrically.' 'But doesn't that make it a little more interesting?' 'No, it can't be done.' I've missed out on that totally. And… my interest in pop music waned after 1972–3. I didn't like *Black Sabbath* and so on. I never understood them. It was strictly for all night dances, drugs and strange cinema venues, that sort of long track.

WR: But in the background of the writing you were doing, there were some senses of rhythm and music that maybe now are more evident to you now than they were then.

BG: As you know I'm very fond of classic piano, I play. And of world music: I played in the '90s in a gamelan orchestra in Durham. I would dearly like to write, as it were, literary symphonies and sonatas; but it seems to me that you cannot translate the experience.

WR: Bunting tries in *Briggflatts* to use a sonata form as statement, variations, return in a different mode.

BG: I don't see how you can have different keys, two contrasting subjects and so on, in language terms.

   I liked the idea of musical structures at one point. The idea, if it doesn't seem too gloomy, of the various sort of sections that form a Mass. Or a trio as three short stanzas. Occasionally I use the word *rondo* and so on, but not in any serious endeavour. I title one piece a *barcarolle* for example. But... there isn't any actual musical input, other than the idea of a structure or a piece in a special mode. For example: *nocturnes*. I decided that they should go with *diurnes*, which are pieces that you write for the daytime. But they're nothing to do with Chopin.

WR: In one of Nuttall's pieces on your work, in *Poetry Information* 15, he says he can hear the syncopations going on in some of the lines from *Cycles*. So he's looking for some sort of musical description. Sort of missed beats.

BG: And that's fair: syncopation in the sense that at one point I deliberately aimed at breaking up standard rhythms. It's tricky though.... Now Stefan Themerson—a friend of Bob's—one of his ideas was a diagram like a triangle with the word 'rhythm' in one corner, 'sound' in another and 'meaning' in the third, which struck me as quite a useful view of it. So that you had to take all of these into account. Except in Bob Cobbing's case you could slur the meaning slightly, and concentrate on the rhythm and sound. But I liked to keep the meaning there.

WR: And that makes me think of Bunting again but clearly he is doing it in a particular context which is not yours.

BG: I remember him saying that Pickard should learn to write in a longer line or some such. As it is, Bunting is much smoother somehow, more lyrical, flowing. It would be nice if I could but I didn't quite get to taking that on board. I thought 'no, I'll stick with a fast change'. (For me, it provides a unity of content and form.)

WR: Bunting's syntax is actually quite complicated and long-winded. I'm not meaning to criticise it. It works over long stretches.

BG: Some of the images suddenly come back and repeat and there's echoes and previous allusions and references back. It's really quite complex.

WR: Something more rapid is what you're talking about.

BG: Yes, a fast rhythm. Goes with fast booklet production. Bob reckoned you could write a poem, cut the stencils, print it, collate and bind it all in one day. With luck...

WR: So when does Pirate Press date from? And what's the...

BG: Just a name I chose—a sort of outlaw tag—when I started getting actual printing capacity through Bob. And he was a very generous man with his time and his facilities. I mean obviously, I bought the paper and made a contribution towards the ink. But basically not just me but many people were free to turn up and take up his time, print pages, collate them all over his tables and expect help getting them into book-shops as well. But that was the weakness, distribution, because even Compendium which was the most sympathetic bookshop had just one clutter of a shelf to wade through. Small press is not bookshop compat-ible, really it's a pity. Peter Finch down in Cardiff was also very helpful with stocking little press material. But again it just ended up packed on shelves in the bookshop...

WR: The book fairs were actually more appropriate.

BG: They could be marvellous and we had some excellent ones at the London Musician's Collective at Regent's Park and one at the Whitechapel Art Gallery, I remember, and various others. Sometimes you could do tremendously well. You'd not only meet interesting people, you'd actually sell items. But as events they were very unpredictable. If it was somewhere that had its own publicity set up you stood a good chance. If you went cold somewhere, which we occasionally tried to do out of London you know, just relying on a bit of local enthusiasm, you might not get it. And then Bob Cobbing had the good idea of combining sales with events.

WR: Readings, exhibitions?

BG: Bookshop and exhibition, bookshop and reading combined. There was a large sound or concrete poetry conference one year in London and that brought in a lot of people. So, obviously yes, that was then combined exhibition with bookshop.

WR: So those are the circumstances in which you got Pirate Press going.

BG: Yes, I still don't understand marketing. It's beyond me. But I mean it was then, in a sense when I was writing and printing an edition of 50 copies, I was thinking of a small audience. I was thinking of friends, of poets and people who might be sympathetic. I wasn't ever imagining that it would be worth going into paperback or hundreds of copies. I was aware that this was not much of a living, but at some point you have to ask yourself what you think you are going to do best. And although I love music very much, I wasn't particularly brilliant or outshining at composition or anything. I could have made more money perhaps. But you then ask what is it that you can make a contribution with, sounds a bit arrogant, but you know, what you are most suited to, what you most want to do becomes at the end what you are going to be best at doing, can contribute most by doing. I decided at some point that this had to be poetry, a very concise use of words, a very tight and concise form of expression. As I said, having the confirmation or approval of Eric Mottram was a very big step to me continuing along that line.

WR: I mean there was associated with Eric and in a different way with Bob, a tremendous intellectual ferment which I guess to some extent is not what gets commented on or remembered when people say 'ah the '70s' and they think of...

BG: Well Jeff Nuttall was closer to that wasn't he, in a way.

WR: I guess.

BG: He was very much a larger than life character and what with his jazz performance reputation and his acting. And he did wonderful plays, which I think have been published since then as scripts, but for one or two performers. They were done in costume in a prepared room, which could be quite a small venue, for a dozen or less audience. They were strange little chamber pieces.

WR: A People Show?

BG: They worked on many levels. They were special events you felt privileged to take part in. And what did appeal particularly to me was the width of techniques that he employed—visual, handwriting, typing, voice interplay. And although, as I said, I tend to stick to a short rhythm, I do when I can try to vary that with other techniques. For me the beauty of cut up texts or a list poem is not that it is progressing you anywhere with language or thought, but that these are wonderful ways of dividing up and varying a poem to produce a sort of more complex structure...

WR: Yeah, that makes sense, more dense.

BG: To give it more scope, in a longer structure, if you can change and vary the expression. I don't like a simple narrative. I've almost never written verse narrative I think. 'Cycles' I used as a title initially to convey this non-time-based progression of stanzas.

WR: When you say list, this takes one to Anglo-Saxon or possibly other languages, it's not typical of Modernism and this is something you got your teeth into fairly early—*Gilgamesh*?

BG: One of the key texts there was...

WR: Not *Beowulf*?

BG: No, no, no the big anthology from Rothenberg... the one that included everything—Eskimo, ancient Egyptian and the whole lot.

WR: *Technicians of the Sacred.*

BG: *Technicians of the Sacred* yes and I think that was perhaps the eye opener it was intended to be, since you had all these different sorts of poetry, small concise expressions or whatever you like to call them from ancient Egypt through to the Bushmen of Africa and so on. It was glorious. It didn't seem to have any particular critical basis, more a scoop collection of anything that could be presented as an alien short poetic text even if it was an action or a description of an event.

WR: With some interesting translation techniques, non-conventional.

BG: Yeah, I quite liked the numbered lists which I take to be anthropologist's way of summarising a longer text; so you could reduce the *Iliad* to one hundred points numbered points—a new text!

WR: Now it might have been 1969 that *Technicians* came out or something like that.

BG: It took a year or two to reach me, but yes that would have been about the right date.

WR: So that came before for you before getting involved with reading Anglo-Saxon.

BG: Yeah, what set that off was actually Peter Finch from Cardiff who kindly sent me a rather battered Victorian copy of the *Gododdin*, which of course was one of the inspirations of *Briggflatts* on the assumption that it had actually been written in the North-East of England at a very early date. And this was a wildly improbable translation because no great work had been done on systematically recovering early Welsh vocabulary at that time. It was an 1870 or so translation and there was this wild confusion of little stanzas which the poet had re-invented into unlikely and improbable short poems. I was very impressed by it and followed that up... which led me on to Old English (Anglo-Saxon), where texts were much better understood and edited.

WR: Just the sheer ways of organising the materials were interesting to you, apart from the materials themselves, the historical aspect.

BG: I mean the *Goddodin* is in effect a list poem, a series of stanzas which are linked, each one celebrating a dead hero but also having linked common lines in various places that carry through. It's fascinating. I've never aspired to duplicate that approach but yes, it's a matter of spreading the possibilities... not thinking of poetry as something that you've got to define and write within a traditional format, but something that you can use to explore, to extend your resources. It's Foucault—the difference between fulfilling a preconceived potential and letting yourself loose on infinite possibilities. I mean you might say the sonnet has got potential in as much as you could redeploy it in interesting ways but there comes a point at which you are no longer interested in that, in simply writing in the framework that other people have considered acceptable and want to go beyond that. And the '70s was particularly a sort of bursting out time of youth culture, well the '60s for that matter, I mean it was an exciting time, almost but not quite revolutionary. And it gave me a great respect for an independent society in that sense, society as a grouping... a voluntary grouping in a way; but on the other hand it diminished my respect for organised political society.

WR: What about 1979 and the counter-revolution, if you like, the Thatcher stuff... whether you thought that what had been discovered and brought about as experiments and experiences in the 60s simply had to be abandoned, because certainly some people took that position after a year of two of Margaret Thatcher. It's a political question.

BG: Yeah, I mean The Poetry Society gave up early in 1976 or '7 and that surprised me and disillusioned me a great deal because I wouldn't have thought that the work we were doing was that revolutionary. I wouldn't have thought that it threatened anyone. I mean compared with some of the advances accepted in other art forms, you know the products of the Poetry Society were really quite ... I won't say respectable, but understandable, you know, unless you absolutely set your standards against anything that didn't rhyme or fit into stanzas. I find it very strange.

WR: The Poetry Society print shop was closed down and the committee in fact effectively expelled... and Bob Cobbing was somebody who kept going and wasn't cowed or however you want to say it.

BG: Well, to my surprise although there were some fairly, well, fairly strong resentments and temptations to blame each other...that didn't happen. And I got on just as well afterwards with Eric Mottram and Bob Cobbing and most of the others as I did before, I'm very glad to say. But of course the potential to do things was changed, we didn't have a centre where you could exhibit, have performances and meet and so on. It was fractured. I tended to keep close with Bob and Paula [Claire] and the logic of that was there were opportunities for international performances, which took us to Toronto and Berlin. And because they actually paid you for performing, it meant that we could carry on writing and publishing for at least a little bit longer.

WR: Just slightly tangential, was the business of working with sound more than with meaning, which is what some of Bob's and Paula's work is about, was that something that set you going with your own writing or would you say that it simply accompanied it as a different kind of work?

BG: I mean, generally I needed to think of working with them in terms of music. My own contributions tended to be visual, various sort of sponge prints, and workings of letraset or found letter shapes... one set was *Dock Poems* with gothic lettering forming cranes and dock fronts, gestures of riverscape as it were. But it influenced my writing also the longer pieces, you mentioned the *Novellas*. (The odd title of the *Second Row* was simply because I was hoping one day to bring out *War w/ Windsor* and other prose as a *First Row* but once things get back to front they're slow to sort.) And...the *Solar System* and *Building the London Hospital*—those weren't pieces that I performed with Bob or Paula but they were written during the period that I was working closely with them and they've got much more found text sound content. These were my first attempts at longer poems, and I wanted to vary content and technique rather than have a plain stretch of all the same. It was one of Jeff Nuttall's ideas to use song lyrics as the basis of found texts and manipulated texts and that comes into the *Solar System*. All these were quite long poems, booklet length; *London Hospital* is a series of 'fragments', but at the same time it was quite an interesting way of building up a longer structure with all sorts of small items a bit as you would a building proper.

WR: So you were using voice you were using rhythm you were using other kinds of patterning which makes you freer in what you can put in.

BG: Yeah... at that time, mid and later '70s, I was become much more inner-city; I was living in Dalston, Stepney, Whitechapel. Not my favourite time (looking back), but places very, very complex in terms of people and the actual society and that contrast of techniques seemed to suit it. Or if you want to look at it another way, when I'm a little more relaxed in the 1980s, the poems become simpler again. I don't know.

WR: So what led you to the more formal study, formal as in institutional I guess, because they don't have to be linked do they, of Anglo-Saxon?

BG: Yeah, Old English…

WR: In other words scholarship and universities don't have to be the same thing.

BG: I mean Eric had very kindly invited me to take his American MA course. But I didn't and don't feel a great deal of sympathy with American literature, before the 1960s. Instead I asked Eric if he would help me get onto a part-time MA at Kings, which was tremendously good value then 'cause you got two years teaching for the price of one and it wasn't very much for that either because they were trying to encourage slightly older people, mature people to return to university…

WR: You got a good deal.

BG: …and I benefited from that I think and of course from teachers like Jane Roberts and Janet Bately. Without wishing to rake up any sad thoughts, quite a tremendous English Department at King's at the time…with Eric making sure none of them fell asleep at the job!

WR: And John Porter you did some work with, co-translations.

BG: Yes, about 1974 or 5. We've put them on the Internet now. It seems like a good way of dealing with texts that you can't quite afford to publish and print.

WR: One of them, maybe more of them had that triple text idea with an original, a literal and a poetic version.

BG: Yes, the Gisli Saga eh… yes, that's quite fascinating late medieval Icelandic verse where the 'kennings' (puzzle compounds that make up new words) become so extreme that you have to have two sets of translations, a literal one and then an explanation of the literal translation to cope with it. John was a tremendous scholar of Icelandic but I guess, a bit like old English, it isn't a field where you are expected to innovate very much. My attempts to do so are severely criticised in some quarters.

WR: Are you saying it was like 19th century philology and therefore you just stuck to the handed down way of doing things?

BG: There is this sort of dark hooded shadow of Christianity overlaying Anglo-Saxon scholarship. It is very gentlemanly/ladylike 99 percent of the time and then it occasionally it flares into violent quarrels over the exact significance of one word in the *Battle of Maldon* or whether Asser really wrote a life of King Alfred. A strange world and not one that I'm tempted to identify with. Which is a pity but there you are.

WR: And you got into Latin, reading Latin, or is that later? When are we talking about?

BG: Well, I read it poorly, from teenage years. It's nice if there is a translation opposite. I still admire Catullus for his immediacy. Another figure that came to me as a surprise later on was Claudian.

WR: Yes, you pointed out some of that in *Liam's Song*.

BG: Yes, he has a strange… he has a tremendous power with words - images that he builds up of dragon banners and armies, or the horses of the sun going back to their stables—quite new, and a new use of Latin I think. And very modern to my ear.

WR: I don't know anything about him, but he is late Latin isn't he?

BG: Very late, yes Rome has more or less fallen already I think. It is his desperate attempt to try and keep together the sandcastles of Rome.
    In the mid-1980s there was a year or two of uncertainty. I should explain that when my father died I moved onto a houseboat at Cowley, near Uxbridge on the Grand Union, which seemed a good solution but… the boat that I was on, a lifeboat, which are notoriously thin hulled, on the basis that you only need to use them once, went into local welders for…

WR: I think it was a ship's lifeboat, that's what you're saying.

BG: Yes, I'm sure proper lifeboats are much sturdier… to have a new steel skin put around the hull. That's how they do it. And unfortunately the welder working got the temperatures too high and it ignited the wooden interior of the boat. Now I wasn't insured at that point so I had to start a lengthy claim on the boatyard's insurers which took I think over two years to settle and at that time I was moving about partly in

Essex where *Morning-Lands*, the book, was written—Alf Harman and his family helped me a lot there. And when I did get the money, it seemed to me that the best use for it was to buy a sensible house, in this case a half a house in what was recently described as one of the ten worst places to live in England, bless them, in the district of Easington in Co. Durham. That was Mayday 1990.

WR: I mean partly that was—I understand from something you wrote—a decision or a response coming out of the dominance in the Southeast by Thatcherism.

BG: Yeah, I was increasingly unhappy living in London in the sense of Central London, Metropolitan London, even cultural London—and notably in Thatcherist London. For example mooring fees went up from £200 a year to a £1000 a year when they discovered that wasn't actually any legal reason that why the British Waterways Board couldn't charge whatever it wanted. So that was dangerous for me. Also I'd known the North, Newcastle especially, since the mid-60s and always admired it so I thought that was the move to make.

WR: You knew Pickard already?

BG: I knew Pickard yes from the '70s and Ric Caddel of course.
    But Seaham was chosen partly for the fact that it was quite a flat town centre and at that point I was still partly responsible for my elderly mother.

WR: So she could visit you?

BG: Yes, so it was somewhere that she could stay and get about the town centre. And apart from a few scrapes it has been a very peaceful place to live.

WR: So it was there you began work on North-East dialect and also dialect literature.

BG: Initially what I did was reform myself into Amra Imprint, partly to qualify for a grant for a publishing project, which would tide me over moving North. And I used that to buy a second hand photocopier and to produce booklets much as I had but with an emphasis on local history to begin with and then there is a series of poem booklets about the coast and then I start to move into dialect study which of course is linked very much with the Old English; it is quite traditional in some of the vocabulary and syntax where I live.

WR: So you were collecting stuff partly in libraries but were you also doing something like fieldwork?

BG: Oh yeah, it was initially all fieldwork, the libraries being used to check etymologies and spellings and so on and so forth. But then it got bigger and the Centre of Northern Studies at Northumberland University agreed to take it on.

WR: This is the dialect…

BG: The dialect dictionary… and we had a parallel 'reader' (anthology) but that has not been so popular. Partly I think because there is no fixed spelling for North-East dialect. It can be difficult for a dialect speaker to actually read dialect notation!

WR: Because that would be your primary audience? …Primary readership.

BG: The dictionary is used like a game locally; somewhere where you can dip in and recognise phrases and words long in use and find out more about them. It has proved to be very popular. And we then got a grant to do a questionnaire, which went remarkably well and produced a whole host of new information, words and phrases and new angles on recognised words, which lead to a larger dictionary and so on.

WR: So it is on-going work over the last 15 or more years.

BG: Yes. Over the last 10 years on a serious basis.

WR: In the '90s when you came to do the book of *Spilt Cities* that was a longish work which was actually, although it is made up of longer or shorter fragments, it is actually a whole book on a single set of themes.

BG: Sort of a set of fractals if I can borrow Allen Fisher's phrase. A sort of overarching structure: in the first part of a pseudo-psychological interrogation of the City as a conscious entity and then an examination of the suburbs. And the last bit is a sort of strange combination of siege of Oxford in the Civil War and local testimony from—at that point, I suppose—southwest London, where good friends from East London had moved to by that time.

WR: Is that the first time you've done a book in that sense that is quite complicated and quite long?

BG: Well, yeah, *Tract against the Giants* doesn't really count because that was just a selection that was put out. What changed that was the kind offer by Invisible Books to do *Rousseau and the Wicked*. I hadn't had much publication in the 1990s except for my own booklets so I quite welcomed the chance to have a wider audience. And I had a mass of poetry accumulated and asked the publisher to select his favourite 98 pages and then I changed the order a bit and so on and so forth. So it was a sort of a consensus there, a little constellation of individual poems within a theme all from the same period, and approximately a theme which was environmental I guess.

And that made me think seriously about structuring a larger book as opposed to just a larger poem; so *Spilt Cities* is actually an attempt to structure a larger book which I could only do by breaking it down and breaking it down again so that each of the three sections has lots of different but hopefully compatible material in it.

WR: That was written while you were working as archivist in the Eric Mottram archive, which was a break from living North.

BG: Well, the main book that I wrote in my spare time then was *Nomad Sense*. It would be nice to think the orderliness of cataloguing led to the highly structured *Spilt Cities*, but maybe it was more a chaotic counter-reaction.

WR: So actually there are a number of books from that time.

BG: Well then it catches on. I get the taste of planning for a larger publication: there was *The Ushabtis* (Talus Editions), *Durham & Other Sequences* (West House)—these are collections within a theme, making one consistent book though not one that you are meant to read through in sequence like *Spilt Cities*.

WR: But when you came to do the selection for Salt I find it quite curious that you will excerpt parts of *Spilt Cities* and so on and then weld them into some sort of slightly thematic sequences.

BG: My original idea for the Salt book was to go for the shorter poems that hadn't been re-published in anthologies. I chose ones from 1985 on because although I'm not discouraged at looking back at earlier poetry, it was a very very different context in the early 70s and mid-70s and it is hard for people now quite to grasp how strange the world was then, slightly dangerous and revolutionary. You know it was a time when miners were able to blockade depots and bring down a government and so on… a very strange exciting period. And without direct experience of that time I don't know if the poems work now. Anyway I aimed to avoid early work and work that had already been reprinted, with only a very few excerpts from the longer poems. Because I thought the shorter poems were more attractive to a reading audience.

Originally I thought of dividing it into subject groups, as a way of organising the contents. And then you could have a bit of a picture at the start of each section. Chris Hamilton-Emery didn't think too much of that. So I thought 'fair enough' but what I did was I kept the same subject groupings but just sort of blurred them into one long sequence.

WR: I mean you can read it through and feel yes, there is some sort of progression.

BG: Slight sort of rainbow chains from subject to subject.

But he was extremely good with the editing. I mean I gave him a draft because I thought this was going to be too much, at the 200 page level, saying 'help me at this point. What do we do? What do we select?' And before I'd virtually heard back, he'd got it all corrected and typeset, and said 'that's fine' which is a delightful way to work.

WR: Really good. So just that period of working with the Mottram archive makes me think of a couple of prose books of yours *The Fams* and *A Pocket History of the Soul*, but they're probably a bit earlier than that.

BG: Yes, they're earlier in the 1990s.

WR: And there were one or two I guess pamphlets to do with politics. I don't want to call them political pamphlets.

BG: Well, *The Fams* and *The History of the Soul* stem from the fact that when I moved North there was quite a bit of spare time for reading and thinking and so on and I was going into these topics. And, I have this strange concept somewhere of a world soul which is sort of equivalent to Michael McClure's sense of galactic unity if you like. (It's there historically in the Neoplatonists and so on.) And then about, just before I took up the Mottram archive work and there was a severe clash with the local councils. They wanted to "regenerate" (put that in as many double quotes as you can spare) the town of Seaham after the pits had closed and the idea was to enlarge the dock company at the expense of the nearby housing.

WR: God!

BG: Having moved up there pitifully in refugee status to find out that my new home was also vulnerable did not please me.

WR: Quite.

BG: So there are a few quite sarcastic pamphlets about that time. And that led to a series of ghost stories in which the offending councillors are picked off one by one in horrifying circumstances I'm glad to say.

WR: You'd been a fan of M.L.R. James way before that?

BG: M.R. James, yes and, of course Le Fanu if you prefer and he's a master of absolutely chilling...
    It is also a mechanism to getting outside the conventional orbit, the conventional ways of expression.

WR: But going back to the *Soul* book and *The Fams*, I mean for a poet to undertake quite a large investigation of the history of culture, is something we kind of got used I guess to the idea in terms of American poets, but it certainly wasn't...

BG: Perhaps what I'm trying to do is break away from the Freudian mould. I'm sure we've discussed this before but it seems to me dangerous in the end that Freud goes for these inherited genetic urges or whatever you like to call them. Because once you do that then you can justify anything by that urge.

WR: Like the First World War?

BG: Well, I mean he was supposed to have divided Eros and Thanatos. But in point of fact, what happens in the popular mind is that Eros is the justification, is the source of anything and everything, the source not only of sexual motivation but the motivation towards violence and power and so forth. So it ends up that once you've established that there is any sort of inherent motivation, then in fact you can use that to justify whatever you like. And what freed me of that obligation to mass murder is Foucault's point that even if you had the most basic urges they would still be so modified by cultural pressure, that really it isn't fair to speak anymore of a basic urge which defines a human. And that's what's great with Foucault. He's saying that our real basic urge is to think that we are human. And the lengths that we go to in order to ensure this safety of identity are quite miraculous. I found that a very liberating approach because you don't have to pay reverence to any idea of a fixed human or a fixed culture or what have you. You can go broader. Hence, this is about the time of *Spilt Cities*, the first part of that is a sort of mock psychoanalysis of the city attempting to get back to its basic urges and motivations which turn out to be those of sacrifice. And it does seem to me ultimately that our culture works to define a human by sacrificing others. And so it seems to me that the First World maintains its priorities both economically and culturally by sacrificing the Third World...which is sad to discover in your 50th year...

≈

WR: Can we go back to an earlier moment, your prison experience? Conrad wrote in *Chance* if you want to find out about a society go inside one of its prisons. As well as this, say, political side to the experience wasn't there also maybe a linguistic shock/violence attached to it—some of which is surely apparent in *Cycles*?

BG: In a sense you have answered the question. Prison both contrasts with the governed society and is its direct consequence. Asked (as I once was by Wandsworth magistrates) if I condoned crime, I would say No, but it doesn't surprise me either. Violence is approved only in the service of the state; and the death count over the last century is unknown millions. In the early 1970s (Nuttall would place it earlier) there was a sense in which the people were reclaiming violence as a political tool, as a group tool, and as a personal tool—in the Miners' strikes, and in Northern Ireland, for example. I was not part of any of that (other than being delayed on a bus one evening as literally hundreds of Irish and police brawled right across the Edgware Road— the sort of scene that features prominently on TV when of another country), but I became involved on a minuscule scale when I joined the protest at 144 Piccadilly, and later agreed to support the Nomad gang in Ruislip as a gesture of local biker solidarity. Their encounters were purely with other chapters—that is, directed against equals—not the public or the state. Having said that, the Angel initiative *was* something different—motorbikes plus awareness? It was a local translation of the American sense of male emancipation (much as the Beatles were); it stopped far short of the assertion of violence (as in *The Clockwork Orange*) as the valid human instinct; and contrasted—this is a major point in the *War w/ Windsor* set—with the professional violence of the state.

WR: How does this affect your poetry?

BG: I should make it clear I have only experienced prison as a prisoner at H.M.P. Brixton. The poems on Dover Borstal were a tribute to Stephen McCarthy, who died [26 Jan 1971] shortly after being recaptured from an escape bid; later work on Michael Dell recorded a case in which the youngster absconded, and drowned while being recaptured. The idea of escape from the state was important to me in the 1970s—as a valid quest even if impossible to achieve. Later poems on behalf of Delvan McIntosh and Ray Gilbert were issued to raise funds for them as prisoners; and celebrate their survival. *The Review of Brian Greenaway* is a contrasting piece—who can claim they would not totally surrender their soul once subjected to the pitiless, malicious regime of prison? Less harmonious characters like Jason Moss and Liam Killigrew feature occasionally. These are 'evidence' poems: that they are mostly written in the first person is necessary, both from a sense of immediacy, and the concept of a universal 'I'—without any intention of claiming their gains or losses for myself.

WR: An on another topic we touched earlier, could you say something about the range of translations you have done and what the work of translations has meant to you?

BG: One point worth explaining is that I have real doubts about the term 'translation' itself. You cannot bring over all the functions of an original into another language—the meaning and the sound and the rhythm and so on. I have always favoured (when I'm allowed) dual text presentation, with the English capable of being used as a key to the original. The appeal of the texts I've worked on has been both their contrast to English and their relevance—Old English, Old Welsh, Anglo-Norman, Medieval Latin, Old Icelandic (through John Porter)—there is a paradox of link here absent in the more alien (classical) Latin or Greek. Publishers though are less interested in dual text editions than what I would call 'replacement translations' or even 'versions'—which come closer to new poems suggested by the base texts.

WR: Have your translations affected your idea of possible poetic forms? Have they affected your sense of what you wanted to do with the language? (After all, one translates, in part, that which is not available in one's 'own' language). And, moving on from those quote marks, would it be accurate to say that you became, in some senses, a multilingual poet, i.e. one who uses more than one language? (I haven't used the word polyglot perhaps because it seems to be associated with Joyce).

BG: We all strive for something new. But the 'new' doesn't just come out of the air, it has a model of some sort or other. For Burroughs, Gysin, Mac Low and so on, it may be that modern technology has been the model—the mathematics, the systems of the random and the nonpersonal. For me the models come from past literature—Biblical, Gilgamesh, Claudian, Euripides, Basho—and to some extent naïve art and gamelan and Western music forms and Etruscan art—the list keeps on growing! The 'borrowing' is seldom direct (but note the balanced line in *Star Fish Jail* and the Fitzgerald-Khayyam stanza structure in *The Bournemouth*—in both these poems the element of pattern and ritual seemed important). Also the conciseness of the haiku (with its width of super-reference) has a tremendous appeal. But in general it is more a question of exploring and establishing resources, a sort of reserve palette, which might influence a phrase here, an allusion there.

As you grow, you collect this width of resources, not just ancient but current like bike culture, science fiction, new ideas of revolution; and work becomes more aware of the cultural maze you live in. There is mythical material in *The Book of Legends*, Etruscan in *The Bournemouth*, sub-Christian in *Review of Brian Greenaway*, regional in *Coal* and so on, but the influences are more often indirect or at least non-structural. I do not usually give a list of references or sources: allusions are part of the palette, not significant in their own right. Similarly, with language, looking at other syntaxes must help expand your own; the simple rules of English are a joy to re-fashion; but I do not aim at the obvious world-pantheon of Pound—larger issues featured in the book *Nomad Sense* but there is enough around me immediately to serve for inspiration.

WR: When did you start doing website work?

BG: I began work on building websites in the late 1990s, when I connected to the internet. The server provided me with some webspace, and I self-taught myself HTML, the mark-up language to format text and pictures for display online. It is tricky and fascinating—not unlike casting a magic spell, for if you get one letter wrong or omit one space or bracket in the HTML, the structure fails. I struggled first with my own website www.billygriff.co.uk—then with space and welcome advice from Bob Trubshaw, and backing from Peter Finch, the quondam Secretary of ALP (Association of Little Presses), we set up a simple listing for little presses—www.the-lollipop.co.uk ('lollipop' standing for List of Little Press Publications). This was to take the place of the deceased ALP printed *Catalogue* of which I had typeset several editions—often they seemed to be out of date before I'd finished the typing. The internet, which can be constantly updated, is ideal for reference material of this kind.

Further informational websites included: www.pitmatic.co.uk (Durham dialect), www.story-of-seaham.com (local history and photos), www.sr7.co.uk (a news and events website for SR7, the postcode for Seaham), and sub-sites covering notes on Old English and versions of drama classics.

The next step forward was to learn CSS (Cascading Style Sheets): this is an extension of HTML that permits accurate setting of font size, though there is always an element of serendipity according to your screen resolution and brand of browser. (The separating of structure from content worries me a bit, but in practice, it comes together neatly enough.)

The internet also copes marvellously with photos and colour—for decades I had been working in black and white text because of printing limitations, and here was an Eldorado of opportunity—as many pictures as you like AND full colour—for text, illustrations, background…

These enriched techniques led to www.opalcoast.co.uk and www.ochrecoast.co.uk; these are mixes of visual, poem, text and sound centring on the Cleveland and Durham coasts respectively. They were begun with Clive Fencott, who had co-operated with me on two-voice texts previous to this. These websites basically work to explore combinations of text and visual. Moving text (scrolling actions—horizontal, vertical, contrasting and wavy) is available in Javascript, frame sequences in 'active gifs'—they are ideal in the realisation of random text and multi-voice combinations.

Next step, getting more experience of using sound on a website... and then maybe video...

Bibliography

Griffiths has published voluminously in both prose works and verse throughout his career, and the large quantity of his literary output presents considerable difficulties in the construction of a bibliography. The instructions for bibliography and reference that are given in the *MHRA Style Book,* used here, are frankly inadequate in providing a description of Griffiths's publications that can be applied consistently over the different range of items that he has produced. In the early years of his career especially, Griffiths's 'publications' could consist of single sheets for free handout or work published in journals with extremely small print runs. Apart from being extremely rare, these works lack ISBN numbers and give few details in regards to their publisher etc.; they are therefore extremely difficult to catalogue.

That the *MHRA* gives quite different instructions for the attribution of texts in journals to pieces that appear in anthologies presents another difficulty. In the early years of Griffiths's publishing career it is extremely difficult to distinguish between what is a journal and what is one of a running series of anthologies. The *MHRA* also provides no examples for multiple entries in journals or anthologies, a strategy that Griffiths uses frequently in presenting new work.

After consulting with Griffiths, the British Library, the Mottram and Little Presses Archives, where many of Griffiths's early works are available, and after reviewing a number of Griffiths's own bibliographies, I am convinced that this is the fullest bibliography of Griffiths's works possible. As such, bearing in mind that this bibliography will be hopefully referred to by interested readers of Griffiths's work in years to come, I have decided to err on the side of including more information rather than less. Thus, I have given more details of Griffiths's works published in journals than is strictly allowed by the *MHRA Style Book*. Where information is missing because the item cannot be traced this fact is acknowledged in square parentheses as [item untraced].

Thus, this bibliography includes all of Griffiths's verse or prose texts that have been distributed for public consumption in any form. Also included are the works of other authors published by Griffiths under the guise of either Pirate or Amra presses, along with critical articles that have been written about Griffiths. What is not included in the bibliography, due to the constantly changing nature of their texts, are any works by or about Griffiths that have been posted on the Internet. For further information about these works as they stand at the present, the reader is advised to consult Griffiths's web site, http://www.billygriff.co.uk Unless otherwise stated Griffiths is the author of all works included here. Abbreviations used include WF Writers Forum, PP Pirate Press, Amra Amra Imprint and COLP Consortium of London Presses.

1971

Bill Compton's Remand Mass (London: Griffiths's Press, 1971) [broadsheet for free distribution]

Black Mass (London: Griffiths's Press, 1971; repr. Pirate Press, 1972) [broadsheet for free distribution]

Cycle on Dover Borstal (London: Griffiths's Press, 1971; repr. PP, 1972, 1973) [broadsheet for free distribution]

Four Early Poems (London: Griffiths's Press, 1971; repr. Pirate Press, 1972) [broadsheet for free distribution]

Mass (London: Griffiths's Press, 1971; repr. Pirate Press, 1972) [broadsheet for free distribution]

Terzetto and *In Gipsy* (London: Griffiths's Press, 1971) [broadsheet for free distribution]

To Tom Saunders on his Imprisonment and *Eliza* (London: Griffiths's Press, 1971; repr. Pirate Press, 1972) [broadsheet for free distribution]

1972

Church Cassation (London: PP, 1972)

'Church Cassation' and 'Animal', *Second Aeon,* 16–17 (Cardiff, 1972), 176–177.

'Cycles on Dover Borstal', 'Terzetto: Brixton Prison' and 'To Johnny Prez. Hells Angels Nomads', *Poetry Review,* 63.3 (London, 1972), 226–231.

[T.E.] *Hulme—Complete Poems,* ed. by Steve Clews (London: PP, 1972)

Remand Mass (London; PP, 1972) [item untraced]
Stamped Poems (London: PP, 1972)

1973

Jeremy Adler, *Tarot Pack*, intro. by Bill Griffiths (London: PP, 1973)
Alex: The Polar Bear (London: PP, 1973)
Mary Anning, *Mary Anning: Letters,* ed. by BillGriffiths (London: PP, 1973)
Steve Clews, *Several Epochs of Agricultural Machinery* (London: PP, 1973)
Cum Permissu: To Commemorate One Year's Free Residence (London: PP, 1973)
'Cycles on Dover Borstal: To Sally', 'Second Cycle: To Michael Keith
     Pascoe, Assistant-Governor Dover Borstal' and 'Third Cycle: H.M.
     Prison Brixton', *Sixpack,* 3–4 (London/New York, 1973)
Elizabeth (London: PP, 1973)
M R James' Ghost Stories (London: PP, 1973; repr. with cover by A&S
     Paxton London: Consortium of London Presses/PP, 1974)
Masses / Texts / Allied Texts (London: PP, 1973)
Miscellany (London: PP, 1973)
'Romany Poems', trans. by Bill Griffiths, *Poetry Review,* 64.1 (London:
     1973), 17–21.
Sets / Lyric Pieces (London: PP, 1973)
'Seven Tarot Cards' and 'Scarab with Gold Circle', in *AB,* ed. by Jeremy
     Adler (London: Poetry Society Press, 1973), pp. 20–21.
Transaxions (1973) [item untraced]
War w/ Windsor (London: PP, *war with windsor; funeraline; vergil; zookeeper;
     october;* repr. [with revisions], illus. by Sean O'Huigin, London:
     COLP/PP/Writers Forum, *War w. Windsor* (1974), *War w/ Windsor*
     (1976). London/WF, 2004)
Work in, *Strange Faeces,* 10.2 (London, 1973) [item untraced]

1974

Cycles 8–16 (London: COLP/PP/WF, 1974)
Forming Four Dock Poems (London: COLP/PP, 1974; repr. [with revisions],
     London: PP/WF, 1977 and as item in *Word Score Utterance* London:
     WF, 1998)
Gisli's Saga—The Verses, trans. by Bill Griffiths and John Porter, cover by
     Bob Cobbing London: COLP/PP, 1974)
The Gododdin, trans. by Bill Griffiths (London: COLP/PP/WF, 1974)
'Mass', 'Bill Compton', 'Harrow', 'And the Lambs', 'Sets / Lyric Pieces',
     'Assembly', 'Settling the Cinque Ports' and 'Bikes', *Poetry Review,*
     65.1 (London, 1974), 26–39.

Musical score, in *WF*100 (London: WF, 1974)

A Note on Democracy (London: PP, 1974)

Work, in *Bob Cobbing & Writers Forum*, ed. by Peter Mayer (Sunderland: Ceolfrith Press, 1974) [item untraced]

1975

Aron's Saga, trans. by John Porter, cover by Jeremy Adler (London: COLP/PP/WF, 1975)

Beowulf: Anglo-Saxon Text with Modern English Parallel, trans. by John Porter, intro. by Bill Griffiths, cover by Jeff Nuttall (London: PP, 1975; repr. [with revisions], 1977)

Andy Clarke, *Day Trip to Boulogne* (London: PP, 1975)

Cycles 1–7 (London: COLP/PP/WF, 1975)

Diptych (London: COLP/PP, 1975)

Eight Poems: Against the Bond and Cement of Civil Society (London: COLP/PP, 1975)

Essay No.1 (London: COLP/PP, c.1975)

Found Sea Texts (London: COLP/PP, 1975)

'Found Text from The Charge of the Light Brigade' and 'Found Text: An Ode to Autumn', in *ABC*, ed. by Jeremy Adler (London: National Poetry Centre Press, 1975), pp. 30–31.

The Gesta Alfredi: Rex Angeli (London: COLP, 1975)

The Grave Stanza of Urien (London: COLP/PP, c.1975)

Idylls of the Dog, King & Other Poems, illus. and cover by A&S Paxton (London: COLP/PP, 1975)

'Industry and Idleness' and '1–7', *Fix*, 2 (Hayes, 1975)

Poems for Ian Hamilton (n.p.; printed privately for Cancer & Cancer by Edwim Halfpenny & Sons, Pepper Street, [c. 1975])

Riddlebook (London: COLP, 1975)

The Story of the Flood from Gilgamesh, trans. by Bill Griffiths, cover by Sean O'Huigin (London: COLP/PP, 1975)

1976

'Approaches to Translation 1', *Modern Poetry in Translation*, 25 (London, 1976), 19–22.

K. Chris Cable, *Hamwell's Book* (London: PP, 1976)

Cycles, cover by Clive Fencott (London: COLP/PP/WF, 1976; repr. [with revisions] London: WF, 1994)

Clive Fencott, *The Spiral Door Stop* (London: PP, c.1976)

'Found Texts', in *Three*, ed. by bpNichol (Toronto: GrOnk Press, 1976)

'The Gesta Alfredi: *Rex Anglie*', in *The Story so Four*, ed. by Steve McCaffery and bpNichol (Toronto: Coach House Press, 1976), pp. 138–145.

Reprinted and Current Poems (1) (London: COLP/PP, c.1976; repr. 1978)

North Atlantic Texts 1, ed. and trans. by Bill Griffiths and John Porter (London: COLP/PP/WF, 1976)

Jeff Nuttall, 'Bill Griffiths-An Appreciation', *Poetry Information*, 15 (London, 1976), 13–16

Sean O Huigin, *Poems* (London: COLP/PP, c.1976)

The Poems on Llwarch Hen, trans. by Bill Griffiths, illus. by Nicholas Parry (Market Drayton: Tern Press, 1976)

Six Walks Around Tenby (London: Earthgrip Press, 1976)

The Song of the Hunnish Victory of Pippin the King (London: Earthgrip Press, 1976)

'The Spider', trans. by Bill Griffiths and John Porter, *Windows*, 4 (East Sussex: East Sussex College of Higher Education Press), 14–15.

Untitled visual piece, in *Curtal Sails* (London: COLP, 1976)

Untitled visual piece, *Kroklok*, 4 (London, 1976), 120.

1977

'Conversation / Bill Griffiths / Chris Cheek', '4 Debates' and 'The Royal Pageant of Chime the Cat', *Saturday Morning*, 4 (London, 1977)

'Hawkstone' and 'Externsteine', *Poetry Wales*, 13.2 (Swansea, 1977), 61–63.

'The Praise Song of Judge John H. Lyle', 'The Praise Song of Justice Melford Stevenson', 'The Connected Praise Songs of Sir John Everest Geodesist and George Everest Esquire Principal Clerk for Criminal Business at the Home Office', 'The Praise Song of William IV', 'Encomium Urbis – Colchester' and 'Thor and the Mist Calf', *Poetry Review*, 67.1–2 (London, 1977), 17–22.

Praise Songs (London: PP, 1977)

'Review: Peter Clive Fencott', *Poetry Information*, 18 (London, 1977–8), 81–82.

Spook Book (London: PP/WF, 1977)

'Towards a Folk Calendar' in *ABCD*, ed. by Jeremy Adler (London: WF, 1977), p.13

Twenty-Five Pages (London: PP/WF, 1977)

Untitled work, in *Mugshots*, ed. by Mike Dobbie (Mike Dobbie, 1977), p.8.

'A Work for Tereus the Hoopoe', 'Line Rearrangement Poems', 'Marvell Advertiser Poems' and 'Corrections to 'Daybreak', *Good Elf*, 5–6 (London, 1977), 6–13.

Work in, *Kontextsound*, ed. by Michael Gibbs (Amsterdam: Tekst in Geluid Festival, 1977) [item untraced]

Zwei Preislieder, trans. by Jeremy Adler and Manfred Sundermann (London: COLP/PP, 1977)

1978

An Account of the End (Cambridge: Lobby Press, 1978)

Pirate Press Book List (London: PP, 1978)

Poem List 1968–1978 (London: PP, 1978)

'Dieu est...', 'Index' and 'Two postcards', *Words Worth*, 1.2 (London, 1978), 45–49.

'At the Grave of a Literary Director', in *bal:le:d curtains*, ed. by Paul Buck (Hebden Bridge: Curtains Press, 1978), pp. 56–59.

A History of the Solar System / Fragments: A History of the Solar System (London: COLP/PP/WF, 1978)

Llywarch Hen: In Welsh/English, trans. and intro. by Bill Griffiths (London: WF, 1978)

Oblong Book (London: PP, 1978; repr. [with revisions], 1979)

A Preliminary Account of Nordrhein-Westfalen etc. (Todmorden, Lancs: Arc Publications, 1978)

Quarto Book (London: PP, 1978; repr. [with revisions], 1979)

For Rediffusion, illus. by R. Clark (London: New London Pride/The Postal Collective, 1978)

'The Runic Poems', in *Alphabetic and Letter Poems: A Chrestomacy*, trans. by Bill Griffiths, ed. by Peter Mayer (London: Menard Press, 1978)

'The Story of the Solar System/Fragments: The Story of the Solar System', *GrOnk 14* (Toronto: 1978)

Small Printings (London: PP, 1978) [a folder of earlier printings, contents variable]

Sun Card Showing Sunrises (London: WF, 1978)

Variations on Morgenroth, Morgenroth, leuchtest mir zur frühem Tod (London: Tapocketa Press, 1978)

Whitechapel: April and May, End and Start Texts (London: PP, 1978)

1979

'Extensteine', 'Hawkstone', 'Four Virtues' and 'The Paderborn Epos', *Ochre*, 3 (Little Clacton, Essex, 1979)

Four Scene-Oramas No.1 [PETE]
Four Scene-Oramas No.2 [ALF]
[untitled] *[= Four Scene-Oramas No.3]* [RAB]
Four Scene-Oramas No.1 [PAULINE]
Four Winds (London: WF, 1979)
'Framework', *Chock,* 5 (Canterbury, 1979)
Gin Chap, [with Paula Claire and Bob Cobbing] (London: WF, 1979)
The Horseshoe Falls (Niagara)
'An Index to the Possibilities of Divination by Urine', *Lobby Press,* 11
    (Cambridge, 1979), 10.
Geraldine Monk, *Long Wake* (London: PP/WF, 1979)
The Moons of Jupiter (London: WF, 1979)
Opal Louis Nations, *The Procreative Habits of Vans, Pick-ups and Macho*
    Heavy Duty Trucks (London: PP, 1979)
'Poetry and the Arts Council of Great Britain', *Lobby Press,* 6
    (Cambridge, 1979), 2–5.

1980

'The Allied Influence on Japan', 'The Influence of Prussia on the U.S.A.',
    'The Influence of Imperial Rome on the Democratic Monarchies',
    'The Influence of the Deep on Mercy', 'The Influence of Corrective
    Environments' and 'The Influence of Plastics on Simile', *Figs,* 3
    (Durham, 1980)
'Building: The New London Hospital', *Loot,* 1.4 (Peterborough, 1980)
The First Three Novellas of the Second Row (London/Trumpington:
    PP/Trumpet Press, 1980)
'Running the Arts', *Poetry and Little Press Information,* 2 (London, 1980),
    27–28.
Work in, *Voix-Off/Angleterre,* ed. by Pierre Jean Buffy (Talence, Bordeaux:
    Editions du Castor Astral, 1980) [item untraced]

1981

Aelfric's Colloquy, trans. and ed. by Bill Griffiths, illus. by Nicholas Parry
    (Market Drayton: Tern Press, 1981)
'The Book', *Poetry & Little Press Information,* 4 (London, 1981), 3–4.
'A Few Jottings on Microfiche', *Reality Studios,* 3.2 (Orpington, Kent,
    1981), 29.
'Joanne-Marie's Swimming Manual', *Heretic,* 1.1 (London, 1981)
'Lament for Charlemagne', 'Variations on a Newcastle Song', '2
    Romany Songs' and 'Thunderclaps', *Lobby Press Newsletter,* 17
    (Cambridge, 1981), 69–72.

The Nine Herb Charm, trans. by Bill Griffiths, illus. by Mary Parry (Market
    Drayton: Tern Press, 1981)
'Pre-Poetry, Poetry and Post-Poetry', *Poetry and Little Press Information,* 7
    (London, 1981), 3–4.

1982

Further Songs & Dances of Death (London: Anarcho Press, 1982)
'Gamelans', *Not Poetry,* 5/6 (Newcastle, 1982)
Poet's Voice (Bath, 1982) 'Six Walks Around Tenby', 'Thames', 'Cycle Two',
    'Cycle Five', 'Cycle Ten', 'Cycle Eleven' and 'Joanne Marie's
    Swimming Lesson' [item untraced]

1983

'The Arts and the GLC: A Mystery', *Poetry and Little Press Information,* 10
    (London, 1983), 25–27.
Eric Mottram, "Every New Book Hacking on Barz': The Poetry of Bill
    Griffiths', *Reality Studios,* 5 (Orpington, Kent, 1983), 45–54.
'Two Summer Poems', *Poet's Voice,* 3 (Bath, 1983), 14.
'Zephaniah's End-Song' [musical score] in *Figs* no. 9 (New Malden,
    Surrey, 1983)

1984

Materia Boethiana (Newcastle/Hay on Wye: Galloping Dog Press/The
    Poetry Bookshop, 1984)
'Nut's Small Poems', from 'Eight Poems', 'Cycle 1: On Dover Borstal',
    'Thor & the Mist-Calf', from 'Forming Four Dock Poems' and 'Setz
    (Oz)', in *Matieres d'Angleterre,* ed. by Pierre Joris and Paul Buck,
    trans. by Pierre Joris and Jean-Pascal Gans (Amiens: Trois Cailloux,
    1984), pp.31–33, pp.157–158, pp.197–199, pp. 231–237, p.321 and
    pp.379–380.
'Peacock Variations', in *Poet's Voice,* 4 (Bath, 1984)
A Tract Against the Giants: Poems and Texts by Bill Griffiths (Toronto: Coach
    House Press,1984)

1985

'Deep Sea Diving', in *Variations: Various Artists* (Peterborough:
    Spectacular Diseases, 1985)

Guthlac B: A Translation by Bill Griffiths of the Old English Poem on the Death of Saint Guthlac, trans. and intro. by Bill Griffiths (Peterborough: Spectacular Disease, 1985)

The Land Ceremonies Charm, trans. by Bill Griffiths, illus. by Mary Parry (Market Drayton: Tern Press, 1985)

Quire Book, (London: WF, 1985; repr. London: WF, 1987)

1986

'The Old English Alcoholic Vocabulary: A Re-examination', *Durham University Journal*, 78 (Durham, 1986), 231–250.

'Sea Shanties', 'In the Coal Year' and 'Invitation', *Figs*, 12 (Matlock, 1986)

1987

The Bournemouth, illus. by Chris Doveton (London: PP/WF, 1987; second edition, 1991)

Judit Kemenczy, 'Opening Game or the No of Gods and Poets', 'Hiakoodzho's Fox' and 'Flags at the Frontier', trans. by Eric Mottram and Miklas Vajda, [with note by Bill Griffiths], *Gare du Nord*, 2 (Paris, 1987), 21–27.

A Text Book of Drama (London: WF, 1987) includes 'Spiller's Boat' and 'At Castleton' by BG (both on p. 90); many of the other playlets are 'arranged' by BG.

'Three Five-Liners' in *First Offense* 2 (Canterbury, 1987)

1988

The Association of Little Presses: ALP The First 22 1/2 Years, [with Bob Cobbing] (London: Association of Little Presses, 1988)

The Book of the Boat: Inland- and Blue-Water Texts with Illustrations by the Author (London: WF, 1988; repr. Seaham: Amra Imprint, 1991)

'Dream of the Rood' [trans. by Bill Griffiths], 'Steve's Garden', 'Cards from Cologne', 'Cook-Book' and Clive Bush, 'Dance Hymns on a Semi-Stable Planet, the Poetry of Bill Griffiths', *Talus*, 3 (London, 1988), 42–88.

'Edmund's Head', trans. by Bill Griffiths, *Figs*, 14 (Matlock, 1988)

Letter in, *Poetry and Little Press Information*, 20 (London, 1988), 7–8.

'To Tom Saunders on his Imprisonment', 'Terzetto: Brixton', 'Animal', 'Into Prison', 'After Stroke', 'For P-Celtic: Found Text from Machen' and 'Compass Poem', in *The New British Poetry*, ed. by Gillian Allnutt and others (London: Paladin, 1988), pp.173–178.

1989

'Ecclesiasticus ch.14', *Mar,* 1 (St Ives, 1989)
'Exposition' and 'The Long Barrow', *Kite,* 3 (Cardiff, 1989)
Morning-Lands (Cowley, Middx.: PP, 1989; repr. second revised edition as
      Morning Lands, Seaham: Amra, 1991)
John Muckle, [Review of *Morning Lands*], *City Limits,* 406, 13–20 July 1989,
      p. 63.
'Peri Eudaimonias', 'The Breed', 'View' and 'Metamorphosis', *Poets Voice,*
      4.2–3 (Bath, 1989), 24–9.
The Rune Poem, ed. and trans. by Bill Griffiths (Market Drayton: Tern
      Press, 1989)
A User-Friendly Dictionary of Old English, ed. by Bill Griffiths (Cowley, Middx.:
      Amra, 1989; repr. 3rd edition, Loughborough: Heart of Albion
      Press, 1993; fifth edition, adding an 'Anglo-Saxon Reader', 2005)
'Zookeeper', 'Cycles 5 10 and 11' and 'The Peacock Variations', in *A
      Mingling of Streams: An Anthology of Poems Selected from 'The Poet's
      Voice' vols.* 1–9, ed. by Fred Beak (Salzburg: University of Salzburg
      Press, 1989), pp.55–64.

1990

An Anglo-Saxon Subject Reader 1. *The Natural World,* ed. by Bill Griffiths
      (Cowley, Middx.: Amra, 1990)
Anglo-Saxon Times: A Study of the Early Calendar (London: Amra, 1990; repr.
      1994)
Bikers, [with John Muckle] (London: Amra, 1990; repr.)
Coal (London: WF, 1990)
The Old English Poem 'Phoenix', trans. by Bill Griffiths (Cowley, Middx.:
      Amra, 1990; repr. 1990)
On Plotinus (Cowley, Middx.: Amra, 1990)
'Recycled Paper', *PALPI,* 26 (London, 1990), 3–4.
*A Short Account of the Residential Moorings on the Grand Union Canal by
      Benbow Bridge Uxbridge,* illus. by Chris Doveton (Cowley, Middx.:
      Amra, 1990)
'Words & Some Warning', *PALPI,* 25 (London, 1990), 30.

1991

Alfred's Metres of Boethius, ed. and intro. by Bill Griffiths (Pinner: Anglo-
      Saxon Books, 1991; repr. 1994)

'Les Assis', in *Soleil + Chair,* ed. by Harry Gilonis (London: WF, 1991)

The Battle of Maldon: Text and Translation, ed., trans. and intro. by Bill Griffiths (Pinner: Anglo-Saxon Books, 1991; repr. 1992, Hockwold-cum-Wilton: Anglo-Saxon Books 1996, [with revisions] 2000; repr. 2003)

A Book of Legends (Seaham/London: Amra/WF, 1991)

Coal 2 (London: WF, 1991)

Coal 3 (London: WF, 1991)

Darwin's Dialogues (London: Amra, 1991; repr.)

Ian Davidson, *The Patrick Poems* (Seaham: Amra, 1991)

John Kemble, *Anglo-Saxon Runes,* ed. by Bill Griffiths (Pinner: Anglo-Saxon Books, 1991)

'Little Scenes', in *Bazzin* (Buxton, Derbyshire: Unknown Press, 1991)

Metrical Cookery (London: Amra, 1991)

A Pocket History of the Soul (Seaham: Amra, 1991)

'Postcards', 'Sandwiches' and 'Unities', *Fragmente,* 3 (Oxford, 1991), 16–18.

The Purple Shepherd: An examination of perfect government according to the best authorities (London: Anarcho Press, 1991)

A Seaham Reader 1: Medieval (Seaham: Amra, 1991)

A Seaham Reader 2: Seaham Hall (Seaham: Amra, 1991)

A Seaham Reader 3: The Harbour (Seaham: Amra, 1991)

A Seaham Reader 4: The 3rd Marquess (Seaham: Amra, 1991)

A Seaham Reader 5: Mines & Miners (Seaham: Amra, 1991)

A Seaham Reader 6: Yearly Bonds etc. (Seaham: Amra, 1991)

The Service of Prime, trans. by Bill Griffiths (Pinner: Anglo-Saxon Books, 1991)

1992

'The Ace & Other Scenes', *Active in Airtime,* 1 (Colchester, 1992), 12–15.

Baking Bread (Seaham: Amra, 1992)

'Calendar Contents', *Spanner* 31, 4.1 (Hereford, 1992)

The Dinosaur Park, [with Clive Fencott] (London: Micro Brigade, 1992)

The Epic of Gilgamesh, Episode 1, trans. by Bill Griffiths, illus. by Nicholas Parry (Market Drayton: Tern Press, 1992)

The Fams: An Investigation into the Concept of Family (Seaham: Amra 1992; repr. 1998)

The Great North Forest (Seaham: Amra, 1992)

Grey Suit Video 3, [with Bob Cobbing, Hugh Metcalfe and Paula Claire] (Cardiff, 1992) [item untraced]

'from Li-Po' [trans.], 'Suncard Showing Sunrises', 'Hodgson's House'
        [extracts], 'Zoo-Keeper', 'Cycle 6', 'A History of the Solar System'
        [extracts], in *verbi visi voco: a performance of poetry*, ed. by Bill
        Griffiths, Bob Cobbing and Jennifer Pike (London: WF, 1992)
Mid North Sea High (Seaham: Amra, 1992)
North Scenes (Seaham: Amra, 1992)
'Petimusque damusque', in *Horace whom I hated so,* ed. by Harry Gilonis
        (London: Five Eyes of Wiwaxia, 1992)
Quotidiania (Seaham: Amra, 1992)
Review of Brian Greenaway and *Notes from Delvan McIntosh,* intro. by Bill
        Griffiths (Seaham: Amra, 1992; repr. 1994)
'Riddle with Goatsbeard' and 'Rat to Boat-Master', *Angel Exhaust,* 8
        (Southend, 1992), 31–33.
Scaffold Hill (Seaham: Amra, 1992)
'Selected Poems, 1969–1989', in *Future Exiles: 3 London Poets: Paladin
        Re/Active Anthology No. 1,* ed. by Iain Sinclair, intro. to Griffiths's
        work by Jeff Nuttall (London: Paladin, 1992), pp.157–334.
*St Cuthbert: Aelfric's Life of the Saint in Old English with Modern English
        Parallel,* ed., trans. and intro. by Bill Griffiths (Seaham: Amra,
        1992; repr. 1996, 2000)
'Steve's Garden' [extracts], in *Six Towns Poetry Festival* (Stoke on Trent:
        Hanley, 1992) [item untraced]
Variations on the Life of Cuthbert, [with Clive Fencott] (Seaham: Amra,
        1992)

1993

Alexander Barrass, *The Pitman's Social Neet,* ed. and intro. by Bill Griffiths
        (Seaham: Amra, 1993; repr. 1994, [with revisions] Newcastle:
        Centre for Northern Studies, 2002)
Janet Batley, [forward acknowledges work by Bill Griffiths], *Anonymous
        OE Homilies: A Preliminary Bibliography* (New York: State University
        Press, 1993)
The Battle of Maldon: A Response to Donald Scragg (Seaham: Amra, 1993)
The Cuddy Anthem: A Mini Dialect Anthology (Seaham: Amra, 1993)
Delvan's Book (Seaham: Amra, 1993)
Durham and Around: A Dialect Reader, ed. by Bill Griffiths (Seaham: Amra,
        1993; repr. [with revisions] 1994)
Essay on Entity (Seaham: Amra, 1993)
Joanne's Book (Seaham: Amra, 1993)

D.R. McIntosh, *A List of Slang Terms from Morden, Surrey* (Seaham: Amra, 1993; repr. [with revisions by Paul Campbell], 1995)

In Praise of Church Street, Seaham (Seaham: Amra, 1993)

Revising Prison: An Essay (Seaham: Amra, 1993)

Satires (Seaham: Amra, 1993)

Seaham: A Provisional Bibliography, ed. and intro. by Bill Griffiths (Seaham: Amra, 1993)

Seventy-Six Day Wanno, Mississippi & Highpoint Journal: From the Work of D.R. MacIntosh & Bill Griffiths, [with Delvan MacIntosh] (Seaham: Amra, 1993)

Skemmies an' Stanes: Two Poems in Dialect (Seaham: Amra, 1993)

Star Fish Jail, intro. by Bill Griffiths (Seaham: Amra, 1993; repr. 1993, repr. [with revisions] 1994)

'On the Tyne', in *Poetry Marathon '93 Charity Anthology*, ed. B.J. Allen (Newcastle: B.J. Allen's Press, 1993), p.40

M.J. Weller, *Carlaverock* or *Le Siege de Karlaverock: An Idea-Gift Found by Bill Griffiths and Treated by M.J. Weller* (London: Visual Associations, 1993)

Work in *Haiku Quarterly*, 10 (Swindon, 1993) Interview with Paul Holman and Bridget Penney, 'let chisel catch coal…', 'Jingle'. [item untraced]

1994

Amra Imprint Book List (Seaham: Amra, 1994)

'Birds & Wind' and 'On the Beach', *Object Permanence*, 2 (Glasgow, 1994), 20–1

'The City of Egypt', in *Motley for Mottram: Tributes to Eric Mottram on his 70th Birthday*, ed. by Bill Griffiths and Bob Cobbing (Seaham/London: Amra/WF, 1994)

The Coast of Durham: A Report on Behalf of the Seaham Environmental Association [with Trevor Charlton] (Seaham: Amra, 1994)

'Detective Notes', in *AND* 7, ed. by Adrian Clarke (London: WF, 1994), pp. 88–89.

'Detective Notes', in *Squad Car Verthragna*, ed. by Mike Weller (London: Visual Associations, 1994)

Durham & Around: Dialect Word List, ed. by Bill Griffiths (Seaham: Amra, 1994; repr. 1995)

Liam's Song, cover by Patricia Farrell, *RWC* 23 (Caversham, Reading, 1994)

Eric Mottram, *Design Origins: Masks* (Seaham: Amra, 1994; repr. 1996)

The Mythology of Seaham: A Review of Tom McNee's Local History Publications
(Seaham: Amra, 1994)

*In Rebuttal of 'The Guardian' on the Role of Solitary Confinement in British
Prisons: A Call for an Enquiry* (Seaham: Amra, 1994)

To the Rescue of Reality (Seaham: Amra, 1994)

The Secret Commonwealth, illus. by Ray Seaford (London: Oasis Books,
1994)

*Some Notes on the Metropolitan Police, London; With Some Footnotes on
Magistrates Courts* (Seaham: Amra, 1994)

1995

'The Alien', in *The Invisible Reader*, ed. by B. Penney and P. Holman
(London: Invisible Books, 1995), pp.30–43.

Jonathan Barker, *Poetry in Britain and Ireland Since 1970: A Select
Bibliography* [makes reference to work by Griffiths] (London: The
British Council Literature Department Press, 1995), p.46.

'The Best Jigsaw', in *Ink Feathers: Six Towns Poetry Festival Anthology*
(Newcastle under Lyme/Bath: Heron Press/The Poets Voice, 1995),
pp.28–31.

*A Century of Self Service?: Aspects of Local Government in the North East with
Special Reference to Seaham* (Seaham: Amra, 1995)

Edward Chicken, *The Collier's Wedding,* ed. and intro. by Bill Griffiths
(Seaham: Amra, 1995)

The Coal World: Murton Tales Re-worked as Dialect Verse, [original text by
Frank Platts], intro. by Bill Griffiths, illus. by Mike Weller
(Seaham: Amra, 1995; repr. 2000)

'Contribution to Kelvin's Project', in *Short Attention Span,* ed. by Kelvin
Corcoran (Cheltenham: Between Meetings, 1995)

The Denes of the Bishopric, [with Trevor Charlton] (Seaham: Amra, 1995;
repr. [with revisions] 2000, Seaham: Story of Seaham, 2003)

An Introduction to Early English Law, ed., trans. and intro. by Bill Griffiths
(Hockwold-cum-Wilton: Anglo-Saxon Books, 1995; repr. 1998)

The Lion Man or Four Poems in One (Seaham: Amra, 1995)

Meet the Dragon: An Introduction to Beowulf's Adversary (Seaham: Amra,
1995; repr. Loughborough: Heart of Albion, 1996)

Myth & Misinformation: A Review of the Drivers Jonas Report Process (Seaham:
Amra, 1995)

Noah's Ark—The Newcastle Mystery Play, ed. by Bill Griffiths (Seaham:
        Amra, 1995)
Now we are Twenty: A Sequel Essay on Reality (Seaham: Amra, 1995)
'Two Poems for Bob in One Style', in *AND* 9, ed. by Adrian Clarke and
        Bob Cobbing (London: WF, 1995), p.75.
Umbro (Cheltenham: Short Run, 1995)
The 'Unnecessary Election': Records of the Local Poll in the South Ward,
        Easington District. 4 May 1995 (Seaham: Amra, 1995)

1996

On the Abuse of Drugs (Seaham: Amra, 1996)
Aspects of Anglo-Saxon Magic, ed. and trans. by Bill Griffiths (Hockwold-
        cum-Wilton: Anglo-Saxon Books, 1996; repr. [with revisions], 2003)
Baldur's Lacrimosa (London: WF, 1996)
'In the Brick Middle Oven', in *Etruscan Jetty* (Newcastle under Lyme:
        Etruscan Books, 1996), p.13
'Coastal Strategy in Co. Durham: Turning the Tide or Lossing the
        Beaches?', *Northern Review,* 4 (Newcastle, 1996), 100–104
'Elvis Sets Sail', 'The Rabbit Hunt' and 'Les Assis', in *Etruscan Reader* 5
        (Newcastle under Lyme: Etruscan Books, 1996) [item untraced]
Fallacies & Ghost Tales of Seaham (Seaham: Amra, 1996)
The Genesis of Iron (Seaham: Amra, 1996)
'How Highpoint is Better than Wandsworth', *Object Permanence,* 6
        (Glasgow, 1996), 15–20.
Histories (Seaham: Amra, 1996)
Hungary (Seaham: Amra, 1996)
M.R. James, *The Experiment: A New Years Eve Ghost Story,* intro. by Bill
        Griffiths (Seaham: Amra, 1996)
Labyrinth (Seaham: Amra, 1996)
Jeff Nuttall, 'Tactics of Disarray', [Review of *Conductors of Chaos*],
        Independent, 20th July 1996, p.7.
On the Platform at Stockton (Seaham: Amra, 1996)
'Quad', 'Anansi' and 'The Durham Coal-Field', *Talisman,* 16 (New Jersey,
        1996) [item untraced]
'Reveries', in *Conductors of Chaos,* ed. and intro. by Iain Sinclair, [Bill
        Griffiths's contribution intro. by Jeff Nuttall] (London: Picador,
        1996), pp.113–126
Rousseau and the Wicked (London: Invisible Books, 1996)
'Some Evidence of Eric', *First Offense,* 10 (1996), 56–58

1997

'Binaries: Not Sonnets', in *Etruscan Reader* 5 (Buckfastleigh: Etruscan
     Books, 1997), pp.33–66
Clive Bush, 'Dance Hymns on a Semi-Stable Planet', in *Out of Dissent: A
     Study of Five Contemporary British Poets* (London: Talus, 1997),
     pp. 211–304
'Cycle 6', 'Five Poems', 'Charm', 'Invite', 'A History of the Solar System/
     Fragments: A History of the Solar System', 'Spiller's Boat', 'The
     Land-Search', 'Nocturnes and Diurnes', 'The Breed', 'For Jeff
     Nuttall', 'On Well-Being', 'Moretum 1', 'Moretum 2', 'Speedway',
     'Bealing Bells', 'Leeds, Kirkstall, Staithes', 'Nutt's Small poems',
     'From the Seventh Sphere, Like Troilus', 'Steve's Garden',
     'November', 'The Hawksmoor Mausoleum', 'Eight Barques for
     the Manifold Soul of G.L. Renfree', 'The Haswell Changeover',
     'MFV Golden Arrow', from 'The Great North Forest', 'Work
     World', 'Pharmacopoeia', from 'Review of Brian Greenaway',
     from 'Star Fish Jail', 'Wandsworth', 'Thirteen Thoughts as
     Though Woken in Caravan Town at Dawn...', 'Words' and
     'Detective Notes', in *Worlds of New Measure: An Anthology of Five
     Contemporary British Poets*, ed. and intro. by Clive Bush (London:
     Talus Editions, 1997), pp.221–322
*The Kid that Carried the Satchel: A Tale of Dering-Do and Dark Pit-Craft, Lazer-
     Published for ye Miners Gala Durham* (Seaham: Amra, 1997)
More Ghostly Tales and Misadventures of Seaville (London: Amra, 1997)
'More on the Coastal Zone of County Durham: The Case of the
     Overlooked Denes', *Northern Review*, 5 (Newcastle, 1997), 47–51
'Paul's Survival Tips', 'Media Studies' and 'Musical Note', *Talus*, 9–10
     (London, 1997), 48–51.
Phantom Tales of Seaville - Three (Seaham: Amra, 1997)

1998

'Basil Bunting and Eric Mottram', *Chicago Review*, 44.3–4 (Chicago,
     1998), 104–113
'The Caller', *Sacrifice Achievement Gratitude - Images of the Great Northern
     Coalfield in Decline* [review] and *Hetton le-Hole: Pitmatic Talk 100 Years
     Ago* [review], *Northern Review*, 7 (Newcastle, 1998), 28–32 and
     87–88.
'Flower Power' and 'The Kid that Carried the Satchel', *Northern Review*, 6
     (1998), 35–42 and 141–7

J. Hilton, 'Review of *Etruscan Reader,* 5 - Revised Edition', *Fire,* 6
    (Kidlington, Oxfordshire, 1998), 3–4.
Nomad Sense (London: Talus Editions, 1998)
The Phoenix, trans. by Bill Griffiths, illus. by Nicholas and Mary Parry
    (Market Drayton: Tern Press, 1998)
'Tha Twa Gleomen' and 'Forming Four Dock Poems', in *Word Score
    Utterance Choreography in Verbal and Visual Poetry,* ed. Bob Cobbing
    and Lawrence Upton (London: WF, 1998)
'Two Mantras', *Chicago Review,* 44.2 (Chicago, 1998), 22–4.

1999

Anonymous review of *A Book of Spilt Cities, Terrible Work* (Plymouth,
    c.1999), 74–75.
Edimilson de Almeida Pereira, 'In the House of Talking' and 'Pierced
    Ear', trans. by Bill Griffiths, *Secure a Lump Sum: Sub Voicive Poetry
    1999,* 11 (Sutton: Sub Voicive Poetry, 1999), 3–4.
A Book of Spilt Cities, intro. by Iain Sinclair, illus. by Robert Clark
    (Buckfastleigh: Etruscan Books, 1999)
Durham: (Poems of a Visit): (Poems of a Visit to Durham Prison), cover by Mike
    Weller (Seaham: Amra, 1999)
'For P-Celtic', from 'Building; the New London Hospital' [extracts],
    'Ship' and 'South Song', in *Other: British and Irish Poetry since 1970,*
    ed. and intro. by Ric Caddel and Peter Quatermain (Hanover and
    London: Wesleyan University Press, 1999), pp.92–98.
Kamandi (Toronto: Red Head Gallery, 1999)
North East Dialect: Survey and Word-List, ed. and intro. by Bill Griffiths
    (Newcastle: Centre for Northern Studies Press, 1999; repr. 2000
    [with revisions] 2001)
Our Winter Game, illus. by Bob Cobbing (London/Seaham: WF/Amra,
    1999)
'Poems of Edimilson de Almeida Pereira', trans. by Bill Griffiths, Will
    Rowe and David Treece, *Journal of Latin American Cultural Studies,*
    8.2 (London, 1999),165–170
'Poems of Entity', *Fire,* 8 (Kidlington, Oxfordshire, 1999), 43–48.
'The Poetry Escape', *Boundary* 2,26.1 (Duke University, North Carolina,
    1999), 125–127.
'The Ringstones', *Gare du Nord,* 2.2 (Paris, 1999), 29–31.
'Room-Mates', *The Gig,* 3 (Willowdale, Ontario, 1999), 3–6.
The Seaham Fishing Fleet (Seaham: Amra, 1999)

Mr Tapscott: A Poem in Nine Sections with Inserts and List of Resources
(Seaham: Amra, 1999)
'The Walkers' and 'Retaking the Language: the Need for Dialect
Initiatives', *Northern Review,* 8 (Newcastle, 1999), 1–17 and
126–132.

2000

'The Abbey', *Fire,* 10 (Kidlington, Oxfordshire, 2000)
Tilla Brading, 'Front Runners', [Review of *A Book of Spilt Cities*], *Poetry
Quarterly Review,* Spring (Nether Stowey, Somerset, 2000), 20–21.
Mark Cox, *Cluck* (Seaham, Amra, 2000)
Mark Cox, *Geek* (Seaham: Amra, 2000)
The Divas: A Fiendish Tale by Bill Griffiths or *A Tale of Unspeakly Transpirations
in the Neglected North* (Seaham: Amra, 2000)
'Exposition—A Madrigal', in *For Bob Cobbing: A Celebration,* ed. by Adrian
Clarke and Lawrence Upton (Sutton: Mainstream Poetry, 2000)
Kaldi: The Goat Secret, illus. by Nicholas Parry (Market Drayton: Tern
Press, 2000)
'Kamandi', 'Glacier', 'Hop Field' and 'The Perception', *Queen Street
Quarterly,* 3/4 (Toronto, 2000), 12–16.
Eric Mottram, *Composition and Performance in the Work of Bob Cobbing: A
Conversation,* [featuring Griffiths], ed. Michael Gibbs, intro. by Eric
Mottram, illus. by Bob Cobbing (London: WF, 2000)
North East Dialect: The Texts, ed. and intro. by Bill Griffiths (Newcastle:
Centre for Northern Studies Press, 2000; repr. 2003)
Readings in Seaham History: Part One, ed. by Bill Griffiths (Seaham: Amra,
2000)
Readings in Seaham History: Part Two, ed. by Bill Griffiths (Seaham: Amra,
2000)
Winter (Market Drayton: Tern Press, 2000)

2001

Ghost Tales, Folk Tales & Tales of Seaville, cover by Darren Brown (Seaham:
Amra, 2001)
*A Historical Account of the Londonderry (Seaham & Sunderland) Railway by the
Late George Hardy,* ed. by Bill Griffiths (Seaham: Story of Seaham,
2001)

'The Last Christmas' and 'The Museum', *Northern Review*, 9/10
(Newcastle, 2001)

'Last word: dialect', in eds Robert Colls and Bill Lancaster, *Newcastle
upon Tyne: A Modern History* (Chichester: Phillimore, 2001),
pp. 361–66

'The Mackerel: An Extended Sequence', in *On Word: Part* 2 (London: WF,
2001)

'The New World', *The Gig*, 9 (Willowdale, Ontario, 2001), 10–13.

Old Seaham: In Anglo-Saxon and Medieval Times (Seaham: The Story of
Seaham/Amra, 2001; repr. 2001, 2002)

'The Psychic Fifth', *The Penniless Press*, 13 (Preston, 2001), 30–34.

'Reekie', in *Anthology of Twentieth Century British and Irish Poetry*, ed. by
Keith Tuma (New York: Oxford University Press, 2001),
pp. 760–765.

'The Seafarer' [trans. by Bill Griffiths], in *The River*, ed. by Paul Burwell
and Harry Palmer (Hull: Paul Burwell and Harry Palmer, 2001)

The Seaham Fishing Fleet (Seaham: Amra, 2001)

Smuggling in Seaham (Seaham: Amra/Story of Seaham, 2001)

The Ushabtis (London: Talus Editions, 2001)

2002

'Bee-Bike' and 'Spiderman', *Neon Highway*, 2 (Liverpool, 2002), 38–42.

Durham and Other Sequences, cover by Robert Clark (Sheffield: West
House Books, 2002)

Market Tales (Seaham: Amra, c.2002)

'From *The Mud Fort*', *Cul-de-Qui*, 1 (London, 2002)

'Haiku', in *Football Haiku*, ed. by Alex Finlay (Edinburgh: Pocket Books,
2002)

'3 Insects', *Tolling Elves Sheet*, 2 (London, 2002)

'Words at the Edge', *Northern Review*, 11 (2002)

2003

'Animals you Might Meet on a Walk', *Northern Review*, 13 (2003/4)

The Battle of Maldon 991, [two separate] trans. by F. Butterfield and Bill
Griffiths (Tonbridge. Kent: Woodcraft Press, 2003)

'Bob Cobbing: Some Performances', *Multi-Storey*, 3 (Manchester, 2003),
17–22.

Andrew Duncan, *The Failure of Conservatism in Modern British Poetry,* [some
  discussion of Griffiths's work], (Cambridge: Salt Publishing, 2003)
James Hay, *Spider and Other Tales of Pit Village Life,* glossary by Bill
  Griffiths (Newcastle/Seaham: Centre for Northern Studies
  Press/Durham & Tyneside Dialect Group Publication, 2003)
The Mud Fort: A Suite (Seaham: Amra, 2003)
*A Preliminary Assessment of Coastal Place-Names in Easington District, Co.
  Durham* (Seaham: Story of Seaham, 2003)
'The Profession of Gipsydom', *Skald,* 18 (Bangor, 2003), 31–35.
[reviews], *Northern Review,* 12 (Newcastle, 2002–2003) [item untraced]
'In the Rush to Man the Shields Lifeboat', in *Morden Poets* 2003, ed. by
  Connie Pickard (Newcastle: Tower Poets, 2003) [item untraced]
Seaham Hall: An Account of the Building and its Owners (Seaham: Story of
  Seaham, 2003)
'At Tynemouth', *Sand,* 1 (Newcastle, 2003), 32–35.

2004

'In the bite snow-crop', in *Onsets: A Breviary (Synopticon) of Poems* 13 *Lines
  or Under* (Willowdale, Ontario: The Gig Press, 2004) [item
  untraced]
Michael Dacre, *The Death of King Edmund…with Historical Note by Bill
  Griffiths* (London: Runetree, 2004)
Dictionary of North-East English (Newcastle: Northumbria University
  Press, 2004)
The Mud Fort (Cambridge: Salt Publishing, 2004)
'Newcastle from a Van Window' in *Tyne Txts,* [with Tom Pickard]
  (Seaham/Newcastle upon Tyne: Amra, in association with
  Morden Poets, dated MMIIIII, 2004)
Northern Sinfonia: 'A Magic of its Own' (Newcastle: Northumbria
  University Press, 2004)
[review], *Northern Review,* 14 (Newcastle, 2004) [item untraced]
Stotty 'n' Spice-Cake: The Story of North East Cooking (Newcastle/Seaham:
  The Centre for Northern Studies Press/Durham & Tyneside
  Dialect Group Publication, 2004)
'A Universal English', in *AND* 12, ed. by Adrian Clarke
  (Sutton/Whitstable: WF, 2004), p.38.
Mike Weller, *Beowulf Cartoon,* intro. by Bill Griffiths (Sutton/
  Whitstable/London: WF/Visual Associations. 2004)

2005

A Dictionary of North East Dialect, ed. by Bill Griffiths (Newcastle: Northumbria University Press, 2005)

"We Farath' Words and Tune', in *The Poetry Buzz: Programme & Souvenir Book of the Buzz* (London: Paige Mitchell, 2005)

Robert Sheppard, *Poetry of Saying, The: British Poetry and its Discontents, 1950–2000*, [some discussion of Griffiths's work], (Liverpool: Liverpool University Press, 2005)

2006

Peter Barry, *Poetry Wars: British Poetry of the 1970s and the Battle of Earls Court*, [discussion of Griffiths's work and of his involvement with the struggles in the Poetry Society], (Cambridge: Salt Publishing, 2006)

Stotty and Spice Cake (Newcastle-upon-Tyne: Northumbria University Press)

'Look it's Loki' (Matchbox no. 2, Manchester)

'Midnight Express', *Square One*, 4, 24–25 (University of Colorado at Boulder)

'Talking to Shim', *10th Muse*, 14, 23–28

Stotty 'n' Spice-Cake: The Story of North East Cooking (Newcastle/Seaham: The Centre for Northern Studies Press/Durham & Tyneside Dialect Group Publication, 2004)

2007

'Cell and Shower', 'Cherry Tree Carol' and 'Monkey' in *Veer Away* (London: Veer Books, 2007), pp. [54–56].

Pitmatic: The Talk of the North East Coalfield compiled by Bill Griffiths (Newcastle upon Tyne: Northumbria University Press, 2007)

Geraldine Monk: *Three Ships for Bill Griffiths* (Sheffield: Gargoyle Editions, 2007).—memorial poem incorporating material by BG from *Morning-Lands*.

This incorporates some corrections and additions on the basis of data provided by Harry Gilonis.

Visuals

'booth photo of BG ca.1982'

1. Work by BG

"Sending you some magic vibes from Autumn waterfall
across from my cottage."

'Autumn Waterfall', typewriter poem by BG ca.1974. The title is a quote
from a letter to BG.

FROM THE CHARGE OF THE LIGHT BRIGADE

INTO
THE

valley of (valley of ((valley of (((valley of ((((valley of (((((val-
ley of ((((((valley of (((((((valley of ((((((((valley of (((((((
(((valley of ((((((((((((valley of ((((((((((valley of ((((((((
of ((((((((((((((valley of (((((((((((((((valley of ((((
((((((((((((valley of (((((((((((((((((valley of (((
((((((((((((((valley of (((((((((((((((((((((valley of (((((((((((((((((((((((valley of (((((((((
(((((((((((((valley of ((((((((((((((((((((((
valley of ((((((((((((((((((((((((valley of (((((((
((((((((((((((((((((valley of ((((((((((((((
(((((((((((valley of ((((((((((((((((((((((((
((valley of ((((((((((((((((((((((((((((((valley
of (((((((((((((((((((((((((((((((((valley of ((
((((((((((((((((((((((((((((((((((valley of ((((
((((((((((((((((((((((((((((((((((((valley
of ((((((((((((((((((((((((((((((((((((((((((((valley

'From The Charge of the Light Brigade', arranged text by BG, ca. 1978
See p. 50.

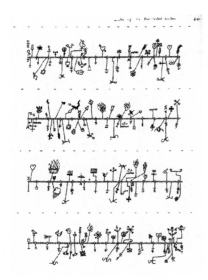

'Clog Calendar' by BG, ca. 1979. The page folded along the dotted lines and was glued into the form of a hollow four-sided baton. See p. 50.

Display of booklets by BG 1977–1980.
Photo from International Concrete Poetry Archive.

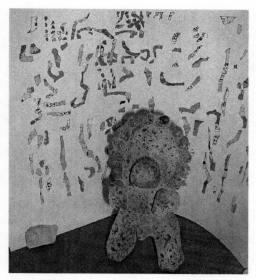

Assemblage related to 'Fire Fiche' (1980). Photo by Paula Claire. See p. 51.

Paula Claire and BG in performance, 1992. Photo from the International Concrete Poetry Archive.
See p. 49.

Bob Cobbing, BG, and Paula Claire

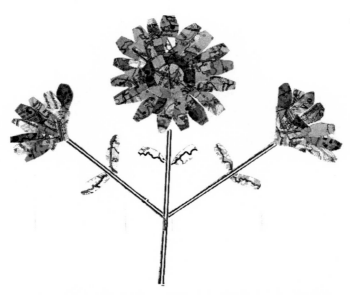

'Flower Map', collage by BG ca.1980 using snips from a coloured atlas.

'Forest Song', collage by BG ca. 1980; text mounted on indian-red background.

'The Cimmerian' (ink and gouache ca.1986; hull coloured bright red)

MID NORTH SEA HIGH

Cover to booklet 'Mid North Sea High', BG (Amra, 1992)

Mᴿ TAPSCOTT

a poem   serts
in nine   & list
sections   of re-
with in-   sources

by

BILL GRIFFITHS

Cover to booklet 'Mr Tapscott' (tinted with yellow/orange gouache). BG (Amra 1999).
The poem is Liverpool-based.

Group 2—by others

*Portrait of BG by Robert Clark, monoprint from ink on glass; reproduced in '
For Rediffusion' (New London Pride, 1978)*

*Image by Sean O Huigin, used in 'War w/ Windsor' (Writers Forum / Pirate Press, 1974);
printed by silkscreen in monastral blue.*

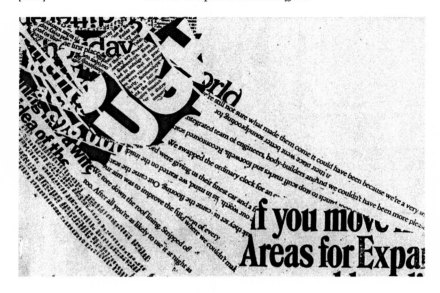

*Front and back cover images by Sean O Huigin for 'The Story of the Flood from Gilgamesh'
trans. BG (Pirate Press, 1975); newsprint collages, printed in black on yellow card.*

DURHAM

Bill Griffiths

Cover image by Michael J. Weller for 'Durham'. BG (Amra, 2001)

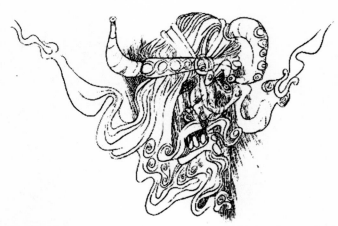

Image by Jeff Nuttall for cover of 'Beowulf' trans. John Porter (Pirate Press, 1975)

Printed in the United Kingdom
by Lightning Source UK Ltd.
125436UK00001B/108/A

9 781844 712496